EMERGENCY
MEDICAL RESPONDER

First Responder in Action

Second Edition

Barbara Aehlert, RN

Mc
Graw
Hill

*Connect
Learn
Succeed™*

EMERGENCY MEDICAL RESPONDER WORKBOOK: FIRST RESPONDER IN ACTION

Published by McGraw-Hill, a business unit of The McGraw-Hill Companies, Inc., 1221 Avenue of the Americas, New York, NY, 10020. Copyright © 2011 by The McGraw-Hill Companies, Inc. All rights reserved. Previous edition © 2007. No part of this publication may be reproduced or distributed in any form or by any means, or stored in a database or retrieval system, without the prior written consent of The McGraw-Hill Companies, Inc., including, but not limited to, in any network or other electronic storage or transmission, or broadcast for distance learning.

Some ancillaries, including electronic and print components, may not be available to customers outside the United States.

This book is printed on acid-free paper.

1 2 3 4 5 6 7 8 9 0 RJE/RJE 1 0 9 8 7 6 5 4 3 2 1 0

ISBN   978-0-07-735223-3
MHID   0-07-735223-8

Vice president/Editor in chief: *Elizabeth Haefele*
Vice president/Director of marketing: *John E. Biernat*
Sponsoring editor: *Barbara Owca*
Director of Development, Business Careers: *Sarah Wood*
Editorial coordinator: *Vincent Bradshaw*
Marketing manager: *Matthew R. McLaughlin*
Lead media producer: *Damian Moshak*
Director, Editing/Design/Production: *Jess Ann Kosic*
Lead project manager: *Rick Hecker*
Senior production supervisor: *Janean A. Utley*
Senior designer: *Srdjan Savanovic*
Senior photo research coordinator: *Lori Hancock*
Media project manager: *Brent dela Cruz*
Outside development house: *Laura Horowitz*
Typeface: *10/12 ITC New Baskerville*
Compositor: *Aptara, Inc.*
Printer: *R. R. Donnelley*
Cover credit: *© Rick Brady*

Unless otherwise credited, all photos © The McGraw-Hill Companies, Inc./Rick Brady, photographer.
Chapter 1: © The McGraw-Hill Companies, Inc./Carin Marter, photographer; Chapter 2: © Courtesy of Tempe Fire Department, Tempe, Arizona; Chapter 25: EMSC Slide Set (CD-ROM). 1996. Courtesy of the Emergency Medical Services for Children Program, administered by the U.S. Department of Health and Human Service's Health Resources and Services Administration, Maternal and Child Health Bureau; Chapter 27: Trauma.org Image; Chapter 28: © The McGraw-Hill Companies, Inc./Carin Marter, photographer; Chapter 29: © David Page; Chapter 39: Courtesy of Charles J. Schubert, MD, from Knoop, et al., Atlas of Emergency Medicine, 2nd edition, McGraw-Hill Company, Inc.; Chapter 41: © Courtesy of Air Evac Services, Phoenix, Arizona; Chapter 42: © David Page.

Medicine is an ever-changing science. As new research and clinical experience broaden our knowledge, changes in treatment are required. The authors and the publisher of this work have checked with sources believed to be reliable in their efforts to provide information that is complete and generally in accord with the standards accepted at the time of publication. However, in view of the possibility of human error or changes in medical sciences, neither the authors nor the publisher nor any other party who has been involved in the preparation or publication of this work warrants that the information contained herein is in every respect accurate or complete, and they are not responsible for any errors or omissions or for the results obtained from use of such information. Readers are encouraged to confirm the information contained herein with other resources.

www.mhhe.com

About the Author

Barbara Aehlert is the President of Southwest EMS Education, Inc., in Phoenix, Arizona, and Pursley, Texas. She has been a registered nurse for more than 30 years, with clinical experience in medical/surgical and critical care nursing and, for the past 23 years, in prehospital education. Barbara is an active CPR, First Aid, ACLS, and PALS instructor.

Contributors

Lynn Browne-Wagner, RN, BSN
EMS Program Director
Northland Pioneer College
Holbrook, AZ

Randy Budd, RRT, CEP
City of Mesa Fire Department
Mesa, AZ

Major Raymond W. Burton (Retired)
Plymouth Academy/Plymouth County
   Sheriff's Academy
Plymouth, MA

Holly Button, CEP
City of Mesa Fire Department
Mesa, AZ

Suzy Coronel, CEP
Sportsmedicine Fairbanks
Fairbanks, AK

Janet Fitts, RN, EMT-P, Educational Consultant
Prehospital and Emergency Medical Services
Pacific, MO

Paul Honeywell, CEP
Southwest Ambulance
Mesa, AZ

Travis Kidd, EMT-P
Orange County Fire/Rescue
Orlando, FL

Andrea Lowrey, RN
Dallas, TX

Terence Mason, RN
City of Mesa Fire Department
Mesa, AZ

Kim McKenna, RN, EMT-P
Director of Education
St. Charles County Ambulance Service
St. Peters, MO

Sean Newton, CEP
City of Scottsdale Fire Department
Scottsdale, AZ

Gary Smith, MD
Medical Director: Apache Junction, Gilbert,
   and Mesa Fire Departments
Apache Junction, Gilbert, and Mesa, AZ

Edith Valladares
Director, Foreign Languages and Academic ESL
Central Piedmont Community College
Charlotte, NC

Reviewers

Paul A. Bishop
Monroe Community College
Rochester, NY

Anthony N. Brown
National Ski Patrol System Emergency Care
*   Advisor/Trainer*
Idaho Falls, ID

Major Raymond W. Burton (Retired)
Plymouth Academy/Plymouth County Sheriff's Academy
Plymouth, MA

David S. Farrow
S.W. EMS
Phoenix, AZ

Janet Fitts, RN, EMT-P
Educational Consultant
Prehospital and Emergency Medical Services
Pacific, MO

Franklin R. Hubbell, DO
SOLO
Conway, NH

Edward Kalinowski, MED, PhD
Department of Emergency Medical Services
University of Hawaii
Honolulu, HI

Barbara Klingensmith, PhD, NREMT-P
Florida State Fire College
San Antonio, FL

Kim McKenna, RN, EMT-P
Director of Education
St. Charles County Ambulance Service
St. Peters, MO

Keith A. Monosky, PhD(c), MPM, EMT-P
Associate Professor
Department of Nutrition, Exercise, and Health Sciences
Central Washington University
Ellensburg, WA

Keith A. Ozenberger, BS, LP
University of Texas Medical Branch
Galveston, TX

Douglas A. Pratt
Weber State University
Ogden UT

William Seifarth
MIEMSS
Baltimore, MD

Jeanne Shepard, CEP
Mesa Fire Department
Mesa, AZ

Tom Vines
Carbon Co. SAR/Mainrod
Red Lodge, MT

Maryalice Witzel, RN, BSN, MSN
Banner Good Samaritan Medical Center
Phoenix, AZ

Technical Editors

Lynn Browne-Wagner, RN, BSN
EMS Program Director
Northland Pioneer College
Holbrook, AZ

Bonnie L. Pastorino, AAS
EMT Department
Northland Pioneer College
Holbrook, AZ

Contents

Preface   viii

Module 1

Preparatory   1

▶ CHAPTER 1
EMS Systems and Research   2

▶ CHAPTER 2
Workforce Safety and Wellness   11

▶ CHAPTER 3
**Legal and Ethical Issues
and Documentation   22**

▶ CHAPTER 4
EMS System Communication   31

▶ CHAPTER 5
Medical Terminology   38

Module 2

**Function and Development
of the Human Body   42**

▶ CHAPTER 6
The Human Body   43

▶ CHAPTER 7
Pathophysiology   52

▶ CHAPTER 8
Life Span Development   58

Module 3

Pharmacology   64

▶ CHAPTER 9
Pharmacology   65

Module 4

**Airway Management, Respiration,
and Ventilation   70**

▶ CHAPTER 10
**Airway Management, Respiration,
and Ventilation   71**

Module 5

Patient Assessment   79

▶ CHAPTER 11
**Therapeutic Communications
and Patient History   80**

▶ CHAPTER 12
Patient Assessment   86

Module 6

Medical Emergencies   97

▶ CHAPTER 13
Medical Overview   100

▶ CHAPTER 14
Neurologic Disorders   103

▶ CHAPTER 15
Endocrine Disorders   112

▶ CHAPTER 16
Respiratory Disorders   118

▶ CHAPTER 17
Cardiovascular Disorders   127

▶ CHAPTER 18
Abdominal and Gastrointestinal Disorders   139

► CHAPTER 19
Genitourinary and Renal Disorders   143

► CHAPTER 20
Gynecologic Disorders   148

► CHAPTER 21
Anaphylaxis   155

► CHAPTER 22
Toxicology   163

► CHAPTER 23
Psychiatric Disorders   170

► CHAPTER 24
Diseases of the Nose   176

Module 7

Shock   179

► CHAPTER 25
Shock   180

Module 8

Trauma   185

► CHAPTER 26
Trauma Overview   187

► CHAPTER 27
Bleeding and Soft Tissue Trauma   193

► CHAPTER 28
Chest Trauma   204

► CHAPTER 29
Abdominal and Genitourinary
Trauma   209

► CHAPTER 30
Trauma to Muscles and Bones   214

► CHAPTER 31
Head, Face, Neck and Spine Trauma   222

► CHAPTER 32
Special Considerations in Trauma   229

► CHAPTER 33
Environmental Emergencies   237

► CHAPTER 34
Multisystem Trauma   243

Module 9

Special Patient Populations   246

► CHAPTER 35
Obstetrics   247

► CHAPTER 36
Neonatal Care   253

► CHAPTER 37
Pediatrics   259

► CHAPTER 38
Older Adults   266

► CHAPTER 39
Patients with Special Challenges   272

Module 10

EMS Operations   277

► CHAPTER 40
Principles of Emergency Response
and Transportation   279

► CHAPTER 41
Incident Management   286

► CHAPTER 42
Multiple-Casualty Incidents   289

► CHAPTER 43
Air Medical Transport   293

► CHAPTER 44
Vehicle Extrication   296

► CHAPTER 45
Hazardous Materials Awareness   301

► CHAPTER 46
Terrorism and Disaster Response   308

Preface

This workbook provides you with an opportunity to review and master the concepts and skills introduced in your textbook, *Emergency Medical Responder: First Responder in Action*, second edition. Chapter by chapter, the workbook provides the following:

Reading Assignment
Provides corresponding textbook page numbers for review prior to completing the workbook exercises.

Sum It Up
A bulleted list of the key information covered in the chapter.

Tracking Your Progress
Readers can check off the objectives they have mastered after learning the chapter content.

Quiz Content
Includes a full range of question types: true or false, multiple choice, sentence completion, matching, and short answer. Each quiz allows the reader to ensure that he or she has mastered the information presented in the text chapter.

Quiz Answers
Provided, by chapter, in one section at the end of the book.

Together, your textbook and this workbook form a complete learning package. *Emergency Medical Responder: First Responder in Action*, second edition, will help you prepare to provide safe and immediate patient care and work effectively as part of an EMS team.

Module 1

Preparatory

▶ CHAPTER **1**

EMS Systems and Research   2

▶ CHAPTER **2**

Workforce Safety and Wellness   11

▶ CHAPTER **3**

Legal and Ethical Issues and Documentation   22

▶ CHAPTER **4**

EMS System Communications   31

▶ CHAPTER **5**

Medical Terminology   38

EMS Systems and Research

READING ASSIGNMENT ▶ Read Chapter 1, pages 1 to 29 in your textbook.

Sum It Up

- The EMS system is a network of resources that provides emergency care and transportation to victims of sudden illness or injury. An EMR is a member of the EMS team who provides prehospital emergency care.
- A healthcare system is a network of people, facilities, and equipment designed to provide for the general medical needs of the population. The EMS system is part of the healthcare system.
- The *National EMS Scope of Practice* is a document that defines four levels of EMS professionals: EMRs, EMTs, advanced EMTs, and paramedics. This document also defines what each level of EMS professional legally can and cannot do. EMRs and EMTs provide basic life support. AEMTs and paramedics provide advanced life support.
- The *National EMS Education Standards* document specifies the objectives that each level of EMS professional must meet when completing his or her education.
- Each state has the authority and responsibility to regulate EMS within its borders and determine how its EMS personnel are certified or licensed. Certification is a designation that ensures a person has met predetermined requirements to perform a particular activity. Licensure is the granting of written permission by the state to perform medical acts and procedures not permitted without authorization. Credentialing is a local process by which an individual is permitted by a specific entity (such as a medical director) to practice in a specific setting (such as an EMS agency).
- Every EMS system must have a medical director. A medical director is a physician who provides medical oversight and is responsible for making sure that the emergency care provided to ill or injured patients is medically appropriate.
- Medical oversight may be on-line or off-line. On-line medical direction is direct communication with a physician by radio or telephone—or face-to-face communication at the scene—before a skill is performed or care is given. Off-line medical direction is the medical supervision of EMS personnel by means of policies, treatment protocols, standing orders, education, and quality management reviews.

- A treatment protocol is a list of steps to be followed when EMS personnel are providing emergency care to an ill or injured patient. Standing orders are written orders that allow EMS personnel to perform certain medical procedures before making direct contact with a physician.
- Quality management is a system of internal and external reviews and audits of all aspects of an EMS system. Quality management is used to identify areas of the EMS system needing improvement. This system helps make sure that the patient receives the highest-quality medical care.
- The phases of a typical EMS response include detection of the emergency, reporting of the emergency (the call made for assistance), dispatch/response (medical resources sent to the scene), on-scene care, care during transport, and transfer to definitive care.
- Characteristics of professional behavior include integrity, empathy, self-motivation, appearance and hygiene, self-confidence, communication, respect, time management, teamwork and diplomacy, patient advocacy, and careful delivery of service.
- Primary duties of the EMR include preparing for the call; ensuring personal safety as well as that of the EMS crew, patient, and bystanders; responding to the call for assistance; performing a scene size-up; gaining access to the patient; performing a patient assessment; providing initial emergency care; transferring patient care; documenting the emergency per local and state requirements; and returning to service.
- Additional duties of the EMR include community involvement and personal professional development.
- Research is essential to determine the effectiveness of new procedures, medications, and treatments in improving patient care and outcome. If you are asked to participate in research, approach this responsibility seriously and complete the task assigned to the best of your ability.

▶ Tracking Your Progress

After reading this chapter, can you:	Page Reference	Objective Met?
• Define the components of Emergency Medical Services (EMS) systems?	1	☐
• Differentiate the roles and responsibilities of the emergency medical responder (EMR) from those of other prehospital care professionals?	10	☐
• Define the terms certification, licensure, credentialing, and scope of practice?	11	☐
• Describe the benefits of EMR continuing education?	12	☐
• Define medical oversight and discuss the emergency medical responder's role in the process?	12	☐
• Discuss the types of medical oversight that may affect the medical care given by an EMR?	13	☐
• Explain quality management and the EMR's role in the quality management process?	16	☐
• Describe the phases of a typical EMS response?	17	☐
• Describe examples of professional behaviors in the following areas: integrity, empathy, self-motivation, appearance and personal hygiene, self-confidence, communication, respect, time management, teamwork and diplomacy, patient advocacy, and careful delivery of service?	19	☐

	Page Reference	Objective Met?
• List the primary and additional responsibilities of the EMR?	22	☐
• Define the role of the EMR relative to the responsibility for personal safety, the safety of the crew, the patient, and the bystanders?	23	☐
• Describe the importance and benefits of research?	27	☐

Chapter Quiz

True/False

Decide whether each statement is true or false. In the space provided, write T for true or F for false.

_____ **1.** A scene size-up is performed to sort patients by the seriousness of their injuries.

_____ **2.** Advanced EMTs and paramedics are often referred to as advanced life support, or ALS, personnel.

Multiple Choice

In the space provided, identify the letter of the choice that best completes each statement or answers each question.

_____ **3.** Which one of the following organizations contributes to the development of professional standards and verifies the skills and knowledge of EMS professionals by preparing and conducting examinations?

  a. The National Association of State EMS Directors
  b. The National Association of Emergency Physicians
  c. The National Registry of emergency medical technicians
  d. The National Council of State EMS Training Coordinators

_____ **4.** You arrive on the scene of a motor vehicle crash involving a minivan. You observe heavy damage to the vehicle. Your *primary* concern at the scene should be

  a. personal safety.
  b. bystander safety.
  c. the well-being of the patient.
  d. determining the total number of patients.

_____ **5.** Before approaching the patient in the crash described in question 4, you should

  a. determine the location of the nearest hospital.
  b. contact a physician for instructions about how to proceed.
  c. put on personal protective equipment and size up the scene.
  d. await the arrival of personnel with more advanced medical training.

_____ **6.** The EMS system is usually activated by using

  a. pagers.
  b. telephones.
  c. citizen band radios.
  d. emergency alarm boxes.

_____ **7.** Which of the following tasks correctly reflects skills that may be performed by an emergency medical responder?

  a. Controlling bleeding
  b. Giving medications into a vein
  c. Identifying abnormal heart rhythms
  d. Performing advanced airway procedures

_____ 8. The process by which a physician directs the emergency care provided by EMS personnel to an ill or injured patient is called
   a. certification.
   b. system regulation.
   c. medical oversight.
   d. resource management.

_____ 9. When medical personnel with more advanced training arrive at the scene of an emergency, you should:
   a. immediately leave the scene.
   b. ask them to obtain information from bystanders.
   c. identify yourself and give a courteous, clear, complete, and concise verbal report.
   d. instruct them to stand back and wait until you have completed your assessment of the patient.

_____ 10. The four nationally recognized levels of prehospital professionals, *from least to most advanced*, are
   a. Paramedic, advanced emergency medical technician, emergency medical technician, and emergency medical responder.
   b. Emergency medical responder, emergency medical technician, advanced emergency medical technician, and paramedic.
   c. Emergency medical technician, emergency medical responder, advanced emergency medical technician, and paramedic.
   d. Emergency medical responder, advanced emergency medical technician, emergency medical technician, and paramedic.

_____ 11. The process of removing structural components from around a patient to facilitate patient care and transport is called
   a. triage.
   b. extrication.
   c. stabilization.
   d. immobilization.

_____ 12. Two patients have been found trapped inside a vehicle. The patients are assessed, and medical direction is then contacted by telephone. This communication is an example of
   a. on-line medical direction.
   b. off-line medical direction.
   c. prospective medical direction.
   d. retrospective medical direction.

_____ 13. One of the patients in question 12, a 30-year-old man, has experienced severe injuries. To which of the following specialty centers should he be transported for definitive care?
   a. Stroke center
   b. Trauma center
   c. Poison center
   d. Rehabilitation center

_____ 14. States use the standards set by which of the following organizations to evaluate the effectiveness of their EMS system?
   a. American College of Surgeons
   b. Federal Communications Commission
   c. American College of Emergency Physicians
   d. National Highway Traffic Safety Administration

_____ 15. Enhanced 9-1-1
   a. prioritizes emergency calls.
   b. locates and dispatches the closest appropriate public safety vehicle.
   c. sends medical personnel to an emergency scene without the assistance of a dispatcher.
   d. routes an emergency call to the 9-1-1 center closest to the caller and displays the caller's phone number and address.

Matching

Match the key terms in the left column with the definitions in the right column by placing the letter of each correct answer in the space provided.

_____ **16.** *National EMS Scope of Practice Model*

_____ **17.** EMRs and EMTs

_____ **18.** Detection

_____ **19.** Vital signs

_____ **20.** Medical oversight

_____ **21.** Empathy

_____ **22.** Prospective medical direction

_____ **23.** Stroke center

_____ **24.** Teamwork

_____ **25.** *National EMS Education Standards*

_____ **26.** Integrity

_____ **27.** Diplomacy

_____ **28.** *National EMS Core Content*

_____ **29.** Retrospective medical direction

_____ **30.** Communication

_____ **31.** Perinatal center

A. Activities performed by a physician after an emergency call

B. Center that specializes in diagnosing and treating diseases of the blood vessels of the brain

C. Tact and skill in dealing with people

D. Identifying with and understanding the feelings, situations, and motives of others

E. The exchange of thoughts, messages, and information

F. Specifies the objectives that each level of EMS professional must meet when completing his or her education

G. Center that specializes in the care of high-risk pregnancies

H. The process by which a physician directs the emergency care provided by EMS personnel to an ill or injured patient

I. Examples of basic life support personnel

J. Telling the truth and providing complete and accurate documentation are examples of this behavior

K. First phase of a typical EMS response

L. Defines four levels of EMS professionals and also defines what each level of EMS professional legally can and cannot do

M. The ability to work with others to achieve a common goal

N. Measurements of breathing, pulse, skin temperature, pupils, and blood pressure

O. The development of treatment protocols and standing orders are examples of this type of medical direction

P. This document defines the domain of prehospital care

Short Answer

Answer each question in the space provided.

32. List the 10 essential components of an Emergency Medical Services (EMS) system.

    1.

    2.

    3.

    4.

    5.

    6.

    7.

    8.

    9.

    10.

33. List six of the primary duties of an emergency medical responder.

    1.

    2.

    3.

    4.

    5.

    6.

34. Explain how the role of a paramedic differs from your role as an emergency medical responder.

35. List the six phases of a typical EMS response.

    1.

    2.

    3.

    4.

    5.

    6.

36. Why is it important to maintain a professional appearance when on duty or when responding to calls?

Answer Section

True/False

1. False

Upon arriving at the scene, EMRs quickly "size-up" the scene to find out if it is safe to enter. A scene size-up is done to:

- Find out if the scene is safe.
- Identify the mechanism of injury or the nature of the illness.
- Identify the total number of patients.
- Request additional help if necessary.

Objective: Define the role of the EMR relative to the responsibility for personal safety, the safety of the crew, the patient, and the bystanders.

2. True

An EMR is a person who has the basic knowledge and skills necessary to provide lifesaving emergency care while waiting for the arrival of additional EMS help. Advanced EMTs (AEMTs) and paramedics can perform all EMT skills and have received additional training in patient assessment, providing IV fluids and medications, advanced airway procedures, and monitoring heart rhythms.

Objective: Differentiate the roles and responsibilities of an EMR from other prehospital care professionals.

Multiple Choice

3. c

The National Registry of EMTs (NREMT) provides examinations for certification and registration that may be required by your state. Recognition as a nationally registered EMR requires successful completion of a written and practical skills examination.

4. a

Although the patient's well-being is an important concern at the scene of an emergency, your personal safety **must** be your primary concern, followed by the safety of your crew, patients, and bystanders.

Objective: Define the role of the EMR relative to the responsibility for personal safety, the safety of the crew, the patient, and the bystanders.

5. c

When you arrive at the scene and before you begin patient care, size up the scene. You should first determine if the scene is safe. You should then identify the mechanism of the injury or the nature of the illness, identify the total number of patients, and request additional help if necessary. Before approaching the patient, put on appropriate personal protective equipment (PPE). This helps reduce your risk of exposure to potentially infectious body fluid substances or other infectious agents.

Objective: Define the role of the EMR relative to the responsibility for personal safety, the safety of the crew, the patient, and the bystanders.

6. b

EMS is usually activated by dialing 9-1-1 using a standard telephone. Other methods of activating an emergency response include emergency alarm boxes, citizen band radios, amateur radios, local access numbers, and wireless telephones.

7. a

Of the skills listed, controlling bleeding can be performed by all levels of prehospital personnel, including an EMR. Giving medications into a vein, identifying abnormal heart rhythms, and performing advanced airway procedures and generally considered advanced life support skills.

Objective: Differentiate the roles and responsibilities of an EMR from other prehospital care professionals.

8. c

EMS personnel to an ill or injured patient. It is also referred to as medical control or medical direction.

Objective: Define medical direction and discuss the EMR's role in the process.

9. c

When medical personnel with more advanced training arrive at the scene of an emergency, you should identify yourself and give a courteous, clear, complete, and concise verbal report.

Objective: List the primary and additional responsibilities of the EMR.

10. b

The four nationally recognized levels of prehospital professionals, *from least to most advanced*, are emergency medical responder, emergency medical technician, advanced emergency medical technician, and paramedic.

Objective: Differentiate the roles and responsibilities of an EMR from other prehospital care professionals.

11. b

Extrication is the process of removing structural components from around a patient to facilitate patient care and transport.

12. a

Medical oversight may be on-line or off-line. On-line medical direction is direct communication with a physician by radio or telephone—or face-to-face communication at the scene—before a skill is performed or care is given. Off-line medical direction is the medical supervision of EMS personnel by means of policies, treatment protocols, standing orders, education, and quality management reviews.

Objective: Discuss the types of medical oversight that may affect the medical care given by an EMR.

13. b

A trauma center is a specialty center where specially trained personnel and equipment are available 24 hours a day to care for patients with serious injuries.

Objective: Define the role of the EMR relative to the responsibility for personal safety, the safety of the crew, the patient, and the bystanders.

14. d

In 1988, NHTSA began a statewide EMS system Technical Assistance Program (TAP). This program identified 10 essential parts of an EMS system and the methods used to assess these areas. States use the standards set by NHTSA to evaluate how effective their EMS system is.

15. d

Enhanced 9-1-1 is a system that routes an emergency call to the 9-1-1 center closest to the caller, and automatically displays the caller's phone number and address.

Matching

16.	L	**24.**	M
17.	I	**25.**	F
18.	K	**26.**	J
19.	N	**27.**	C
20.	H	**28.**	P
21.	D	**29.**	A
22.	O	**30.**	E
23.	B	**31.**	G

Short Answer

32. Regulation and policy, resource management, human resources and training, transportation, facilities, communications, public information and education, medical oversight, trauma systems, evaluation

Objective: Define the components of Emergency Medical Services (EMS) systems.

33. Primary duties of the EMR include preparing for the call; ensuring personal safety as well as that of the EMS crew, patient, and bystanders; responding to the call for assistance; performing a scene size-up; gaining access to the patient; performing a patient assessment; providing initial emergency care; transferring patient care; documenting the emergency per local and state requirements; and returning to service.

Objective: List the primary and additional responsibilities of the EMR.

34. An emergency medical responder is the first person with medical training who arrives at the scene of an emergency. An emergency medical responder provides initial emergency care, including assessing for life-threatening conditions. A paramedic is the most advanced level of EMS professional. A paramedic has received additional education in patient assessment, intravenous fluid and medication administration, advanced airway procedures, assessment of heart rhythms, diseases, physical examination techniques, and invasive procedures. A paramedic can perform all the skills of an emergency medical responder, an emergency medical technician, and an advanced emergency medical technician.

Objective: Differentiate the roles and responsibilities of the emergency medical responder (EMR) from those of other prehospital care professionals.

35. The six phases of a typical EMS response are:

1. Detection of the emergency
2. Reporting of the emergency (the call made for assistance)
3. Dispatch/response (medical resources sent to the scene)
4. On-scene care
5. Care during transport
6. Transfer to definitive care

Objective: Describe the phases of a typical EMS response.

36. Presenting a neat, clean, and professional appearance invites trust, instills confidence, enhances cooperation, and brings a sense of order to an emergency situation.

Objective: Describe examples of professional behaviors in the following areas: integrity, empathy, self-motivation, appearance and personal hygiene, self-confidence, communication, respect, time management, teamwork and diplomacy, patient advocacy, and careful delivery of service.

CHAPTER

2

Workforce Safety and Wellness

READING ASSIGNMENT Read Chapter 2, pages 30 to 78 in your textbook.

Sum It Up

- As an EMR, you will encounter many stressful situations. A stressor is any event or condition that has the potential to cause bodily or mental tension. To be an effective EMR, you must learn to recognize the physical, behavioral, mental, or emotional signs of stress.

- You should manage stress through lifestyle changes. These changes include developing good dietary habits, exercising, and practicing relaxation techniques. You should also seek to create balance in your life, including time with family and friends.

- Professional help may be needed to help you cope with stress. Many organizations have employee assistance programs that offer confidential counseling to prehospital professionals.

- An EMR is responsible for ensuring the safety of the crew, the patient, and bystanders. However, an EMR's first priority is ensuring his or her own safety at all scenes. This responsibility includes protecting oneself against disease transmission, including using personal protective equipment and having the proper vaccinations. It also involves safety at hazardous materials scenes, motor vehicle crashes and rescue scenes, and violent scenes.

- As an EMR, you will most often give initial emergency care to a patient in the position in which the patient is found. You will need to be able to distinguish an emergency from a nonemergency situation. Your role will also include positioning patients to prevent further injury and assisting other EMS professionals in lifting and moving patients.

- Body mechanics is the way we move our bodies when lifting and moving. Body mechanics includes body alignment, balance, and coordinated body movement. Good posture is key to proper body alignment.

- To lift safely, you should use the power grip (underhand grip). To perform this grip, you should position your hands a comfortable distance apart (about 10 inches). With your palms up, grasp the object you are preparing to lift. The power grip allows you to take full advantage of the strength of your hands, forearms, and biceps.

- Safely lifting patients requires that you use good posture and good body mechanics. You should consider the weight of the patient and call for additional help if needed. Plan how and where you will move the patient. It is also important to remember to lift with your legs and not your back. When you are lifting with other EMS professionals, communication and planning are key.

- An emergency move is used when there is an immediate danger to you or the patient. These dangers include scene hazards, the inability to reach patients who need lifesaving care, and a patient location or position that prevents you from giving immediate and lifesaving care.

- Drags are one type of emergency move. When dragging a patient, remember to stabilize the patient's head and neck as much as possible before beginning the move. Also, always remember to pull along the length of the spine. *Never* pull the patient's head away from his neck and shoulders. You should also never drag a patient sideways. Carries are the second major type of emergency move. As an EMR, you should become familiar with the different types of carries.

- An urgent move is used to move a patient when there is an immediate threat to life, such as in the following situations: altered mental status, inadequate breathing, or shock. Rapid extrication is an example of an urgent move. It must be accomplished quickly, without compromise or injury to the spine. This skill is performed by emergency medical technicians and advanced life support personnel.

- Nonurgent moves are used to move, lift, or carry patients with no known or suspected injury to the head, neck, spine, or extremities. The direct ground lift and the extremity lift are the two main types of nonurgent moves.

- The direct carry and the draw sheet method are the two primary methods used to transfer a supine patient to a bed or stretcher. In both transfer types, you will be assisting hospital personnel or another EMS professional. Therefore, teamwork and coordination are essential.

- Patient positioning is an important part of the patient care you provide. In some cases, simply changing a patient's position can improve her condition. As an EMR, you should become familiar with the different types of positions and when to use them.

- Many different types of equipment are used to assist in stabilizing and moving patients. In your role as an emergency care provider, it is important to become familiar with the equipment used in your area. Commonly used equipment includes various types of stretchers and backboards as well as the stair chair.

- Avoid restraining a patient unless the patient is a danger to you, himself, or others. When using restraints, have police present, if possible, and get approval from medical direction. If you must use restraints, apply them with the help of law enforcement and other EMS personnel.

- Critically ill or injured patients may experience grief, which is a normal response to a loss of any kind. The five stages of grief are denial, anger, bargaining, depression, and acceptance. Remember that a person going through grief may skip a stage, go through more than one stage at the same time, or go through each stage more than once. Cultural factors influence how a person experiences grief.

- Patients may experience any number of emotions in response to their illness or injury. As an EMR, you must be respectful of each patient. Listen with empathy to the patient's concerns but do not give the patient false hope or false reassurance. In dealing with the patient's family or friends or with bystanders, you may need to use many of the same approaches you use in dealing with patients.

- Some patients may not want aggressive efforts aimed at reviving them when they are dying. These patients may have an advance directive or a DNR order. An advance directive is a legal document that details a person's healthcare wishes when she becomes unable to make decisions for herself. A DNR order is written by a physician. It instructs medical professionals not to provide medical care to a patient who has experienced a cardiac arrest.

- The signs of obvious death include decapitation (beheading), putrefaction (decomposition), dependent lividity, and rigor mortis. If a person shows signs of obvious death, do not disturb the body or scene. The police or medical examiner will need to authorize removing the body. You should document the victim's position and injuries. You should also document the conditions at the scene as well as statements of persons at the scene.

▶ Tracking Your Progress

After reading this chapter, can you:	Page Reference	Objective Met?
• Discuss the concept of wellness?	33	☐
• Define the components of wellness?	33	☐
• Discuss the components of wellness associated with physical well-being?	33	☐
• Define stress?	33	☐
• Discuss the benefits of physical fitness?	33	☐
• Discuss the importance of obtaining adequate rest?	33	☐
• Define stressor and name common stressors associated with working in Emergency Medical Services?	34	☐
• Give examples of stressful situations that may be encountered in EMS?	34	☐
• Describe the body's fight-or-flight response?	35	☐
• Give examples of physical, behavioral, mental, and emotional signs of stress?	36	
• State the possible steps that EMS professionals may take to help reduce or alleviate stress?	37	☐
• State the possible reactions that members of the EMS professional's family may exhibit due to their outside involvement in EMS?	37	☐
• Define traumatic incident and give examples of traumatic incident situations?	38	☐
• Recognize the signs and symptoms of traumatic incident stress?	38	☐
• Define infection, pathogen, and communicable disease?	38	☐
• Describe methods of disease transmission?	39	☐
• Define infectious disease exposure?	39	☐
• Discuss the classification of communicable diseases?	39	☐
• Discuss the importance of standard precautions?	40	☐
• Describe the steps EMS professionals should take for personal protection from airborne and bloodborne pathogens?	41	☐
• Describe how to document and manage an infectious disease exposure?	45	☐
• Distinguish among the terms cleaning, disinfection, and sterilization?	45	☐
• Describe how to clean or disinfect items following patient care?	45	☐
• Define hazardous material and list the personal protective equipment necessary in a hazardous materials situation?	46	☐
• List the personal protective equipment necessary during rescue operations?	48	☐
• List the personal protective equipment necessary at a violent scene?	48	☐

After reading this chapter, can you:	Page Reference	Objective Met?
• List possible warning signs of danger at residences, street scenes, and highway encounters?	49	☐
• List methods to avoid disturbing evidence at a crime scene?	49	☐
• Describe the indications for an emergency move, urgent move, and nonurgent move?	50	☐
• Describe the steps for performing an emergency move, urgent move, and nonurgent move?	50	☐
• Define body mechanics?	50	☐
• Discuss the guidelines and safety precautions that need to be followed when lifting a patient?	52	☐
• Describe the guidelines and safety precautions for carrying patients and/or equipment?	52	☐
• Describe correct and safe carrying procedures on stairs?	54	☐
• State the guidelines for reaching and their application?	54	☐
• Describe correct reaching for log rolls?	54	☐
• State the guidelines for pushing and pulling?	54	☐
• Discuss positioning patients with different conditions such as unresponsiveness, chest pain/discomfort or difficulty breathing, suspected spine injury, shock (hypoperfusion), and pregnancy?	60	☐
• Discuss the various devices associated with moving a patient in the prehospital setting?	67	☐
• Describe how to restrain a patient safely?	71	☐
• Describe the information that must be documented regarding the use of restraints?	72	☐
• Give examples of changes in circumstances that can cause an individual to go through the grieving process?	72	☐
• Describe the stages of grief?	72	☐
• List signs of obvious death?	75	☐
• Discuss the EMS professional's approach to a patient who is dying?	75	☐
• Discuss how an EMS professional should convey the news of a death to concerned survivors?	76	☐
• Discuss the possible reactions that a patient's family member may exhibit when confronted with death and dying?	76	☐

Chapter Quiz

Multiple Choice

In the space provided, identify the letter of the choice that best completes each statement or answers each question.

_____ 1. You respond to a residence for a possible drowning. You arrive to find law enforcement personnel performing CPR on a 3-year-old boy. The child was found floating facedown in the pool. He was last seen 10 or 15 minutes ago. Before approaching the patient, you should

    a. take a moment to wash your hands before beginning patient care.

    b. locate the child's parents and ask about the child's medical history.

    c. contact the closest hospital to let them know they will be receiving a patient.

    d. quickly survey the scene for possible hazards and put on appropriate personal protective equipment.

_____ **2.** How should you approach the mother of the child in question 1?
  a. Ask her how she could have let something like this happen.
  b. Calmly but firmly tell her that it appears her son will not survive.
  c. Let her know that everything that can be done to help will be done.
  d. Using a gentle tone of voice, tell her that everything is going to be okay.

_____ **3.** Standard precautions include
  a. self-protection against all body fluids and substances.
  b. procedures used by EMS personnel when dealing with a violent patient.
  c. the rescue equipment that should be worn at the scene of a motor vehicle crash.
  d. procedures used by EMS personnel when relaying the news about a patient's death.

_____ **4.** Which of the following is an example of a situation requiring an emergency move?
  a. An 88-year-old man who is sitting in a chair in his home and is confused
  b. A 57-year-old woman who is in a supermarket complaining of difficulty breathing
  c. A 5-year-old boy who is sitting on the bench in the park complaining of stomach pain
  d. A 72-year-old woman who is sitting in a chair and is unresponsive, not breathing, and has no pulse

_____ **5.** The single most important method you can use to prevent the spread of communicable disease is
  a. washing your hands.
  b. following a balanced diet.
  c. wearing vinyl or latex gloves.
  d. keeping your immunizations current.

_____ **6.** Which of the following may be used in a high-angle rescue?
  a. Wheeled stretcher, basket stretcher
  b. Basket stretcher, flexible stretcher
  c. Portable stretcher, wheeled stretcher
  d. Flexible stretcher, scoop stretcher

_____ **7.** Hepatitis B virus (HBV) is an example of a(n)
  a. airborne disease.
  b. foodborne disease.
  c. bloodborne disease.
  d. sexually transmitted disease.

_____ **8.** Which of the following is an example of an emergency move?
  a. Direct ground lift
  b. Extremity lift
  c. Direct carry
  d. Blanket drag

_____ **9.** You should wear a high-efficiency particulate air (HEPA) mask when providing care to a patient known to be or suspected to be infected with
  a. tetanus.
  b. measles.
  c. hepatitis B.
  d. tuberculosis.

_____ **10.** Which of the following statements is true regarding safe lifting techniques?
  a. Place your feet close together.
  b. Know your physical abilities and limitations.
  c. Use the large muscles of your back to lift.
  d. Keep the weight a minimum of 20 to 30 inches from your body.

Matching

Match the key terms in the left column with the definitions in the right column by placing the letter of each correct answer in the space provided.

_____ 11. Terminal illness

_____ 12. Physical well-being

_____ 13. Do not resuscitate order

_____ 14. Pathogens

_____ 15. Stress

_____ 16. Airborne disease

_____ 17. Empathy

_____ 18. Grief

_____ 19. Rigor mortis

_____ 20. Communicable disease

_____ 21. Sleep deprivation

_____ 22. Dependent lividity

_____ 23. Cumulative stress

_____ 24. Advance directive

_____ 25. Exposure

_____ 26. Cleaning

_____ 27. Traumatic incident

_____ 28. Stressor

_____ 29. Occupational Safety and Health Administration

_____ 30. Disinfecting

_____ 31. Standard precautions

_____ 32. Sterilizing

_____ 33. Hazardous material

_____ 34. Personal protective equipment

A. Cleaning with chemical solutions such as alcohol or chlorine

B. Repeated exposure to smaller stressors that build up over time

C. To understand, be aware of, and be sensitive to the feelings, thoughts, and experiences of another

D. A normal response that helps people cope with the loss of someone or something that had great meaning to them

E. A legal document that specifies a person's healthcare wishes when he or she becomes unable to make decisions for him or herself

F. A condition caused by disturbances in the amount, quality, and consistency of sleep

G. The process of washing a contaminated object with soap and water

H. The settling of blood in areas on which the body has been resting

I. Any event or condition that has the potential to cause bodily or mental tension

J. An illness or injury for which there is no reasonable expectation of recovery

K. A component of wellness

L. Any substance that causes or may cause adverse effects on the health or safety of employees, the general public, or the environment

M. An infection that can be spread from one person to another

N. A situation that causes a healthcare provider to experience unusually strong emotions and may interfere with the provider's psychological ability to cope and function immediately or later

O. Germs capable of producing disease

P. Using boiling water, radiation, gas, chemicals, or superheated steam to destroy all the germs on an object

Q. The stiffening of body muscles that occurs after death

R. A branch of the federal government responsible for safety in the workplace

Continued

S. Self-protection against all body fluids and substances

T. Specialized clothing or equipment worn by an individual for protection against a hazard

U. Contact with infected blood, body fluids, tissues, or airborne droplets, either directly or indirectly

V. A chemical, physical, or emotional factor that causes bodily or mental tension

W. A written physician order that instructs medical professionals not to provide medical care to a patient who has experienced a cardiopulmonary arrest

X. An infection spread by droplets produced by coughing or sneezing

Short Answer

Answer each question in the space provided.

35. List six examples of stressful situations you may encounter as an emergency medical responder.
    1.
    2.
    3.
    4.
    5.
    6.

36. A 62-year-old man was the unrestrained driver of a vehicle that struck a power pole at approximately 80 miles per hour. What is the greatest danger in moving this patient, if you determine that an emergency move is necessary?

37. The mother of a 3-year-old boy has just been informed that her son drowned in the backyard pool. Describe the possible reactions of the child's mother to this situation.

38. You are called to the scene of a motor vehicle crash. A patient requires extrication from one of the vehicles involved in the crash. List four items of protective clothing that should be worn during this situation.

1.

2.

3.

4.

39. List three lifestyle changes you can make to help reduce stress.

1.

2.

3.

40. List the five stages of the grief process.

1.

2.

3.

4.

5.

41. List the information that must be documented when restraints are used.

42. You are preparing to transfer a patient from a stretcher to a bed using a direct carry. Where should you place the stretcher?

Answer Section

Multiple Choice

1. d

When you arrive at the scene and before you begin patient care, size up the scene to find out if it is safe to enter. Before approaching the patient, put on appropriate personal protective equipment to help reduce your risk of exposure to potentially infectious body fluid substances or other infectious agents.

Objective: Define the role of the EMR relative to the responsibility for personal safety, the safety of the crew, the patient, and the bystanders.

2. c

Allow the child's mother to express her feelings and listen empathetically. Let her know that everything that can be done to help will be done, but do not falsely reassure. Use a gentle tone of voice and a reassuring touch, if appropriate.

Objective: Discuss the EMS professional's approach to a patient who is dying.

3. a

Standard precautions refer to self-protection against all body fluids and substances. These fluids and substances include blood, urine, semen, feces, vaginal secretions, tears, and saliva. Standard precautions include handwashing and using personal protective equipment. They also include the proper cleaning, disinfecting, and disposing of soiled materials and equipment.

Objective: Discuss the importance of standard precautions.

4. d

In general, a patient should be moved immediately (an emergency move) when one of the following situations exists: (1) presence of scene hazards, (2) the inability to reach other patients who need lifesaving care, or (3) the inability to provide immediate, lifesaving care because of the patient's location or position.

Objective: Describe the indications for an emergency move, urgent move, and nonurgent move.

5. a

Handwashing is the single most important method you can use to prevent the spread of communicable disease. Frequent handwashing removes germs picked up from other people or from contaminated surfaces. Wash your hands before and after contact with a patient (even if gloves were worn), after removing your gloves, and between patients.

Objective: Describe the steps EMS professionals should take for personal protection from airborne and bloodborne pathogens.

6. b

A basket stretcher is used for moving patients over rough terrain, in water rescues, or in high-angle rescues. A basket stretcher that has a solid bottom can also be pulled over snow and ice (and other terrain), much like a sled.

Objective: Discuss the various devices associated with moving a patient in the prehospital setting.

7. c

Bloodborne diseases are spread by contact with the blood or body fluids of an infected person. Examples include hepatitis B virus (HBV), hepatitis C, human immunodeficiency virus (HIV), and syphilis.

Objective: Discuss the classification of communicable diseases.

8. d

A blanket drag is an example of an emergency move.

Objective: Describe the indications for an emergency move, urgent move, and nonurgent move.

9. d

Wear a surgical-type face mask to protect against the possible splatter of blood or other body fluids. Also wear a face mask in situations in which an airborne disease is suspected. The mask should be changed if it becomes moist. If you know or suspect that your patient has tuberculosis, wear an N95 or high-efficiency particulate air (HEPA) mask.

Objective: Describe the steps EMS professionals should take for personal protection from airborne and bloodborne pathogens.

10. b

To prevent injury when lifting, know your physical ability and limitations. Make sure that enough help is available, using at least two people to lift. If possible, always use an even number of people to lift to maintain balance. Use your legs to lift, not your back. Your legs are much stronger than your back. Position your feet a comfortable distance apart (usually a shoulder's width) on a firm surface. Wear proper footwear to protect your feet and maintain a firm footing. Keep the patient's weight as close to you as possible. "Hug the load." Doing so moves your center of gravity closer to the patient, helps maintain balance, and reduces muscle strain.

Objective: Discuss the guidelines and safety precautions that need to be followed when lifting a patient.

Matching

11.	J	**23.**	B
12.	K	**24.**	E
13.	W	**25.**	U
14.	O	**26.**	G
15.	V	**27.**	N
16.	X	**28.**	I
17.	C	**29.**	R
18.	D	**30.**	A
19.	Q	**31.**	S
20.	M	**32.**	P
21.	F	**33.**	L
22.	H	**34.**	T

Short Answer

35. Examples of stressful situations follow:

- Mass-casualty incident
- Infant and child trauma
- Death, terminal illness
- Amputation
- Violence
- Death of a child
- Infant, child, elder, or spousal abuse
- Death or injury of a coworker or other public safety personnel
- Emergency response to illness or injury of a friend or family member

Objective: Give examples of stressful situations that may be encountered in EMS.

36. The greatest danger in moving a patient quickly is the possibility of aggravating a spinal injury. Always drag the patient in the direction of the length (the long axis) of the body. This action will provide as much protection as possible to the patient's spine. Never push, pull, or drag a patient sideways.

Objective: Describe the indications for an emergency move, urgent move, and nonurgent move.

37. People react differently to situations involving illness and injury. The child's mother may express anger, rage, despair, crying, or feelings of guilt or may show little reaction.

Objective: Discuss the possible reactions that a patient's family member may exhibit when confronted with death and dying.

38. Protective clothing that should be worn during this situation includes:

- Puncture-proof gloves
- Turnout gear
- Helmet
- Eye protection (such as heavy goggles)
- Boots with steel toes

Objective: List the personal protective equipment necessary during rescue operations.

39. You should manage stress through lifestyle changes. These changes include developing good dietary habits, exercising, and practicing relaxation techniques. You should also seek to create balance in your life, including time with family and friends. Professional help may be needed to help you cope with stress. Many organizations have employee assistance programs that offer confidential counseling to prehospital professionals.

Objective: State the possible steps that EMS professionals may take to help reduce or alleviate stress.

40. Critically ill or injured patients may experience grief, which is a normal response to a loss of any kind. The five stages of grief are denial, anger, bargaining, depression, and acceptance. Remember that a person going through grief may skip a stage, go through more than one stage at the same time, or go through each stage more than once.

Objective: Describe the stages of grief.

41. When caring for a patient in restraints, document the following information:

- The reason for the restraints
- The number of personnel used to restrain the patient

- The type of restraints used
- The time the restraints were placed on the patient
- The status of the patient's airway, breathing, circulation (ABCs), and distal pulses before and after the restraints were applied
- Reassessment of the patient's ABCs and distal pulses

Objective: Describe the information that must be documented regarding the use of restraints.

42. The stretcher should be placed at a 90-degree angle to the bed, with the head end of the stretcher at the foot of the bed.

Objective: Describe the guidelines and safety precautions for carrying patients and/or equipment.

Legal and Ethical Issues and Documentation

READING ASSIGNMENT ▶ Read Chapter 3, pages 79 to 103 in your textbook.

Sum It Up

- The U.S. government is made up of three branches: legislative, executive, and judicial. Law made by the legislative branch of government is called statutory or legislative law. The rules and regulations made by the executive branch of government are called administrative law. The court system makes up the judicial branch of government. Courts hear cases that challenge or require explanation of the laws passed by the legislative branch of government and approved by the executive branch.
- In a lawsuit, the plaintiff (also called the complainant) is the party that files a formal complaint with the court. The defendant is the party being sued or accused.
- The maximum period within which a plaintiff must begin a lawsuit (in civil cases) or a prosecutor must bring charges (in criminal cases) or lose the right to file the suit is called the statute of limitations.
- Criminal law is the area of law in which the federal, state, or local government prosecutes individuals on behalf of society for violating laws designed to safeguard society.
- Civil law is a branch of law that deals with complaints by individuals or organizations against a defendant for an illegal act or wrongdoing (tort).
- A lawsuit begins when an incident occurs and an individual or organization find that the problems resulting from the incident require the involvement of the courts. The plaintiff's attorney gathers pertinent facts, prepares documents, and files a written statement (the complaint) with the court. After the complaint is filed, copies of the court documents and a summons (notice) are delivered (served) to the defendant (or the defendant's attorney) notifying her that a lawsuit has been filed against her. The defendant's attorney prepares a response to the complaint and files it with the court. A copy of the defendant's answer is sent to the plaintiff's attorney. After a lawsuit is filed, discovery begins. To find out more details about the claim, one party may send written questions (interrogatories) to the other party. Depositions may be taken by either party during discovery; this involves asking individuals oral questions while they are under oath. After discovery is completed, the judge will hold a pretrial conference with the attorneys to further narrow the issues to be decided during the trial. After the trial is finished, a decision is handed down by a judge or jury. The decision determines guilt or liability and the damages and award, if any, to the plaintiff.

- The scope of practice includes the emergency care and skills an EMR is legally allowed and expected to perform. These duties are set by state laws and regulations. As an EMR, you have the ethical responsibilities of treating all patients with respect and giving each patient the best care you are capable of giving. You must also determine if patients are competent (that is, if they can understand the questions you ask and the consequences of the decisions they make about their care).

- A competent patient must give you consent (permission) before you can provide emergency care. Expressed consent is one in which a patient gives specific permission for care and transport to be provided. Expressed consent may be given verbally, in writing, or nonverbally. Implied consent is consent assumed from a patient requiring emergency care who is mentally, physically, or emotionally unable to provide expressed consent.

- Mentally competent adults have the right to refuse care and transport. As an EMR, you must make sure that the patient fully understands your explanation and the consequences of refusing treatment or transport. In high-risk situations in which the patient's injuries may not be obvious, you must contact medical direction or call ALS personnel to the scene to assess the patient.

- An advance directive is a form filled out by the patient. It outlines the patient's wishes for care if the patient is not able to express these wishes. A do not resuscitate order is written by a physician and details the patient's wishes for care when terminally ill.

- Assault is considered to be threatening, attempting, or causing a fear of offensive physical contact with a patient or another person. Battery is the unlawful touching of another person without consent. Because each state has its own definitions of assault and battery, you should check your local protocols concerning these terms.

- Abandonment is terminating patient care without making sure that care will continue at the same level or higher. You can also be charged with abandonment if you stop patient care when the patient still needs and desires additional care.

- A healthcare professional is negligent if he or she fails to act as a reasonable, careful, similarly trained person would act under similar circumstances. Negligence includes the following four elements: (1) the duty to act, (2) a breach of that duty, (3) injury or damages (physical or psychological) that result, and (4) a proximate cause (the actions or inactions of the healthcare professional that caused the injury or damages).

- A medical identification device is used to alert healthcare personnel to a patient's particular medical condition. This identification device may be in the form of a bracelet, a necklace, or an identification card.

- If you are sent to a crime scene, you must wait for law enforcement personnel to declare that the scene is safe to enter. After you are certain the scene is safe and you ensure your safety, your first priority will be patient care. You should be alert and document anything unusual on the call.

- An organ donor is a person who has signed a legal document to donate his organs in the event of death. The patient may have an organ donor card or may have indicated the intent to be a donor on a driver's license.

- Good documentation is complete, clear, concise, objective, timely, accurate, and legible.

- A PCR has many important functions.
  - *Continuity of care.* The PCR may be used by receiving-facility staff to help determine the direction of treatment following the EMS treatments given.
  - *Legal document.* Good documentation reflects the emergency medical care provided, the status of the patient on arrival at the scene, and any changes on arrival at the receiving facility.

- *Education and research.* The PCR can be used to show proper documentation and illustrate how to handle unusual or uncommon situations, as well as to identify training needs for the EMS providers.
- *Administrative.* The PCR is used for billing and EMS service statistics.
- *Quality management.* Completed reports are typically evaluated for adequacy of documentation, compliance with local rules and regulations, compliance with agency documentation standards, and appropriateness of medical care.
- A PCR generally consists of an administrative section, patient and scene information section, and patient assessment (narrative) section.
  - The administrative section includes data pertaining to the EMS call, such as the date, times, service, unit, and crew information.
  - The patient and scene information section includes data such as the patient's name, age, gender, weight, address, date of birth, and insurance information.
  - The patient assessment section includes the patient's chief complaint, mechanism of injury or nature of illness, location of the patient, treatment given before arrival of EMS, patient signs and symptoms, care given, vital signs, medical history, and changes in condition.
- The PCR form and the information on it are considered confidential. Local and state protocols and procedures determine where the different copies of the PCR should be distributed.
- Falsification of information on the PCR may lead not only to suspension or revocation of the EMR's certification and/or license but also to poor patient care because it gives other healthcare professionals a false impression of which assessment findings were discovered or what treatment was given.
- When a documentation error occurs, do not try to cover it up. Instead, document what did or did not happen, include the time and date, and initial your change.

▶ Tracking Your Progress

After reading this chapter, can you:	Page Reference	Objective Met?
• Describe the basic structure of the legal system in the United States?	81	☐
• Define the terms plaintiff, defendant, statute of limitations, criminal law, civil law, and tort?	81	☐
• Differentiate between criminal and civil law?	81	☐
• Discuss the steps in a lawsuit?	81	☐
• Differentiate between the scope of practice and the standard of care for emergency medical responder practice?	82	☐
• Discuss the concept of medical oversight, including off-line medical direction and on-line medical direction, and its relationship to the EMR?	83	☐
• Define ethics?	83	☐
• Describe the ethical responsibilities of the EMR?	83	☐
• Describe a three-part test used for determining a patient's competence?	84	☐
• Define consent and discuss the methods of obtaining consent?	84	☐
• Differentiate between expressed and implied consent?	84	☐
• Explain the role of consent of minors in providing care?	85	☐
• Discuss the implications for the emergency medical responder in patient refusal of transport?	85	☐

After reading this chapter, can you:	Page Reference	Objective Met?
• Explain the purpose of advance directives relative to patient care and how the EMR should care for a patient who is covered by an advance directive?	88	☐
• Define and give examples of comfort care?	89	☐
• Differentiate between assault and battery and describe how to avoid each?	90	☐
• Describe what constitutes abandonment?	90	☐
• Define negligence and describe the four elements that must be present in order to prove negligence?	90	☐
• State the conditions necessary for the emergency medical responder to have a duty to act?	91	☐
• Explain the importance, necessity, and legality of patient confidentiality?	92	☐
• List the actions that an emergency medical responder should take to assist in the preservation of a crime scene?	93	☐
• State the conditions that require an emergency medical responder to notify local law enforcement officials?	94	☐
• Discuss the responsibilities of the EMR relative to emergency care for patients who are potential organ donors?	94	☐
• Describe the legal implications associated with the written report?	94	☐
• Identify the various sections of the written report?	95	☐
• Describe what information is required in each section of the prehospital care report and how it should be entered?	95	☐

Chapter Quiz

True/False

Decide whether each statement is true or false. In the space provided, write T for true or F for false.

_____ 1. The emergency care and skills an emergency medical responder is legally allowed and expected to perform are set by state laws and regulations.

_____ 2. Individuals who violate rules regarding a patient's protected health information may face criminal and civil penalties.

_____ 3. Implied consent requires that the patient be of legal age and be able to understand the consequences of a decision.

_____ 4. You must have written consent from the patient to discuss his health information with other healthcare professionals involved in the medical care of that patient.

_____ 5. A potential organ donor should not be treated differently from any other patient who requires your care.

_____ 6. Criminal law is a branch of law that deals with complaints by individuals or organizations against a defendant for an illegal act or wrongdoing.

Multiple Choice

In the space provided, identify the letter of the choice that best completes each statement or answers each question.

_____ 7. Terminating patient care without making sure that care will continue at the same level or higher is called

    a. damages.

    b. abandonment.

    c. failure to act.

    d. breach of duty.

Questions 8–9 pertain to the following scenario:

You are dispatched to a private residence of an "ill man." You arrive to find a 40-year-old man unresponsive on the living room floor. The patient's 14-year-old daughter states that she arrived home a few minutes ago and found her father in this condition. She immediately called 9-1-1 and then called her mother, who is at work. Your general impression is that the patient appears to be unresponsive. You can see that he is breathing. There are no obvious signs of trauma.

_____ 8. Select the *correct* statement about this situation:
   a. You may provide care for this patient using implied consent.
   b. You may provide care for this patient only if the medical director authorizes you to do so.
   c. You cannot provide care for this patient if he is unable to give you verbal consent to treat him.
   d. You can provide care for this patient based on the child's request that you provide care to her father.

_____ 9. When assessing the patient and attempting to learn the reason he is unresponsive, you should
   a. see if you can locate a neighbor who might have information that will help you.
   b. attempt to locate the patient's wife to find out the patient's medical history.
   c. immediately contact medical direction for any information about the patient in hospital records.
   d. look for a medical identification device; look in the immediate area for signs of a fall, drug overdose, or alcohol use; and ask the patient's daughter about the patient's medical history.

_____ 10. The area of law in which the federal, state, or local government prosecutes individuals on behalf of society for violating laws designed to safeguard society is called
   a. criminal law.
   c. legislative law.
   b. statutory law.
   d. administrative law.

Sentence Completion

In the blanks provided, write the words that best complete each sentence.

11. _____ _____ _____ consists of the emergency care and skills an emergency medical responder is legally allowed and expected to perform when necessary.

12. A written document that specifies a person's healthcare wishes when the person becomes unable to make decisions for him- or herself is known as a(n) _____ _____ .

Matching

Match the key terms in the left column with the definitions in the right column by placing the letter of each correct answer in the space provided.

_____ 13. Assault

_____ 14. Advance directive

_____ 15. Negligence

_____ 16. Abandonment

_____ 17. Battery

_____ 18. Implied consent

_____ 19. Expressed consent

_____ 20. Duty to act

A. The unlawful touching of another person without consent

B. Terminating care of a patient without ensuring that care will continue at the same level or higher

C. Consent in which a patient gives specific authorization for the provision of care and transport

D. A formal contractual or an implied legal obligation to provide care to a patient requesting services

E. Threatening, attempting, or causing fear of offensive physical contact with a patient or another individual

F. A deviation from the accepted standard of care, resulting in further injury to the patient

Continued

G. Consent based on the assumption that the patient would consent to lifesaving interventions if he was able to do so

H. A legal document that specifies a person's healthcare wishes when the person becomes unable to make decisions for him- or herself

Short Answer

Answer each question in the space provided.

21. When can patient care be transferred to another healthcare professional?

22. List the four elements that must be proved in a negligence case.

    1.
    2.
    3.
    4.

23. A 48-year-old man is involved in a high-speed motor vehicle crash. The patient was not restrained. He is alert and oriented to person, place, time, and event. Obvious injuries include minor bleeding from a cut on his forehead and a large bruise on his chest. The patient is refusing treatment and transport to the hospital. Advanced life support personnel are en route to the scene. What information must you give the patient regarding his refusing care?

24. Briefly explain how you should obtain expressed consent from a patient.

25. What is meant by the phrase *statute of limitations?*

Answer Section

True/False

1. True

   The scope of practice includes the emergency care and skills an emergency medical responder is legally allowed and expected to perform. These duties are set by state laws and regulations.

   Objective: Differentiate between the scope of practice and the standard of care for emergency medical technician practice.

2. True

   The Health Insurance Portability and Accountability Act (HIPAA) went into effect in 2003. This law was passed by Congress in 1996, in part, to ensure the confidentiality of a patient's health information. Individuals who disobey HIPAA privacy rules face criminal and civil penalties.

   Objective: Explain the importance, necessity, and legality of patient confidentiality.

3. False

   Objective: Differentiate between expressed and implied consent.

4. False

   You may freely discuss all aspects of your patient's medical condition, the treatment you gave, and any of the patient's health information you have with others involved in the patient's medical care. However, when discussing patient information with another healthcare professional, take a moment to look around you. Be sensitive to your level of voice. Make sure that persons who do not need to know this information are not able to hear what is said.

   Objective: Explain the importance, necessity, and legality of patient confidentiality.

5. True

   An organ donor is a person who has signed a legal document to donate organs in the event of death. This document may be an organ donor card that the patient carries in a wallet. Alternately, the patient may have indicated the intent to be a donor on a driver's license. Family members may also tell you that the patient is an organ donor. A patient who is a potential organ donor should not be treated differently from any other patient who requires your care.

   Objective: Discuss the responsibilities of the EMR relative to emergency care for patients who are potential organ donors.

6. False

   Criminal law is the area of law in which the federal, state, or local government prosecutes individuals on behalf of society for violating laws designed to safeguard society. Civil law is a branch of law that deals with complaints by individuals or organizations against a defendant for an illegal act or wrongdoing (tort).

   Objective: Differentiate between criminal and civil law.

Multiple Choice

7. b

   Abandonment is terminating patient care without making sure that care will continue at the same level or higher. You can be charged with abandonment if you turn the patient over to another healthcare professional with less medical training than you. You can also be charged with abandonment if you stop patient care when the patient still needs and desires additional care.

   Objective: Describe what constitutes abandonment.

8. a

Implied consent is consent assumed from a patient requiring emergency care who is mentally, physically, or emotionally unable to provide expressed consent. Implied consent is sometimes called the *doctrine of implied consent*. Implied consent is based on the assumption that the patient would consent to lifesaving treatment if able to do so. It is effective only until the patient no longer requires emergency care or regains competence to make decisions.

Objective: Differentiate between expressed and implied consent.

9. d

If a patient is unresponsive, look for a medical identification device; look in the immediate area for signs of a fall, drug overdose, or alcohol use; and ask the patient's daughter about the patient's medical history in an attempt to learn the reason he is unresponsive. An identification device may be in the form of a bracelet, a necklace, or an identification card. Medical identification is used to alert healthcare personnel to a patient's particular medical condition. For example, the patient may have diabetes, epilepsy, a heart condition, or a specific allergy. You must consider this information while performing your assessment and patient interview.

10. a

Criminal law is the area of law in which the federal, state, or local government prosecutes individuals on behalf of society for violating laws designed to safeguard society.

Objective: Differentiate between criminal and civil law.

Sentence Completion

11. **Scope** of **practice** (also called scope of care) consists of the emergency care and skills an emergency medical responder is legally allowed and expected to perform when necessary.

Objective: Define the terms certification, licensure, credentialing, and scope of practice.

12. A written document that specifies a person's healthcare wishes when the person becomes

unable to make decisions for him- or herself is known as an **advance** **directive**.

Objective: Explain the purpose of advance directives relative to patient care and how the EMR should care for a patient who is covered by an advance directive.

Matching

13.	E	**17.**	A
14.	H	**18.**	G
15.	F	**19.**	C
16.	B	**20.**	D

Short Answer

21. Patient care may be transferred to another healthcare professional if that person accepts the patient and his medical qualifications are equal to or greater than yours.

Objective: Describe what constitutes abandonment.

22. The four elements that must be proved in a negligence case are the following:

- You had a duty to act
- You breached that duty
- Injury/damages were inflicted
- Your actions or lack of actions caused the injury/damage

Objective: Define negligence, and describe the four elements that must be present in order to prove negligence.

23. You must inform the patient of the following:

- The nature of his injury
- The treatment that needs to be performed
- The benefits of that treatment
- The risks of not providing that treatment
- Any alternatives to treatment
- The dangers of refusing treatment (including transport)

Objective: Discuss the implications for the emergency medical responder in patient refusal of transport.

24. To obtain expressed consent:

- Identify yourself and your level of medical training
- Explain all treatments and procedures to the patient

- Identify the benefits of each treatment or procedure
- Identify the risks of each treatment or procedure

Objective: Differentiate between expressed and implied consent.

25. The statute of limitations is the maximum period within which a plaintiff must begin a lawsuit (in civil cases) or a prosecutor must bring charges (in criminal cases) or lose the right to file the suit. The length of the statute of limitations varies by state and may differ for cases involving adults and children.

Objective: Define the terms plaintiff, defendant, statute of limitations, criminal law, civil law, and tort.

EMS System Communications

READING ASSIGNMENT ▶ Read Chapter 4, pages 104 to 115 in your textbook.

Sum It Up

- Communication is the process of sending and receiving information. As an EMR, you must be able to communicate effectively with crewmembers, emergency dispatchers, medical direction, and other healthcare professionals; law enforcement personnel and other public safety workers; the patient; and the patient's family.
- The Federal Communications Commission (FCC) is the U.S. government agency responsible for the development and enforcement of rules and regulations pertaining to radio transmissions.
- Very high frequency (VHF) radio frequencies can be subdivided into low band and high band. Low-band frequencies generally have a greater range than high-band VHF frequencies. Radio waves in the low-band frequency range bend and follow the curvature of the Earth, allowing radio transmission over long distances. Radio waves in the high-band frequency range travel in a straight line. This straight-line quality means that the radio wave is easily blocked by topography such as a hill, mountain, or large building.
- Ultrahigh frequency (UHF) radio waves travel in a straight line but do have an ability to reflect off or bounce around buildings. The 800-megahertz frequencies are UHF radio signals that use computer technology to make transmissions more secure than the other types of radio transmission.
- A base station is a transmitter/receiver at a stationary site such as a hospital, mountaintop, or public safety agency. A radio signal generated by the base station may be sent directly to a receiving unit or to a repeater as needed. A mobile two-way radio is a vehicular-mounted communication device. A portable radio is a handheld communication device. A repeater is a device that receives a transmission from a low-power portable or mobile radio on one frequency and then retransmits it at a higher power on another frequency so that it can be received at a distant location.
- Mobile data computers, or MDCs (also called mobile data terminals, or MDTs) are computers mounted in emergency vehicles that display information pertaining to the calls for which EMS personnel are dispatched. The computer is also used to send and receive text messages between the EMS crew and the dispatch center.

- An EMS communications network must provide a means by which a citizen can reliably access the EMS system (usually by dialing 9-1-1). To ensure adequate EMS system response and coordination, there must also be a means for communication from dispatch center to emergency vehicle, communication between emergency vehicles, communication from the emergency vehicle to the hospital, communication between hospitals, and communication between agencies, such as between EMS and law enforcement personnel.
- The sequence 9-1-1 is the official national emergency number in the United States and Canada. When the numbers 9-1-1 are dialed, the caller is quickly connected to a single location called a Public Safety Answering Point (PSAP). Although EMS is usually activated by dialing 9-1-1 from a standard telephone, other methods of activating an emergency response include emergency alarm boxes, citizen band radios, and wireless telephones. Enhanced 9-1-1, or E9-1-1, is a system that routes an emergency call to the 9-1-1 center closest to the caller and automatically displays the caller's phone number and address. Voice over Internet Protocol (VoIP, also known as Internet Voice) is technology that allows users to make telephone calls by means of a broadband Internet connection instead of using a regular telephone line.
- Emergency medical dispatchers (EMDs) are trained professionals who are responsible for verifying the address of the incident, asking questions of the caller, assigning responders to the incident, alerting and activating responders to the incident, providing prearrival instructions to the caller, communicating with responders, and recording incident times.
- After being dispatched to the call, dispatch should be notified when the EMS crew is responding to the call, arriving at the scene, leaving the scene for the receiving facility, arriving at the receiving facility, leaving the hospital for the station, returning to service, and arriving at the station.
- When communicating with individuals from other agencies, be organized, concise, thorough, and accurate.
- It may be necessary to contact medical direction for advice or receive other orders. The information given to the physician must be accurate. Repeat orders back to the physician, word for word.
- Use a standardized reporting format when relaying a verbal report to medical direction or to the staff of the receiving facility.
- The Health Insurance Portability and Accountability Act (HIPAA) limits the medical information that may be shared about an individual.

▶ Tracking Your Progress

After reading this chapter, can you:	Page Reference	Objective Met?
• Define communications?	105	☐
• Describe the role of the Federal Communications Commission in EMS system communications?	105	☐
• Describe the following components of an EMS communications system: base station, mobile two-way radio, portable radio, repeater, digital radio equipment, cellular telephone?	106	☐

After reading this chapter, can you:	**Page Reference**	**Objective Met?**
• Discuss the role of an emergency medical dispatcher in a typical EMS event?	109	☐
• List the proper methods of initiating and terminating a radio call?	110	☐
• List the correct radio procedures during each phase of a typical EMS call?	111	☐
• Discuss the communication skills that should be used when interacting with individuals from other agencies?	111	☐
• Identify the essential components of the verbal report?	112	☐
• Explain the importance of effective communication of patient information in the verbal report?	113	☐
• State legal aspects to consider in verbal communication?	114	☐

Chapter Quiz

Multiple Choice

In the space provided, identify the letter of the choice that best completes each statement or answers each question.

_____ 1. Which of the following radio transmission frequencies has the clearest reception ability combined with the shortest range?

    a. UHF frequencies
    b. 800-MHz frequencies
    c. VHF low-band frequencies
    d. VHF high-band frequencies

_____ 2. When transmitting patient information, it is important to be an advocate for patient privacy and confidentiality. Which of the following devices provides protection against eavesdropping by persons with scanners?

    a. Cellular telephone technology
    b. VHF low-band radio transmission
    c. VHF high-band radio transmission
    d. None of the above

_____ 3. Which of the following radio communications devices typically has a range of 10 to 15 miles and operates at 20 to 50 watts?

    a. Portable radio
    b. Handheld radio
    c. Base station transmitter/receiver
    d. Vehicle-mounted mobile two-way radio

_____ 4. Which of the following devices is typically mounted on a stationary site, such as a hospital or mountaintop, and is capable of transmitting and receiving radio communications?

    a. A base station
    b. A cellular phone
    c. A mobile two-way radio
    d. A multiple-channel portable radio

_____ 5. Which of the following receives transmissions on one frequency and then retransmits the transmission on a different frequency so that it will travel farther?

    a. A repeater

    b. A base station

    c. A multichannel portable radio

    d. A VHF low-band radio frequency

_____ 6. Which of the following lists the proper procedure to follow when transmitting radio communications?

    a. Depress the push-to-talk (PTT) button and immediately begin speaking with the microphone 1 to 2 feet from your mouth.

    b. Depress the PTT button and immediately begin speaking with the microphone 10 to 12 inches from your mouth.

    c. Depress the PTT button, wait 1 second, and then begin talking with the microphone 2 to 3 inches from your mouth.

    d. Depress the PTT button, wait 4 seconds, and then begin talking with the microphone 10 to 12 inches from your mouth.

_____ 7. Which of the following is an advantage of a public safety answering point (PSAP)?

    a. It allows a longer range of radio transmission.

    b. It allows security from eavesdropping via scanner.

    c. It allows rapid access to fire, police, and EMS agencies.

    d. It allows the maximum amount of radio frequencies from which to choose.

_____ 8. The primary advantage of enhanced 9-1-1 (E9-1-1) over standard 9-1-1 is

    a. E9-1-1 routes the call directly to the closest responding rescue unit.

    b. E9-1-1 displays the caller's telephone number and address for the call taker.

    c. E9-1-1 can be used effectively from hotel rooms and other buildings with switchboards.

    d. E9-1-1 does not require the caller to state the problem in order to get an appropriate response.

_____ 9. When communicating via radio, you should

    a. keep your transmissions to 1-minute bursts of information.

    b. be courteous and say "Please" and "Thank You" when appropriate.

    c. use as many codes as possible to speed transmission of information.

    d. use the terms "affirmative" and "negative" in place of "yes" and "no."

_____ 10. What radio transmission band would be ideal for use in metropolitan areas where building penetration is needed?

    a. UHF

    b. VHF low band

    c. VHF high band

    d. VHF medium band

_____ 11. Which of the following characteristics is true regarding low-band VHF frequencies?

    a. They are very effective in metropolitan areas.

    b. They require the use of a repeater due to their short range.

    c. They have an ability to reflect off or bounce around buildings.

    d. The radio waves bend and follow the curvature of the Earth.

Matching

Match the key terms in the left column with the definitions in the right column by placing the letter of each correct answer in the space provided.

_____ **12.** Global Positioning System

_____ **13.** Public Safety Answering Point

_____ **14.** Mobile two-way radio

_____ **15.** Portable radio

_____ **16.** Computer-aided dispatch (CAD)

_____ **17.** Band

_____ **18.** Repeater

_____ **19.** Mobile data computer

_____ **20.** Base station

_____ **21.** Multiplex system

_____ **22.** Transmitter

_____ **23.** Federal Communications Commission

A. A device that sends out data on a given radio frequency

B. A transmitter/receiver at a stationary site such as a hospital, mountaintop, or public safety agency

C. A computer system that aids dispatch personnel in handling and prioritizing emergency calls

D. A vehicular-mounted communication device that usually transmits at a lower power than do base stations

E. A device that receives a transmission from a low-power portable or mobile radio on one frequency and then retransmits it at a higher power on another frequency so that it can be received at a distant location

F. The U.S. government agency responsible for regulation of interstate and international communications by radio, television, wire, satellite, and cable

G. A computer mounted in an emergency vehicle that displays information pertaining to the calls for which EMS personnel are dispatched

H. A facility equipped and staffed to receive and control 9-1-1 access calls

I. A mode of radio transmission that permits simultaneous transmission of voice and other data using one frequency

J. Technology that uses a system of satellites and receiving devices to compute the receiver's geographic position on the Earth

K. A group of radio frequencies close together

L. A handheld communication device used for radio communication away from the emergency vehicle

Answer Section

Multiple Choice

1. b

The 800-MHz technology allows high clarity of transmission; however, this technology is dependent upon repeaters to ensure that messages meet their intended recipient.

2. d

Any nonencrypted radio device is subject to eavesdropping via scanner. A general rule of message transmission is do not transmit something you, your agency, or your patient wouldn't want printed in the local newspaper.

Objective: State legal aspects to consider in verbal communication.

3. d

The mobile two-way radio operates at 20–50 watts and generally has a transmission range of 10–15 miles. The local terrain can influence the range of transmission. Handheld portable radios operate at a much lower power (1–5 watts) and have a lower transmission range. Base station radio transmissions are much more powerful and have a farther range.

4. a

Base station devices are typically mounted at the highest local elevation, such as a tall building or a close mountain peak. Cellular phones are mobile devices that depend on local networks within cells to route their transmissions. As their names imply, mobile two-way radios and multiple-channel portable radios are not stationary devices.

Objective: Describe the following components of an EMS communications system: base station, mobile two-way radio, portable radio, repeater, digital radio equipment, cellular telephone.

5. a

Repeaters greatly enhance the performance of portable radios. Most portable radios operate at low wattage and hence have limited transmission range. Repeaters are located throughout the transmission area (county boundaries, for example) and receive the transmissions from low-wattage devices. The repeater then retransmits the intended message with greater power and range on a different frequency.

Objective: Describe the following components of an EMS communications system: base station, mobile two-way radio, portable radio, repeater, digital radio equipment, cellular telephone.

6. c

The proper procedure for radio transmission is, first, depress the push-to-talk (PTT) button and wait a second or two. This "opens" the transmission at the repeater (if one is present in your system), thus decreasing the chance that your first words will be lost. You should then speak clearly in a normal tone and volume with the microphone held about 2–3 inches from your mouth.

Objective: List the proper methods of initiating and terminating a radio call.

7. c

The PSAP system allows rapid access to emergency agencies since it centralizes emergency calls for assistance. Calls may in turn be routed to different agencies depending on the origin and type of call.

8. b

Enhanced 9-1-1 uses telephone company records to provide additional information to the call processing agency. If the 9-1-1 call goes through a switchboard, the ability to pinpoint the origin of the call is lost. With E9-1-1, callers must still state the problem (medical emergency, fire, police situation). The ability to route a call to the closest appropriate response unit is a separate system, sometimes referred to as Automatic Vehicle Locator (AVL). AVL uses satellite technology to select response units based on geography.

9. d

The words "yes" and "no" are often difficult to understand in radio transmissions. Transmissions should be kept to 30 seconds or less to allow the listener an opportunity to interact in the transmission (such as, "We didn't copy the pulse rate, Rescue 204; could you repeat"). Courtesy is assumed in radio transmissions. "Please," "thank you," and "you're welcome" are generally implied. Finally, use plain English in your transmissions (unless local protocol dictates otherwise). Codes may be misunderstood by the person on the other end of the radio transmission.

Objective: List the correct radio procedures during each phase of a typical EMS call.

10. a

UHF band transmissions offer strong penetrating power into densely populated areas. Like the 800-MHz systems, UHF systems necessitate the use of repeaters due to short transmission distances.

11. d

Radio waves in the low-band frequency range bend and follow the curvature of the Earth, allowing radio transmission over long distances. These radio waves are subject to interference by atmospheric conditions including weather disturbances and electrical equipment. These waves do not penetrate solid structures (such as buildings) well, making VHF low band less effective for use in metropolitan areas.

Matching

12. J

13. H

14. D

15. L

16. C

17. K

18. E

19. G

20. B

21. I

22. A

23. F

5 Medical Terminology

READING ASSIGNMENT Read Chapter 5, pages 116 to 129 in your textbook.

Sum It Up

- Healthcare professionals use medical terms to communicate information about a patient's illness or injury. To correctly relay what you are seeing and what the patient is saying in your written and verbal reports, you must know medical terms and their meanings. You must also spell medical terms correctly because a spelling error may completely alter the meaning of the word.

- Medical terms are made up of three main parts: a root word, prefix, and suffix. A root word is the main part of a word and conveys the body system, part, disease, or condition being discussed. A prefix is a syllable placed at the beginning of a root word to modify its meaning. A suffix is a syllable placed at the end of a root word to modify its meaning.

- A vowel is often added between a root word and suffix or between two word roots to make the new term easier to pronounce. The vowel used is called a combining vowel. The root word plus the combining vowel is called a combining form.

- In your role as an EMR, it is important to know the terms used to describe body positions and directions. You must be able to use these terms correctly so that you can describe the position in which a patient is found and transported. You will also need to know body positions so that you can place a patient in a specific position on the basis of the patient's condition.

- Abbreviations and acronyms are used to save time and space when documenting. Use abbreviations and acronyms only if they are standard and approved by your EMS system.

▶ Tracking Your Progress

After reading this chapter, can you:	Page Reference	Objective Met?
• Identify and define the main parts of a medical term?	117	☐
• Identify and define a combining vowel and combining form?	118	☐
• Describe the standard anatomical position?	121	☐
• Identify and define terms that describe directions and positions of the body?	121	☐
• Identify and define commonly used medical abbreviations and acronyms?	124	☐

Chapter Quiz

Matching

Match the key terms in the left column with the definitions in the right column by placing the letter of each correct answer in the space provided.

_____ 1. tachy-

_____ 2. U/A

_____ 3. -rrhage

_____ 4. algesia

_____ 5. TRX

_____ 6. -ostomy

_____ 7. -partum

_____ 8. SNT

_____ 9. a-, an-

_____ 10. proximal

_____ 11. sternum

_____ 12. -cutane/o

_____ 13. -ictal

_____ 14. TPR

_____ 15. carp/o

_____ 16. -itis

_____ 17. anti-

_____ 18. gluc/o

_____ 19. bilateral

_____ 20. brady-

A. Skin

B. Closer to the midline or center area of the body

C. Inflammation

D. Soft, nontender

E. Transport

F. Breastbone

G. Pertaining to both sides

H. Fast

I. Temperature, pulse, respiration

J. Sensitivity to pain

K. Without, from, absence of

L. Against, opposing

M. Upon arrival

N. Sugar

O. Wrist

P. Seizure, attack

Q. Slow

R. Creation of an opening

S. Rapid flow or discharge

T. Birth, labor

Short Answer

Answer each question in the space provided.

21. Based on your knowledge of medical terminology, what does the term *hypodermic* mean?

22. Define *dyspnea*.

23. What is the medical term that means inflammation of a joint?

24. What is the medical term for red blood cell?

25. Define *hematoma*.

Answer Section

Matching

1.	H	**11.**	F
2.	M	**12.**	A
3.	S	**13.**	P
4.	J	**14.**	I
5.	E	**15.**	O
6.	R	**16.**	C
7.	T	**17.**	L
8.	D	**18.**	N
9.	K	**19.**	G
10.	B	**20.**	Q

Short Answer

21. *Hypo-* means "beneath or below normal; *derm* means "the skin"; and *-ic* means "pertaining to." Thus, *hypodermic* means "pertaining to the area beneath the skin."

22. *Dyspnea* means "difficulty breathing" (*dys-* = difficult, bad, painful, abnormal; *-pnea* = breathing).

23. *Arthritis* (*arth* = joint, *-itis* = inflammation).

24. *Erythrocyte* (*erythr/o-* = red, *-cyte* = cell).

25. *Hemat* = blood, *-oma* = swelling. Thus, a *hematoma* is swelling because of a collection of blood.

Module **2**

Function and Development of the Human Body

▶ CHAPTER **6**

The Human Body   43

▶ CHAPTER **7**

Pathophysiology   52

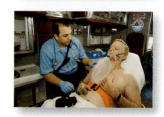

▶ CHAPTER **8**

Life Span Development   58

CHAPTER

6 The Human Body

cell
↓
tissue
↓
organ
↓
body system

READING ASSIGNMENT ▶ Read Chapter 6, pages 130 to 160 in your textbook.

Sum It Up

- The body's most basic building block is a cell. The human body contains billions of cells. Clusters of cells form tissues. Specialized types of tissues form organs such as the brain and the liver. An organ system (also called a body system) consists of tissues and organs that work together to provide a specialized function. The circulatory and respiratory systems are examples of organ systems.

- Organ systems work together to maintain a state of homeostasis (balance). These systems need a constant internal environment to perform the required functions of the body.

- In your role as an EMR, it is important to know the terms used to describe body positions and directions. You must be able to use these terms correctly so that you can describe the position in which a patient is found and transported. You will also need to know body positions so that you can place a patient in a specific position on the basis of the patient's condition.

- A body cavity is a hollow space in the body that contains internal organs. Knowing the body cavities and the organs found within each cavity will help you describe the location of the injury or symptoms of a sick or injured patient.

- The musculoskeletal system gives the human body its shape and ability to move and protects the major organs of the body. It consists of the skeletal system (bones) and the muscular system (muscles).

- The respiratory system supplies oxygen from the air we breathe to the body's cells. It also removes carbon dioxide (a waste product of the body's cells) from the lungs when we breathe out. This system is made up of an upper and a lower airway. The upper airway includes the nose, the pharynx (throat), and the larynx (voice box). The lower airway consists of structures found mostly within the chest cavity, such as the trachea (windpipe) and the lungs.

- The circulatory system is made up of the cardiovascular and lymphatic systems. This system has three main functions: (1) to deliver oxygen-rich blood and nutrients to body tissues, (2) to help maintain body temperature, and (3) to protect the body against infection. The cardiovascular system consists of the heart, blood, and blood vessels. The lymphatic system consists of lymph, lymph nodes, lymph vessels, tonsils, the spleen, and the thymus gland.

- The nervous system is a collection of specialized cells that transfer information to and from the brain. The two main functions of the nervous system are to control the voluntary (conscious) and involuntary (unconscious) activities of the body and to provide for higher mental function (such as thought and emotion). The nervous system has two divisions: (1) the CNS and (2) the PNS. The PNS has two divisions. The somatic (voluntary) division has receptors and nerves concerned with the external environment. It influences the activity of the musculoskeletal system. The autonomic (involuntary) division has receptors and nerves concerned with the internal environment. It controls the involuntary system of glands and smooth muscle and functions to maintain a steady state in the body. The autonomic division is divided into the sympathetic and parasympathetic divisions. The sympathetic division mobilizes energy, particularly in stressful situations. This is called the fight-or-flight response. Its effects are widespread throughout the body. The parasympathetic division conserves and restores energy; its effects are localized in the body.

- The integumentary system is made up of the skin, hair, nails, sweat glands, and oil (sebaceous) glands. The skin is the largest organ of the body. It protects the body from the environment, bacteria, and other organisms and plays an important role in temperature regulation.

- The digestive system brings nutrients, water, and electrolytes into the body (ingestion). It chemically breaks down food into small parts so that absorption can occur (digestion). It moves nutrients, water, and electrolytes into the circulatory system so that they can be used by body cells (absorption). It also eliminates undigested waste (defecation). The primary organs of the digestive system are the mouth, pharynx, esophagus, stomach, small intestine, large intestine, rectum, and anal canal. The accessory organs are the teeth and tongue, salivary glands, liver, gallbladder, and pancreas.

- The endocrine system is a system of glands that secrete chemicals (hormones) directly into the circulatory system. It influences body activities and functions. The endocrine system works closely with the nervous system to maintain homeostasis.

- The reproductive system makes cells (sperm, eggs) that allow continuation of the human species. The urinary system produces and excretes urine from the body.

▶ Tracking Your Progress

After reading this chapter, can you:	Page Reference	Objective Met?
• Define anatomy and physiology?	133	☐
• Name the levels of organization of the body and explain each?	133	☐
• Name the organ systems of the body?	133	☐
• Define homeostasis and give an example of a typical homeostatic mechanism?	133	☐
• Name the body cavities and some organs within each cavity?	133	☐
• Explain the four quadrants of the abdomen and name the organs in those areas?	134	☐
• List the functions of the musculoskeletal system?	134	☐
• Identify the two major subdivisions of the skeleton and list the bones in each area?	135	☐

After reading this chapter, can you:

	Page Reference	Objective Met?
• Explain how bones are classified and give an example of each?	135	☐
• Name the bones of the skull and face?	136	☐
• Describe the structure of the vertebral column?	137	☐
• Explain the purpose of muscles and the basic differences between skeletal, smooth, and cardiac muscles?	140	☐
• Explain the purpose of tendons and ligaments?	141	☐
• State the general function of the respiratory system?	142	☐
• Describe the anatomy and function of the upper and lower airways?	142	☐
• State the pathway of the respiratory system including nasal cavities, pharynx, and larynx?	143	☐
• Describe the structure and function of the larynx, trachea, and epiglottis?	143	☐
• Describe the changes in air pressure within the chest cavity during ventilation?	145	☐
• Explain the relationship between pulmonary circulation and respiration?	146	☐
• Describe the components and functions of the circulatory system?	148	☐
• Name the chambers of the heart and their function?	148	☐
• Trace the flow of blood through the heart's chambers and valves?	148	☐
• Describe the primary functions of blood?	148	☐
• List the formed elements of blood and state the primary functions of each?	149	☐
• Describe the structure and function of each of the blood vessels: arteries, arterioles, capillaries, venules, and veins?	149	☐
• Name the major arteries and describe their location and the parts of the body they nourish?	150	☐
• Name the major veins and describe their location and the parts of the body they drain of blood?	150	☐
• Define pulse and differentiate between a central pulse and a peripheral pulse, giving examples of each?	152	☐
• Define blood pressure, systolic blood pressure, and diastolic blood pressure?	152	☐
• Define perfusion and hypoperfusion?	152	☐
• Name the divisions of the nervous system and state the general functions of each?	152	☐
• Describe the location and function of the meninges and cerebrospinal fluid?	153	☐
• State the functions of the parts of the brain and locate each part on a diagram?	153	☐
• Compare the functions of the sympathetic and parasympathetic divisions of the autonomic nervous system?	154	☐
• State the functions of the integumentary system?	154	☐
• Describe the layers of the skin and, where applicable, the structures contained within them?	154	☐
• Describe the functions and components of the digestive system?	155	☐
• Describe the functions and components of the endocrine system?	156	☐
• Describe the functions and components of the male and female reproductive systems?	157	☐
• Describe the functions and components of the urinary system?	158	☐

Chapter Quiz

True/False

Decide whether each statement is true or false. In the space provided, write T for true or F for false.

_____ **1.** Hemoglobin is an oxygen-carrying protein in red blood cells.

_____ **2.** The spleen is the largest internal organ of the body.

_____ **3.** The chambers of the heart that have the thickest walls are the ventricles.

_____ **4.** The salivary glands release chemicals (enzymes) that begin the breakdown of food and also moisten and lubricate food so that it can be swallowed.

Multiple Choice

In the space provided, identify the letter of the choice that best completes each statement or answers each question.

_____ **5.** The oropharynx
- **a.** is the lowermost part of the throat.
- **b.** is located directly behind the nasal cavity.
- **c.** opens into the mouth and serves as a passageway for both food and air.
- **d.** is a small piece of tissue that looks like a mini punching bag and hangs down in the back of the throat.

_____ **6.** Which of the following are bones of the forearm?
- **a.** Radius and ulna
- **b.** Tibia and radius
- **c.** Fibula and humerus
- **d.** Humerus and femur

_____ **7.** Select the correct statement about the heart.
- **a.** The lower chambers of the heart are called the atria.
- **b.** The walls of the heart are made up of skeletal muscle.
- **c.** The upper chambers of the heart are called the ventricles.
- **d.** The heart contains four valves that make sure blood flows in the proper direction.

_____ **8.** White blood cells
- **a.** are also called erythrocytes.
- **b.** help the body fight infection.
- **c.** are irregularly shaped blood cells that have a sticky surface.
- **d.** gather at the site of an injured blood vessel and stop the flow of blood.

_____ **9.** Which of the following arteries is found in the upper extremity?
- **a.** Carotid artery
- **b.** Brachial artery
- **c.** Femoral artery
- **d.** Posterior tibial artery

_____ **10.** The exchange of oxygen and carbon dioxide between the air and blood occurs in the
- **a.** larynx.
- **b.** alveoli.
- **c.** trachea.
- **d.** bronchioles.

_____ **11.** Which of the following are parts of the upper airway?
- **a.** Nose, pharynx, larynx
- **b.** Lungs, larynx, pharynx
- **c.** Trachea, bronchioles, lungs
- **d.** Nose, bronchioles, pharynx

_____ **12.** The thyroid cartilage
- **a.** is the largest cartilage of the larynx.
- **b.** can be felt on the posterior surface of the neck.
- **c.** is the only complete ring of cartilage in the larynx.
- **d.** forms the base of the larynx on which the other cartilages rest.

_____ 13. The meninges
  a. is the largest part of the human brain.
  b. is the part of the brain that contains the thalamus and hypothalamus.
  c. are a very thick bundle of nerve fibers that joins the two hemispheres of the brain.
  d. are three layers of connective tissue coverings that surround the brain and spinal cord.

_____ 14. Which of the following is the largest organ system in the human body?
  a. Digestive system
  b. Respiratory system
  c. Reproductive system
  d. Integumentary system

Matching

Match the key terms in the left column with the definitions in the right column by placing the letter of each correct answer in the space provided.

_____ 15. Thoracic cavity

_____ 16. Abdominal cavity

_____ 17. Body cavity

_____ 18. Pelvic cavity

_____ 19. Pleural cavities

_____ 20. Spinal cavity

_____ 21. Cranial cavity

_____ 22. Pericardial cavity

A. Surrounds the heart

B. Surrounds the lungs

C. Located in the head; contains the brain

D. Extends from the bottom of the skull to the lower back; contains the spinal cord

E. A hollow space in the body that contains internal organs

F. Located below the diaphragm and above the pelvis

G. Body cavity below the abdominal cavity

H. Located below the neck and above the diaphragm; contains the heart, major blood vessels, and lungs

Match the key terms in the left column with the definitions in the right column by placing the letter of each correct answer in the space provided.

_____ 23. Pulse

_____ 24. Appendicular skeleton

_____ 25. Homeostasis

_____ 26. Tissue

_____ 27. Aorta

_____ 28. Physiology

_____ 29. Cerebellum

_____ 30. Systolic blood pressure

_____ 31. Cells

_____ 32. Xiphoid process

_____ 33. Perfusion

_____ 34. Corpus callosum

A. The largest artery in the body

B. The basic building blocks of the body

C. Upper and lower extremities (arms and legs), shoulder girdle, and pelvic girdle

D. A thick bundle of nerve fibers that joins the two hemispheres of the brain

E. The second-largest part of the human brain

F. The pressure in an artery when the heart is pumping blood

G. The regular expansion and recoil of an artery caused by the movement of blood from the heart as it contracts

H. "Steady state"

I. Cells that cluster together to perform a specialized function

J. The flow of blood through an organ or a part of the body

K. The study of the normal functions of an organism

L. The inferior portion of the breastbone

Short Answer

Answer each question in the space provided.

35. List the formed elements of the blood.

36. List the parts of the central nervous system.

37. Explain the purpose of tendons and ligaments.

38. What is hemoglobin?

39. List at least four effects of stimulation of the sympathetic division of the autonomic nervous system.
   1.
   2.
   3.
   4.

40. What is a pulse, and where can a pulse be felt?

Answer Section

True/False

1. True

   Red blood cells (erythrocytes) contain hemoglobin. Each red blood cell has about 250 million hemoglobin molecules. Hemoglobin is an iron-containing protein that chemically bonds with oxygen. Thus, hemoglobin is the part of the red blood cell that picks up oxygen in the lungs and transports it to the body's cells. Hemoglobin is red and therefore gives blood its red color.

   Objective: List the formed elements of blood, and state the primary functions of each.

2. False

   The skin is the largest organ system of the human body. In a 150-pound man, the skin weighs about 9 pounds and covers an area of about 18 square feet.

3. True

   The ventricles are larger and have thicker walls than the atria (the heart's upper chambers) because the job of the ventricles is to pump blood to the lungs and body.

   Objective: Name the chambers of the heart and their function.

4. True

   The mouth, teeth, and salivary glands begin the process of digestion. The tongue manipulates food for chewing and swallowing. Chemicals (enzymes) in the salivary glands begin the breakdown of food. The salivary glands also moisten and lubricate food so it can be swallowed. The teeth mince food into small pieces so it can be swallowed when mixed with saliva.

   Objective: Describe the functions and components of the digestive system.

Multiple Choice

5. c

   The nasopharynx is located directly behind the nasal cavity. The oropharynx is the middle part of the throat. It opens into the mouth and serves as a passageway for both food and air. It is separated from the nasopharynx by the soft palate. The uvula is the small piece of tissue that looks like a mini punching bag and hangs down in the back of the throat. The laryngopharynx is the lowermost part of the throat.

   Objective: Describe the anatomy and function of each of the structures in the upper and lower airways.

6. a

   The humerus is the largest bone of the upper extremity and is the second longest bone in the body. The forearm contains two bones, the radius (lateral, thumb side), and ulna (medial side). The ulna is the longer of the two bones. The femur (thigh bone) is the longest, heaviest, and strongest bone of the body. The knee is the joint that lies between the femur and the two lower leg bones, the tibia (shinbone) and fibula.

   Objective: Identify the two major subdivisions of the skeleton, and list the bones in each area.

7. d

   The heart has four hollow chambers. The two upper chambers are the right and left atria. The job of the atria is to receive blood from the body and lungs. The two lower chambers of the heart are the right and left ventricles. The ventricles are larger and have thicker walls than the atria because their job is to pump blood to the lungs and body.

   The heart contains four one-way valves that make sure blood flows in the proper direction. Cardiac muscle, found in the walls of the heart, produces the heart's contractions and pumps blood. Cardiac muscle is found only in the heart and has its own supply of blood through the coronary arteries.

Objective: Trace the flow of blood through the heart's chambers and valves.

8. b

White blood cells (leukocytes) attack and destroy germs that enter the body. Red blood cells (erythrocytes) deliver oxygen to the cells, gather carbon dioxide and then transport it to the lungs, where it is removed from the body when we exhale. Platelets are irregularly shaped blood cells that have a sticky surface. When a blood vessel is damaged and starts to bleed, platelets gather at the site of injury. The platelets begin sticking to the opening of the damaged vessel and seal it, stopping the flow of blood.

Objective: List the formed elements of blood, and state the primary functions of each.

9. b

The subclavian arteries branch into the axillary and brachial arteries in the upper arm. A brachial pulse can be felt on the inside of the arm between the elbow and the shoulder. This artery is used when determining a blood pressure with a blood pressure cuff and stethoscope.

Objective: Name the major arteries, and describe their location and the parts of the body they nourish.

10. b

The trachea (windpipe) is located in the front of the neck. It is kept permanently open by C-shaped cartilages. The trachea branches into large airway tubes called the right and left primary bronchi. Each bronchus is joined to a lung, so 1 tube leads to the right lung and the other leads to the left lung. The primary bronchi branch into bronchioles. Bronchioles end in microscopic tubes called alveolar ducts. Each alveolar duct ends in several alveolar sacs. At the end of each alveolar duct, the collections of air sacs (alveoli) looks like a cluster of grapes. Alveoli are the sites where gases—oxygen and carbon dioxide—are exchanged between the air and blood.

Objective: Differentiate between ventilation and respiration.

11. a

The respiratory system is divided into the upper and lower airways. The upper airway is made up of structures outside the chest cavity. These structures include the nose, the pharynx (throat), and the larynx (voice box). The lower airway consists of parts found almost entirely within the chest cavity, such as the trachea (windpipe) and the lungs.

Objective: Describe the anatomy and function of each of the structures in the upper and lower airway.

12. a

The thyroid cartilage (Adam's apple) is the largest cartilage of the larynx and is shaped like a shield. It can be felt on the front surface of the neck. The cricoid cartilage is the lowermost cartilage of the larynx. It is the only complete ring of cartilage in the larynx. The cricoid cartilage forms the base of the larynx on which the other cartilages rest.

Objective: Describe the anatomy and function of each of the structures in the upper and lower airway.

13. d

Meninges (literally, "membranes"), are three layers of connective tissue coverings that surround the brain and spinal cord. The pia mater (literally, "gentle mother") forms the delicate inner layer that clings gently to the brain and spinal cord. It contains many blood vessels that supply the nervous tissue. The arachnoid (literally, "resembling a spider's web") layer is the middle layer with delicate fibers resembling a spider's web; it contains few blood vessels. The dura mater (literally, "hard" or "tough mother") is the tough, outermost layer that sticks to the inner surface of the skull.

Objective: Describe the location and function of the meninges and cerebrospinal fluid.

14. d

The skin (integumentary system) is the largest organ system of the human body.

Objective: Name the organ systems of the body.

Matching

15.	H	25.	H
16.	F	26.	I
17.	E	27.	A
18.	G	28.	K
19.	B	29.	E
20.	D	30.	F
21.	C	31.	B
22.	A	32.	L
23.	G	33.	J
24.	C	34.	D

Short Answer

35. Red blood cells, white blood cells, platelets

    Objective: List the formed elements of blood, and state the primary functions of each.

36. Brain and spinal cord

    Objective: Name the divisions of the nervous system, and state the general functions of each.

37. Tendons are strong cords of connective tissue that firmly attach the end of a muscle to a bone. The tendons of many muscles cross over joints, and this helps to stabilize the joint. Ligaments are tough groups of connective tissue that attach bones to bones and bones to cartilages. They provide support and strength to joints and restrain excessive joint movement.

Objective: Explain the purpose of tendons and ligaments.

38. Hemoglobin is an iron-containing protein that chemically bonds with oxygen. About 97% of the oxygen in the body is bound to hemoglobin molecules. The remaining 3% of the body's oxygen is dissolved in the liquid portion of the blood called plasma.

    Objective: Describe the primary functions of blood.

39. Effects of stimulation of the sympathetic division of the autonomic nervous system include:

    - Heart rate increases.
    - Heart's force of contraction increases.
    - Pupils widen.
    - Digestion decreases.
    - Mouth and nose secretions decrease.
    - Bronchial muscles relax.
    - Urine secretion decreases.

    Objective: Compare the functions of the sympathetic and parasympathetic divisions of the autonomic nervous system.

40. A pulse is the regular expansion and recoil of an artery caused by the movement of blood from the heart as it contracts. A pulse can be felt anywhere an artery passes near the skin surface and over a bone.

    Objective: Define pulse and differentiate between a central pulse and a peripheral pulse, giving examples of each.

7 Pathophysiology

▶ Read Chapter 7, pages 161 to 169 in your textbook.

Sum It Up

- Disease is an abnormal condition in which the body's steady state (homeostasis) is threatened or cannot be maintained. Pathology is the study of disease. Pathophysiology is the study of the physical, chemical, and mechanical processes that cause or are caused by disease or injury, producing changes in the structure and function of the body.

- The basic building block of the human body is the cell. Cell metabolism is the sum of the chemical reactions that occur within cells, enabling them to maintain a living state.

- Most diseases start with an injury to the cell. Although cells have the ability to adapt to their environment to protect themselves from injury, cellular injury can occur if the cell is changed or damaged to the point that normal function is negatively affected or permanently impaired.

- Hypoxia, which is a lack of adequate oxygen, is the most common cause of cellular injury. Hypoxia deprives the cell of oxygen and interferes with energy (ATP) production. Ischemia, which is a reduced blood supply, is the most common cause of hypoxia. Death of tissue due to ischemia is called an infarct.

- The respiratory system delivers oxygen from the atmosphere to the blood where it gets distributed to body cells and removes carbon dioxide produced by the body cells to the atmosphere. Your patient must have an open airway in order for these essential processes to occur. A blocked airway, or an injury or disease that affects oxygenation or ventilation, can lead to hypoxia (a lack of oxygen) and/or hypercarbia (an increase in carbon dioxide).

- Perfusion is the circulation of blood through an organ or a part of the body. Perfusion depends on cardiac output (CO), peripheral vascular resistance (PVR), and the transport of oxygen. Cardiac output is the amount of blood the heart pumps each minute. Cardiac output is determined by multiplying stroke volume (SV) by heart rate (HR). Stroke volume is the amount of blood ejected by the ventricles of the heart with each contraction.

- The amount of blood returning to the ventricles is called venous return. In a healthy heart, an increase in the volume of blood in the ventricles causes the fibers in the heart muscle to stretch, resulting in a more forceful contraction. Hemorrhage (also called major bleeding), an extreme loss of blood from a blood vessel, is one cause of decreased venous return.

- Peripheral vascular resistance (PVR), also called systemic vascular resistance (SVR), is the opposition that blood encounters in the blood vessels as it travels away from the heart. The smallest arteries, arterioles, are made up of smooth muscle. They provide the greatest resistance to blood flow through the arterial circulation because the lumen of an arteriole is narrower than that of medium and large arteries. Narrowing of a vessel (vasoconstriction) increases peripheral resistance. Widening of a vessel (vasodilation) decreases peripheral resistance.

- Blood pressure is the force exerted by the blood on the inner walls of the heart and arteries. It is affected by cardiac output (heart) and peripheral vascular resistance (blood vessels).

- Shock is the inadequate circulation of blood through an organ or a part of the body. Shock is also called hypoperfusion. Because the presence of shock affects the body's ability to oxygenate and perfuse cells, shock can lead to death if it is not corrected.

- Conditions that may increase a person's chance of developing a disease are called risk factors or predisposing factors. Examples of risk factors include age, gender, lifestyle, environment, and heredity.

- Some diseases develop in stages. The incubation period is the interval between the exposure to a disease-causing agent and the appearance of signs and symptoms. A sign is a medical or trauma condition of the patient that can be seen, heard, smelled, measured, or felt by the examiner. A symptom is a condition described by the patient. Symptoms are subjective findings because they are dependent on (subject to) the patient's interpretation and description of the complaint. A syndrome is a group of signs and symptoms that together are characteristic of a specific disease or disorder.

▶ Tracking Your Progress

After reading this chapter, can you:	Page Reference	Objective Met?
• Define disease, pathology, and pathophysiology?	162	☐
• Define cell metabolism?	162	☐
• Define hypoxia and ischemia and explain their effects on the body?	162	☐
• Define perfusion?	163	☐
• Describe the structure of blood vessel walls?	163	☐
• Describe the function of large- and medium-sized arteries, arterioles, capillaries, venules, and veins?	163	☐
• Discuss shock (hypoperfusion)?	165	☐
• Define sign, symptom, and syndrome and then differentiate between a sign and a symptom?	167	☐

Chapter Quiz

True/False

Decide whether each statement is true or false. In the space provided, write T for true or F for false.

_____ **1.** A thrombus is a blood clot.

_____ **2.** The process of the heart muscle dying is called a myocardial infarction.

_____ **3.** Interruption of the body's oxygen supply and/or removal of carbon dioxide can lead to shock.

_____ **4.** Perfusion affects the speed with which oxygen and nutrients are delivered to body cells, tissues, organs, and organ systems and the speed of waste removal.

Multiple Choice

In the space provided, identify the letter of the choice that best completes each statement or answers each question.

_____ **5.** Cells within which of the following areas of the body are the most rapidly affected by hypoxia because of their high demand for oxygen?

    a. Eyes, ears, and nose

    b. Brain, heart, and kidneys

    c. Bones, ligaments, and tendons

    d. Skeletal muscle, liver, and pancreas

_____ **6.** Shock caused by a severe infection is called

    a. septic shock.

    b. cardiogenic shock.

    c. anaphylactic shock.

    d. hypovolemic shock.

_____ **7.** An abnormal condition in which the body's steady state (homeostasis) is threatened or cannot be maintained is called

    a. a disease.

    b. hypercarbia.

    c. an infarction.

    d. cell metabolism.

_____ **8.** The opposition that blood encounters in the blood vessels as it travels away from the heart is called

    a. perfusion.

    b. venous return.

    c. cardiac output.

    d. peripheral vascular resistance.

Sentence Completion

In the blanks provided, write the words that best complete each sentence.

9. _____ _____ is the sum of the chemical reactions that occur within cells, enabling them to maintain a living state.

10. A blocked airway, or an injury or disease that affects oxygenation or ventilation, can lead to _____ (a lack of oxygen) and/or _____ (an increase in carbon dioxide).

11. Capillaries connect to _____ .

12. Changing the diameter of the arterioles alters their resistance to blood flow. For example, if arterioles widen, peripheral resistance is _____ (*increased* or *decreased*), which means there is _____ (*more* or *less*) resistance to blood flow.

Matching

Match the key terms in the left column with the definitions in the right column by placing the letter of each correct answer in the space provided.

_____ **13.** Capillaries

_____ **14.** Large arteries

_____ **15.** Arterioles

_____ **16.** Veins and venules

_____ **17.** Medium arteries

A. Distributing vessels

B. Resistance vessels

C. Capacitance vessels

D. Exchange vessels

E. Conductance vessels

Short Answer

Answer each question in the space provided.

18. List three possible causes of hypoxia.

1.

2.

3.

19. List three possible causes of a blocked airway.

1.

2.

3.

20. What is the difference between hypoxia and ischemia?

Answer Section

True/False

1. True

   A thrombus is a blood clot. A common cause of ischemia is narrowing of arteries and blockage of the vessel by plaque or a thrombus. For example, ischemia of the heart muscle can occur if a coronary artery is blocked. If the vessel is partially blocked, medications such as nitroglycerin may be used to dilate the affected vessel, allowing blood flow to resume and oxygenation to be restored. If the vessel is completely blocked, ischemia can lead to cell and tissue death, which is called necrosis.

2. True

   The process of the heart muscle dying is called a myocardial infarction or heart attack.

3. True

   Interruption of the body's oxygen supply and/or removal of carbon dioxide can lead to shock. Unless adequate perfusion is quickly restored, death may soon follow.

   Objective: Discuss shock (hypoperfusion).

4. True

   Perfusion is the circulation of blood through an organ or a part of the body. Perfusion affects the speed with which oxygen and nutrients are delivered to body cells, tissues, organs, and organ systems and the speed of waste removal. Adequate perfusion requires a properly functioning heart, intact blood vessels, and adequate blood flow.

   Objective: Define perfusion.

Multiple Choice

5. b

   Hypoxia, which is a lack of oxygen available to the tissues, is the most common cause of cellular injury. Cells within the brain, heart, and kidney are the most rapidly affected by hypoxia because of their high demand for oxygen. Hypoxia deprives the cell of oxygen and interferes with energy (ATP) production.

   Objective: Define hypoxia and ischemia, and explain their effects on the body.

6. a

   Shock caused by a severe infection is called septic shock. Cardiogenic shock is a condition in which the heart fails to function effectively as a pump. Shock due to a severe allergic reaction is called anaphylactic shock. Hypovolemic shock is a condition in which there is a loss of blood, plasma, or water from the body resulting in an inadequate volume of fluid in the circulatory system to maintain adequate perfusion. This type of shock may occur because of bleeding, vomiting, diarrhea, or burns, among other causes.

   Objective: Discuss shock (hypoperfusion).

7. a

   Disease is an abnormal condition in which the body's steady state (homeostasis) is threatened or cannot be maintained.

   Objective: Define disease, pathology, and pathophysiology.

8. d

   Peripheral vascular resistance (PVR), also called systemic vascular resistance (SVR), is the opposition that blood encounters in the blood vessels as it travels away from the heart. Because the resistance to flow in the venous circulation is very low, peripheral vascular resistance generally refers to the opposition to flow encountered in the arterial circulation.

Objective: Describe the structure of blood vessel walls.

Sentence Completion

9. <u>Cell</u> <u>metabolism</u> is the sum of the chemical reactions that occur within cells, enabling them to maintain a living state.

   Objective: Define cell metabolism.

10. A blocked airway, or an injury or disease that affects oxygenation or ventilation, can lead to **hypoxia** (a lack of oxygen) and/or **hypercarbia** (an increase in carbon dioxide).

    Objective: Define hypoxia and ischemia, and explain their effects on the body.

11. Capillaries connect to **venules,** which are the smallest branches of veins.

    Objective: Describe the function of large- and medium-sized arteries, arterioles, capillaries, venules, and veins.

12. Changing the diameter of the arterioles alters their resistance to blood flow. For example, if arterioles widen, peripheral resistance is **decreased,** which means there is **less** resistance to blood flow.

    Objective: Describe the structure of blood vessel walls.

Matching

13. D
14. E
15. B
16. C
17. A

Short Answer

18. Hypoxia deprives the cell of oxygen and interferes with energy (ATP) production. It may result from decreased amounts of oxygen in the air, loss of hemoglobin or hemoglobin function, decreased production of red blood cells, poisoning of substances within the cells, or diseases of the respiratory or cardiovascular system.

    Objective: Define hypoxia and ischemia, and explain their effects on the body.

19. A blocked airway, or an injury or disease that affects oxygenation or ventilation, can lead to hypoxia (a lack of oxygen) and/or hypercarbia (an increase in carbon dioxide). Possible causes of a blocked airway include the presence of a foreign body, the tongue blocking the airway in an unconscious patient, blood or secretions, swelling, and trauma to the neck.

20. Hypoxia, which is a lack of adequate oxygen, is the most common cause of cellular injury. Hypoxia deprives the cell of oxygen and interferes with energy (ATP) production. Ischemia, which is a reduced blood supply, is the most common cause of hypoxia. If the cause of the ischemia is not reversed and blood flow restored to the affected area, ischemia may lead to cellular injury and, ultimately, cell death.

    Objective: Define hypoxia and ischemia, and explain their effects on the body.

CHAPTER
8 Life Span Development

READING ASSIGNMENT Read Chapter 1, pages 170 to 184 in your textbook.

Sum It Up

- Life span is the period during which something is functional. In humans, life span is the period from birth to death.

- Human development is the process of growing to maturity. Stages of human development include the following:
  - Infancy   birth to 12 months
  - Toddler   12 to 36 months
  - Preschooler   3 to 5 years
  - School-age   6 to 12 years
  - Adolescence   13 to 19 years
  - Early adulthood   20 to 40 years
  - Middle adulthood   41 to 60 years
  - Late adulthood   61 years and older

- Each stage of human development is accompanied by physiologic, cognitive, and psychosocial milestones. Physiologic milestones pertain to growth, body system changes, and changes in vital signs. Vital signs are measurements of breathing, pulse, skin temperature, pupils, and blood pressure. Cognitive changes pertain to mental processes such as reasoning, imagining, and problem solving. Psychosocial milestones pertain to personality, emotions, social interactions and expectations.

- Maximum life expectancy is the oldest age to which any person lives. At present, maximum life expectancy for humans is about 120 years. Average life expectancy is the age at which half of the people born in a particular year will have died. A baby born in 2004 in the United States would have an average life expectancy of 77.9 years.

▶ Tracking Your Progress

After reading this chapter, can you:	Page Reference	Objective Met?
• Discuss the physiologic, cognitive, and psychosocial characteristics of an infant?	171	☐
• Discuss the physiologic, cognitive, and psychosocial characteristics of a toddler?	174	☐
• Discuss the physiologic, cognitive, and psychosocial characteristics of a preschool child?	175	☐
• Discuss the physiologic, cognitive, and psychosocial characteristics of a school-age child?	177	☐
• Discuss the physiologic, cognitive, and psychosocial characteristics of an adolescent?	178	☐
• Discuss the physiologic, cognitive, and psychosocial characteristics of an early adult?	180	☐
• Discuss the physiologic, cognitive, and psychosocial characteristics of a middle-aged adult?	181	☐
• Discuss the physiologic, cognitive, and psychosocial characteristics of an older adult?	181	☐

Chapter Quiz

Multiple Choice

In the space provided, identify the letter of the choice that best completes each statement or answers each question.

_____ 1. Which age group is most likely to play "doctor"?

    a. Toddler
    b. Preschooler
    c. School-age child
    d. Adolescent

_____ 2. The onset of menstruation during puberty is called

    a. menses.
    b. menarche.
    c. menopause.
    d. reproduction.

_____ 3. In which age group does a child learn to run, ride a bicycle, climb, jump, hop, and skip?

    a. Toddler
    b. Preschooler
    c. School-age child
    d. Adolescent

_____ 4. In which age group do all body systems function at optimal performance?

    a. School-age child
    b. Adolescent
    c. Early adult
    d. Late adult

Sentence Completion

In the blanks provided, write the words that best complete each sentence.

5. A toddler's heart rate is usually between _____ and _____ beats per minute and respiratory rate is about _____ to _____ breaths per minute.

6. Measurements of breathing, pulse, skin temperature, pupils, and blood pressure are called _____.

7. Parents and researchers have identified three unique types of infant cries: the _____ cry, the _____ cry, and the _____ cry.

8. Middle adults may experience _____ syndrome, which is a feeling of sadness and loneliness when one or more of their children leaves home.

Matching

Match the key terms in the left column with the definitions in the right column by placing the letter of each correct answer in the space provided.

_____ 9. Newly born

_____ 10. 2 months

_____ 11. 3 months

_____ 12. 4 months

_____ 13. 5 months

_____ 14. 6 months

_____ 15. 7 months

_____ 16. 8 months

_____ 17. 9 months

_____ 18. 10 months

_____ 19. 11 months

_____ 20. 12 months

A. Rolls over

B. Plays "peek-a-boo"

C. Is fearful of strangers

D. Crawls well

E. Can follow large moving objects

F. Helps dress self

G. Coos and babbles, laughs aloud

H. Attempts to walk without assistance

I. May be soothed by rocking

J. Makes one-syllable sounds such as "ba" and "da"

K. Waves "bye-bye"

L. Sleeps throughout the night without food

Short Answer

Answer each question in the space provided.

21. Why are older adults at increased risk of experiencing a heat- or cold-related emergency?

22. What is human development?

23. Why are falls common in older adults?

24. Each stage of human development is accompanied by physiologic, cognitive, and psychosocial milestones. What are cognitive milestones?

25. Explain what is meant by the term *elder speak.*

Answer Section

Multiple Choice

1. b

   Preschoolers explore their bodies and find playing doctor an interesting activity.

   Objective: Discuss the physiologic, cognitive, and psychosocial characteristics of a preschool child.

2. b

   Menarche is the onset of menstruation during puberty. In the United States the average age of menarche is 12.5 years.

3. c

   The school-age child can run, ride a bicycle, climb, jump, hop, and skip.

   Objective: Discuss the physiologic, cognitive, and psychosocial characteristics of a school-age child.

4. c

   Peak physical conditioning occurs between 19 and 26 years of age, and adults develop lifelong habits and routines during this time. All body systems function at optimal performance.

   Objective: Discuss the physiologic, cognitive, and psychosocial characteristics of an early adult.

Sentence Completion

5. A toddler's heart rate is usually between **80** and **130** beats per minute and respiratory rate is about **20** to **30** breaths per minute.

   Objective: Discuss the physiologic, cognitive, and psychosocial characteristics of a toddler.

6. Measurements of breathing, pulse, skin temperature, pupils, and blood pressure are called **vital signs.**

7. Parents and researchers have identified three unique types of infant cries: the **basic** cry, the **angry** cry, and the **pain** cry.

   Objective: Discuss the physiologic, cognitive, and psychosocial characteristics of an infant.

8. Middle adults may experience **empty nest** syndrome, which is a feeling of sadness and loneliness when one or more of their children leaves home.

   Objective: Discuss the physiologic, cognitive, and psychosocial characteristics of a middle-aged adult.

Matching

9. E
10. I
11. G
12. A
13. L
14. J
15. C
16. B
17. K
18. D
19. H
20. F

Short Answer

21. Older adults have less subcutaneous tissue, inefficient blood vessel constriction, diminished shivering and sweating, diminished perception of temperature, and diminished thirst perception. These factors increase an older adult's likelihood of experiencing a heat- or cold-related emergency.

    Objective: Discuss the physiologic, cognitive, and psychosocial characteristics of an older adult.

22. Human development is the process of growing to maturity.

23. Falls are common in older adults. They occur because of vision and/or balance problems, physical weakness, environmental hazards (such as

poor lighting and throw rugs), urinary problems, and the effects of taking multiple medications.

Objective: Discuss the physiologic, cognitive, and psychosocial characteristics of an older adult.

24. Cognitive milestones pertain to mental processes such as reasoning, imagining, and problem solving.

25. Elder speak, often unknowingly used by young adults when speaking to an older adult, is a style of speech that resembles baby talk and contains the following features:

- A slower rate of speaking
- A patronizing tone
- High pitch
- Increased volume
- Increased repetition
- Simpler vocabulary and grammar than in normal adult speech
- Statements that sound like questions
- Exaggeration of words

Elder speak does not communicate appropriate respect. Its use implies that the older adult is dependent and incompetent, lacking the ability to understand and respond.

Objective: Discuss the physiologic, cognitive, and psychosocial characteristics of an older adult.

Module 3

Pharmacology

► CHAPTER 9

Pharmacology   65

CHAPTER

9

Pharmacology

READING ASSIGNMENT Read Chapter 9, pages 185 to 197 in your textbook.

Sum It Up

- A drug's chemical name is a description of its composition and molecular structure. The generic name (also called the nonproprietary name) is the name given to a drug by the company that first manufactures it. A drug's trade name is also known as its brand name or proprietary name.
- A local effect of a drug usually occurs only in a limited part of the body (usually at the site of drug application). Drugs with systemic effects are absorbed into the bloodstream and distributed throughout the body.
- Each drug is in a specific medication form to allow properly controlled concentrations of the drug to enter the bloodstream where the drug has an effect on the target body system.
- Before giving a drug, an EMR must know the following:
  —The drug's mechanism of action—the desired effects the drug should have on the patient
  —Indications for the drug's use, including the most common uses of the drug in treating a specific illness
  —Contraindications—situations in which the drug should not be used because it may cause harm to the patient or offer no possibility of improving the patient's condition or illness
  —Correct dose (amount) of the drug to be given
  —The proper route by which the drug is given
  —Adverse effects—undesired effects of a drug. Some adverse effects may be predictable.
- Before giving a drug, use the six "rights" of drug administration: right patient, right drug, right dose, right route, right time (frequency), and right documentation. After giving a drug, document the time you gave the drug, document the patient's response to the drug, monitor the patient for possible adverse (harmful) effects, and reassess and record the patient's vital signs.
- Medications an EMR can assist a patient in taking with approval by medical direction may include an epinephrine autoinjector, if state law and your agency policy permit. Medications an EMR can self-administer or administer to a peer with approval by medical direction include atropine, pralidoxime chloride, and possibly diazepam.

► Tracking Your Progress

After reading this chapter, can you:	Page Reference	Objective Met?
• List the main sources of medications?	187	☐
• Differentiate among the chemical, generic, and trade names of a drug?	187	☐
• Give examples of reputable sources of drug information?	188	☐
• Discuss the forms in which medications may be found?	188	☐
• Differentiate between local and systemic effects of medications?	188	☐
• List and differentiate routes of drug administration?	190	☐
• State the medication form, dose, and action for oxygen administration?	192	☐
• State the generic and trade names, medication form, dose, administration, action, indications, and contraindications for the epinephrine autoinjector?	192	☐ ☐
• Explain what a nerve agent is and give examples?	193	☐
• Define antidote?	193	☐
• Describe the signs and symptoms of nerve agent exposure?	194	☐
• Identify the medications contained in the Mark I and DuoDote autoinjectors?	194	☐
• Describe the generic and trade names, medication form, dose, administration, action, indications, and contraindications for the medications contained in the Mark I and DuoDote autoinjectors?	194	☐
• State the generic and trade names, medication form, dose, administration, action, indications, and contraindications for the diazepam autoinjector?	196	☐

Chapter Quiz

Multiple Choice

In the space provided, identify the letter of the choice that best completes each statement or answers each question.

_____ 1. Before administering any medication, you must
  a. assess the patient's physical status.
  b. obtain a drug history from the patient.
  c. obtain permission to administer the medication from medical direction.
  d. all of the above.

_____ 2. A drug's effect that usually occurs in a limited part of the body is known as
  a. a side effect.
  b. a local effect.
  c. an adverse effect.
  d. a systemic effect.

_____ 3. Oxygen is an example of which type of drug form?
  a. Liquid   **c.** Gas
  b. Solid   **d.** Suspension

_____ 4. A drug's mechanism of action is
  a. the route by which a drug is administered.
  b. an exaggerated response to a drug by an individual.
  c. how a drug exerts its effect on body cells and tissues.
  d. the condition(s) for which a specific drug has documented usefulness.

_____ **5.** Your state law and agency policy permit EMRs to assist a patient in using a prescribed autoinjector. You contact your medical direction physician to get approval to assist a patient in using his epinephrine autoinjector. After the physician confirms the medication to be used, the dose of the medication, and its route into the body, you should

    a. immediately give the medication.

    b. reply "10-4, copy" and give the medication.

    c. repeat the orders back to the physician.

    d. contact your dispatcher and request that a paramedic unit be sent to your location before you give the medication.

_____ **6.** An autoinjector delivers medication via which route?

    a. Inhalation   **b.** Sublingual

    c. Subcutaneous   **d.** Intramuscular

Short Answer

Answer each question in the space provided.

7. When is an emergency medical responder permitted to administer a nerve agent autoinjector?

8. List five adverse effects of epinephrine administration.

9. Briefly explain the difference between a Mark I and a DuoDote kit.

10. Explain the mechanism of action of epinephrine.

11. List six signs or symptoms of severe nerve agent exposure.

Answer Section

Multiple Choice

1. d

Assessing the patient's physical status is essential to ensuring that a correct treatment plan is developed. You must be knowledgeable about each drug you may administer. Obtaining a patient's drug history should include prescription medications, over-the-counter medications, and medication allergies. Finally, as an EMR, you must gain approval from medical direction before administering a medication. Approval may be in the form of on-line medical direction (speaking with the physician via phone or radio) or off-line medical direction (through standing orders).

2. b

A local effect of a drug usually occurs only in a limited part of the body (usually at the site of drug application). For instance, if you apply calamine lotion to a rash on your arm or leg, the effects of the drug are limited to the extremity to which the drug was applied.

Objective: Differentiate between local and systemic effects of medications.

3. c

Drugs that are in a gas form are breathed in and absorbed through the respiratory tract. Oxygen is an example of a drug that is given in gas form.

Objective: Discuss the forms in which the medications may be found.

4. c

A drug's mechanism of action refers to how the drug exerts its effect on body cells and tissues.

5. c

Before giving any drug, you must assess the patient and obtain a medication history from the patient.

Then consult with medical direction. When speaking with medical direction, be sure to relay relevant information about the patient, including the patient's age, chief complaint, vital signs, signs and symptoms, allergies, current medications, and pertinent past medical history. The physician's order will include the name, dose, and route of the drug to be given. Repeat the orders back to the physician including the name of the drug, the dose, and the route of administration.

6. d

An autoinjector is a drug delivery system that is designed to work through clothing. Applying firm, even pressure to the injector propels a spring-driven needle into the patient's skin (usually the thigh) and then injects the drug into the muscle.

Objective: List and differentiate routes of drug administration.

Short Answer

7. Administer a nerve agent autoinjector kit if you or a peer has serious signs or symptoms that indicate the presence of nerve agent poisoning and you are authorized to do so by medical direction.

Objective: Describe the generic and trade names, medication form, dose, administration, action, indications, and contraindications for the medications contained in the Mark I and DuoDote autoinjectors.

8. Adverse effects of epinephrine administration include:

- Rapid heart rate
- Anxiety
- Excitability
- Nausea, vomiting
- Chest pain or discomfort
- Headache
- Dizziness

Objective: State the generic and trade names, medication form, dose, administration, action, indications, and contraindications for the epinephrine autoinjector.

9. Nerve agent antidotes are available in two types. The Mark I kit contains two separate autoinjectors—one for atropine and one for pralidoxime chloride. DuoDote, approved by the FDA in 2007, is a prefilled autoinjector that delivers atropine and pralidoxime chloride in one intramuscular injection.

   Objective: Describe the generic and trade names, medication form, dose, administration, action, indications, and contraindications for the medications contained in the Mark I and DuoDote autoinjectors.

10. Epinephrine works by relaxing the passages of the airway and constricting the blood vessels. The opening of the airway allows the patient to move more air into and out of the body, and this will increase the amount of oxygen in the bloodstream. Constriction of the blood vessels slows the leakage of fluid from the blood vessels into the space around the cells of the body.

   Objective: State the generic and trade names, medication form, dose, administration, action, indications, and contraindications for the epinephrine autoinjector.

11. Signs or symptoms of severe nerve agent exposure include:

   - Strange or confused behavior
   - Severe difficulty breathing or severe secretions from the airway
   - Muscle twitching, jerking, staggering
   - Drowsiness
   - General weakness
   - Headache
   - Involuntary urination
   - Involuntary defecation (bowel movement)
   - Seizures
   - Apnea
   - Unconsciousness

   Objective: Describe the signs and symptoms of nerve agent exposure.

Module 4

Airway Management, Respiration, and Ventilation

▶ CHAPTER **10**

Airway Management, Respiration, and Ventilation   71

CHAPTER 10
Airway Management, Respiration, and Ventilation

READING ASSIGNMENT Read Chapter 10, pages 199 to 233 in your textbook.

Sum It Up

- As an EMR, you must maintain an open airway in order to allow a free flow of air `into and out of the patient's lungs. You must be familiar with the structures of the upper and lower airways. You must also understand the mechanisms of breathing.

- One of the most important actions that you can perform is opening the airway of an unresponsive patient. You must become familiar with the two main methods of opening an airway: the head tilt–chin lift and the modified jaw-thrust maneuver. The head tilt–chin lift maneuver is used to open the airway if trauma to the head or neck is not suspected. When trauma to the head or neck of an unresponsive patient is suspected, you should use the modified jaw-thrust maneuver to open the patient's airway. However, use a head tilt–chin lift maneuver if the jaw thrust does not open the airway.

- You should always have suction equipment with arm's reach when you are managing a patient's airway or assisting a patient's breathing. Suctioning is a procedure used to vacuum vomitus, saliva, blood, food particles, and other material from the patient's airway.

- If you see foreign material in the patient's mouth, you must remove it immediately. If foreign material is seen in an unresponsive patient's upper airway, a finger sweep may be used to remove it. A "blind" finger sweep is never performed. Performing a blind finger sweep may cause the object to become further lodged in the patient's throat.

- In some situations, the recovery position can be used to help maintain an open airway in an unresponsive patient. This position involves positioning a patient on his side. As an EMR, you must become familiar with placing a patient in this position. You must also remember not to place a patient with a known or suspected spinal injury in the recovery position.

- After you have opened a patient's airway, you may need to use an airway adjunct to keep it open. After the airway adjunct is inserted, maintain the proper head position while the device is in place.
  - An oral airway (also called an oropharyngeal airway, or OPA) is a device that is used only in unresponsive patients without a gag reflex. An OPA is inserted

into the patient's mouth and used to keep the tongue away from the back of the throat.

— A nasal airway (also called a nasopharyngeal airway, or NPA) is a device that is placed in the patient's nose. An NPA keeps the patient's tongue from blocking the upper airway. It also allows air to flow from the hole in the NPA down into the patient's lower airway.

- After making sure that the patient's airway is open, you must check for breathing. If the patient is breathing, you must determine if the patient is breathing adequately or inadequately. You must also be able to recognize the sounds of noisy breathing, which include stridor, snoring, gurgling, and wheezing.

- You may need to give patients supplemental oxygen. Become familiar with the features and functioning of oxygen cylinders. Remember to always keep combustible materials away from oxygen equipment and never position any part of your body over the cylinder.

- The two most common oxygen delivery devices are the nonrebreather mask and the nasal cannula. In most situations, the nonrebreather mask is the preferred method of oxygen delivery. It allows the delivery of high-concentration oxygen to a breathing patient. At 15 L/min, the oxygen concentration delivered is about 60% to 95%. The nasal cannula is used for patients who are breathing adequately. A nasal cannula can deliver an oxygen concentration of 25% to 45% at 1 to 6 L/min.

- If your patient's breathing is inadequate or absent, you will need to assist the patient by forcing air into the patient's lungs during inspiration. This action is called positive-pressure ventilation and includes the following: mouth-to-mask ventilation, mouth-to-barrier ventilation, and bag-mask ventilation. As an EMR, you must be familiar with performing all of these ventilation methods. You must also learn how to remove foreign body airway obstructions in patients of every age.

▶ Tracking Your Progress

After reading this chapter, can you:	Page Reference	Objective Met?
• Name and label the major structures of the respiratory system on a diagram?	201	☐
• Discuss how the airway of infants and young children differs from that of older children and adults?	203	☐
• List the signs of an adequate airway?	204	☐
• List the signs of an inadequate airway?	204	☐
• Describe the steps in the head tilt–chin lift?	205	☐
• Relate mechanism of injury to opening the airway?	205	☐
• Describe the steps in performing the jaw-thrust maneuver?	206	☐
• Describe the assessment findings and symptoms of a foreign body airway obstruction?	207	☐
• State the importance of having a suction unit ready for immediate use when providing emergency medical care?	208	☐
• Describe the techniques of suctioning?	208	☐
• Describe how to measure and insert an oral airway?	210	☐
• Describe how to measure and insert a nasal airway?	211	☐
• List the signs of adequate breathing?	214	☐

After reading this chapter, can you:

	Page Reference	Objective Met?
• List the signs of inadequate breathing?	216	☐
• Differentiate among respiratory distress, respiratory failure, and respiratory arrest?	216	☐
• Define the components of an oxygen delivery system?	217	☐
• Identify a nonrebreather face mask and state the oxygen flow requirements needed for its use?	219	☐
• Identify a nasal cannula and state the flow requirements needed for its use?	223	☐
• Describe the technique of giving blow-by oxygen?	224	☐
• Describe differences between normal ventilation and positive-pressure ventilation?	224	☐
• Describe the purpose of cricoid pressure and explain how to perform this procedure?	224	☐
• Describe how to ventilate a patient with a resuscitation mask or barrier device?	226	☐
• List the parts of a bag-mask system?	228	☐
• Describe the steps for one and two rescuers in artificially ventilating a patient with a bag-mask?	228	☐
• Describe the signs of adequate artificial ventilation using the bag-mask?	230	☐
• Describe the signs of inadequate artificial ventilation using the bag-mask?	230	☐
• List the steps in performing mask-to-stoma ventilation?	231	☐
• Describe how ventilating an infant or child is different from ventilating an adult?	232	☐

Chapter Quiz

True/False

Decide whether each statement is true or false. In the space provided, write T for true or F for false.

_____ 1. An oral airway can be used in responsive, semiresponsive, and unresponsive patients.

_____ 2. A finger sweep may be used on responsive patients or unresponsive patients who have a gag reflex.

Multiple Choice

In the space provided, identify the letter of the choice that best completes each statement or answers each question.

_____ 3. Do not suction an adult for more than
   a. 3 seconds.
   b. 5 seconds.
   c. 15 seconds.
   d. 30 seconds.

_____ 4. Which of the following are signs of a severe airway obstruction?
   a. Wheezing between coughs
   b. Absence of cough, speech, or breathing
   c. Able to speak and can cough forcefully
   d. Coughing and a high-pitched noise on inhalation

_____ **5.** A 6-year-old child is found unresponsive in the living room by his mother. No spinal injury is suspected. You should open the child's airway using the

    a. head tilt–chin lift maneuver.

    b. modified jaw-thrust maneuver.

    c. tongue–jaw lift maneuver.

    d. Sellick maneuver.

_____ **6.** Select the correct statement regarding the airway of an infant or child.

    a. The narrowest part of a child's airway is at the vocal cords.

    b. The tongue of an infant or child is large in size relative to the size of the mouth.

    c. The supporting cartilage of a child's trachea is more developed than that of an adult's.

    d. An infant less than 6 months of age breathes primarily through his mouth.

_____ **7.** A 92-year-old man has a tracheal stoma. If it is necessary to provide positive-pressure ventilation for this patient, the preferred method is to use

    a. your mouth directly over the stoma.

    b. a nasal cannula aimed at the stoma.

    c. a nonrebreather mask placed over the stoma.

    d. a pediatric pocket mask placed over stoma.

_____ **8.** A 35-year-old woman is choking in a restaurant. She is awake but unable to cough or speak. She is quickly turning blue. Your first action should be to

    a. tell her you are going to help her and perform abdominal thrusts.

    b. apply a pocket mask to her face and begin rescue breathing.

    c. check for a pulse and prepare to perform chest compressions.

    d. place her on the floor and perform a jaw-thrust maneuver.

Sentence Completion

In the blanks provided, write the words that best complete each sentence.

  9. The largest cartilage of the larynx is the thyroid cartilage, also called the _____ _____.

 10. OPA stands for _____ _____.

 11. The _____ is the most common cause of upper-airway obstruction in an unresponsive patient.

 12. When providing rescue breathing for an infant or child, give one breath every _____ seconds, which is _____ breaths/min.

 13. When providing rescue breathing for an adult, give one breath every _____ to _____ seconds, which is _____ to _____ breaths/min.

 14. The gases that are exchanged during the process of breathing are _____ and _____.

Matching

Match the key terms in the left column with the definitions in the right column by placing the letter of each correct answer in the space provided.

_____ **15.** Nasal septum

_____ **16.** Aspiration

_____ **17.** Patent

_____ **18.** Airway adjuncts

_____ **19.** Glottis

_____ **20.** Diaphragm

_____ **21.** Epiglottis

_____ **22.** Suctioning

A. A piece of cartilage that closes off the trachea during swallowing

B. The primary muscle of respiration

C. Breathing a foreign substance into the lungs

D. The space between the vocal cords

E. A wall of tissue that separates the right and left nostrils

F. Open

G. A procedure used to vacuum material from the patient's airway

H. Devices used to help keep a patient's airway open

Short Answer

Answer each question in the space provided.

23. Describe how to select an oral airway of the correct size for a patient.

24. List five signs of inadequate ventilation.

1.

2.

3.

4.

5.

25. Describe the differences between normal ventilation and positive-pressure ventilation.

Answer Section

True/False

1. False

   An oral airway is inserted into the patient's mouth and used to keep the tongue away from the back of the throat. It may only be used in unresponsive patients *without* a gag reflex. If you try to use an oral airway in a patient with a gag reflex, she may vomit and aspirate the vomitus into her lungs.

2. False

   You should use a finger sweep only when you can see solid material blocking the upper airway of an unresponsive patient. A finger sweep is not performed on responsive patients or on unresponsive patients who have a gag reflex.

Multiple Choice

3. c

   If the patient's airway is open and a need for suction has been identified, attempt to provide 100% oxygen for 2 to 3 minutes before suctioning. This is called preoxygenation. Preoxygenating the patient is important because oxygen levels will drop during suctioning. The maximum length of time allowed for suctioning is 10 to 15 seconds for adults and 10 seconds for children and infants.

   Objective: Describe the techniques of suctioning.

4. b

   A patient who is alert and talking clearly or crying without difficulty has an open airway. If you suspect a foreign body airway obstruction but the patient is responsive, can speak or make sounds, and can cough forcefully, he has a mild airway obstruction. You may hear wheezing between coughs. If the patient is unable to speak, cry, cough, or make any other sound, he has a severe airway obstruction. Death due to suffocation will follow rapidly if you do not take prompt action.

   Objective: Describe assessment findings and symptoms of a foreign body airway obstruction.

5. a

   The head tilt–chin lift maneuver is the most effective method for opening the airway in a patient with no known or suspected trauma to the head or neck. It requires no equipment and is simple to perform. When done correctly, the base of the tongue will be displaced from blocking the back of the throat.

   Objective: Relate mechanism of injury to opening the airway.

6. b

   The narrowest part of a child's airway is at the cricoid cartilage, which is lower in the child's airway than it is in an adult's. A small change in airway size (because of conditions such as swelling or inflammation) can result in significant breathing problems. The tongue is larger in proportion to the airway in the infant and child than in the adult. The trachea is softer and more flexible in infants and children. The supporting cartilage of a child's trachea is less developed than that of an adult's, making it prone to compression with improper neck positioning. Infants less than 6 months of age breathe primarily through the nose, not the mouth.

   Objective: Discuss how the airway of infants and young children differs from that of older children and adults.

7. d

   To ventilate a patient with a stoma, the use of a bag-mask or pediatric face mask or barrier device is recommended. Remove any garment (scarf, necktie) covering the stoma. Place a pediatric face mask or barrier device on the patient's neck over the stoma. Make an airtight seal around the stoma and then slowly blow into the one-way valve on the mask until the chest rises. Remove your mouth from the mask to allow the patient to exhale. If a bag-mask is available, connect oxygen to the BM device. If the patient has a tracheostomy tube in place, remove the mask from the device. Connect the bag-mask device to the patient's tracheostomy tube and squeeze the bag while watching for chest rise. Allow the patient to exhale passively. If a stoma is present (but no tracheostomy tube), attach a pediatric mask to the BM device. Center the mask over the stoma, and make an airtight seal around the stoma. If the chest does not rise and fall, seal the patient's mouth and nose and try again to ventilate. Release the seal to allow the patient to exhale.

Objective: List the steps in performing mask-to-stoma ventilation.

8. a

Based on the information provided, the patient has a severe airway obstruction. Since this patient is awake but cannot cough or speak, perform abdominal thrusts. Stand behind the patient and wrap your arms around her waist. Make a fist with one hand. Place your fist, thumb side in, just above the patient's navel. Grab your fist tightly with your other hand. Pull your fist quickly inward and upward. Continue performing abdominal thrusts until the foreign body is expelled or the patient becomes unresponsive. Perform each abdominal thrust with the intent of relieving the obstruction. If abdominal thrusts are not effective, consider the use of chest thrusts to relieve the obstruction. If the patient is obese or in the later stages of pregnancy, perform chest thrusts instead of abdominal thrusts: Place your arms around the patient's chest, directly under the armpits. Press your hands backward, giving quick thrusts into the middle of the breastbone. Do not place your hands on the patient's ribs or on the bottom of the breastbone (xiphoid process). The xiphoid process can easily be broken off the breastbone and can cut underlying organs, such as the liver.

Objective: Describe assessment findings and symptoms of a foreign body airway obstruction.

Sentence Completion

9. The largest cartilage of the larynx is the thyroid cartilage, also called the **Adam's apple.**

   Objective: Name and describe the locations and functions of the organs of the respiratory system.

10. OPA stands for **oropharyngeal airway.**

11. The **tongue** is the most common cause of upper-airway obstruction in an unresponsive patient.

    Objective: Describe assessment findings and symptoms of a foreign body airway obstruction.

12. When providing rescue breathing for an infant or child, give one breath every **3** seconds, which is **20** breaths/min.

    Objective: Describe the steps for one and two rescuers in artificially ventilating a patient with a bag-mask.

13. When providing rescue breathing for an adult, give one breath every **5** to **6** seconds, which is **10** to **12** breaths/min.

    Objective: Describe the steps for one and two rescuers in artificially ventilating a patient with a bag-mask.

14. The gases that are exchanged during the process of breathing are **oxygen** and **carbon dioxide.**

    Objective: Describe the anatomy and function of the upper and lower airways.

Matching

15. E	19. D
16. C	20. B
17. F	21. A
18. H	22. G

Short Answer

23. OPAs are available in a variety of sizes. To select the correct size, hold the OPA against the side of the patient's face. Select an OPA that extends from the corner of the patient's mouth to the tip of the earlobe, or the angle of the jaw.

    Objective: Describe how to measure and insert an oral airway.

24. Signs of inadequate ventilation include:
    - Anxious appearance, concentration on breathing
    - Confusion, restlessness

- Inability to speak in complete sentences
- Abnormal work (effort) of breathing (retractions, nasal flaring, accessory muscle use, sweating, tripod position, flared nostrils, or pursed lips)
- Abnormal breathing sounds (stridor, wheezing)
- Depth of breathing that is unusually deep or shallow
- A breathing rate that is too fast or slow for the patient's age
- An irregular breathing pattern
- Inadequate chest wall movement or damage due to trauma
- Pain with breathing

Objective: List the signs of inadequate breathing.

25. During normal ventilation, negative pressure is created inside the chest and air is sucked into the lungs. During positive-pressure ventilation, a healthcare professional is pushing air into the patient's lungs. During normal ventilation, blood returns to the heart from the body, and blood is pulled back to the heart during normal breathing. During positive-pressure ventilation, blood return to the heart is decreased when the lungs are inflated. As a result, less blood is available for the heart to pump, and the amount of blood pumped out of the heart is reduced. During normal ventilation, the esophagus remains closed, and no air enters the stomach. During positive-pressure ventilation, air is pushed into the stomach during ventilation. Excess air in the stomach may lead to vomiting. An excessive rate or depth of positive-pressure ventilation can harm the patient. For example, ventilating too fast or too deep may cause low blood pressure, vomiting, and decreased blood flow when the chest is compressed during CPR.

Objective: Describe differences between normal ventilation and positive-pressure ventilation.

Patient Assessment

▶ CHAPTER **11**

Therapeutic Communications and Patient History   80

▶ CHAPTER **12**

Patient Assessment   86

11 Therapeutic Communications and Patient History

READING ASSIGNMENT ▶ Read Chapter 11, pages 235 to 248 in your textbook.

Sum It Up

- The communication process involves six basic elements: source, encoding, message, channel, receiver (decoder), and feedback. The source of verbal communication is spoken or written words. A message is the information to be communicated. The sender decides the message he wants to send and then encodes it. Encoding is the act of placing a message into words or images so that it is understood by the sender and receiver. The sender selects the path (channel) for transmitting the message to the receiver. The receiver is the person or group for whom the sender's message is intended. When a message is received, the receiver must interpret (decode) the sender's message. Noise is anything that obscures, confuses, or interferes with the communication. Feedback is the response from the receiver (verbal or nonverbal) that allows the sender to know how his message is being received.

- When communicating with a patient, identify yourself and explain that you are there to provide assistance. Recognize the patient's need for privacy, preserve the patient's dignity, and treat the patient with respect.

- When talking with family members, friends, and bystanders, avoid interrupting when they are talking. Speak clearly and use common words (avoid using medical terms). Speak at an appropriate speed or pace, not too rapidly and not too slowly.

- The patient history is part of the patient assessment during which you find out pertinent facts about the patient's medical history. Components of the patient history include the chief complaint, history of the present illness, past medical history (pertinent to the medical event), and current health status (pertinent to the medical event).

- When asking questions to find out the patient's medical history, use open-ended questions when possible. Open-ended questions require that the patient answer with more than a yes or no. Questions that require a yes or no answer are called closed or direct questions.

- The chief complaint is the reason the patient called for assistance. The history of the present illness is a chronological record of the reason the patient is seeking medical assistance. It includes the patient's chief complaint and the patient's answers to questions about the circumstances that led up to the request for medical help. The conclusion you reach about what is wrong with your patient is called a field impression.
- OPQRST is a memory aid that may help identify the type and location of a patient's pain or discomfort. OPQRST stands for **O**nset, **P**rovocation/palliation/position, **Q**uality, **R**egion/radiation, **S**everity, and **T**ime.
- The Wong-Baker FACES Pain Rating Scale is a tool used to assess pain in children 3 years or older.
- SAMPLE is a memory aid used to standardize the approach to history taking. SAMPLE stands for **S**igns and symptoms, **A**llergies, **M**edications, **P**ast medical history, **L**ast oral intake, and **E**vents leading to the injury or illness. It is important to obtain a SAMPLE history from all responsive patients. A sign is any medical or trauma condition displayed by the patient that can be seen, heard, smelled, measured, or felt. A symptom is any condition described by the patient.

▶ Tracking Your Progress

After reading this chapter, can you:	Page Reference	Objective Met?
• Discuss the basic elements of the communication process?	236	☐
• Identify nonverbal behaviors that are used in patient interviewing?	236	☐
• Discuss common patient responses to illness or injury?	237	☐
• Discuss the communication skills that should be used to interact with the patient?	238	☐
• Discuss developmental considerations of various age groups that influence patient interviewing?	241	☐
• Discuss techniques that may be necessary when interviewing patients who have special needs?	242	☐
• Discuss the communication skills that should be used to interact with family members and bystanders?	244	☐
• Identify and explain each of the components of the patient history?	244	☐
• Provide examples of open-ended and closed or direct questions?	244	☐
• Discuss the need to search for additional medical identification?	245	☐
• Give examples of pertinent positive and pertinent negative findings?	245	☐
• Explain the standardized approach to history taking using the OPQRST and SAMPLE acronyms?	245	☐
• Differentiate between a sign and a symptom?	248	☐

Chapter Quiz

True/False

Decide whether each statement is true or false. In the space provided, write T for true or F for false.

_____ 1. During the communication process, the feedback received may be verbal or nonverbal.

_____ 2. OPQRST is a memory aid used to determine a patient's level of responsiveness.

_____ 3. "Do you have any allergies?" is an example of a direct question.

Multiple Choice

In the space provided, identify the letter of the choice that best completes each statement or answers each question.

_____ 4. In which zone of interpersonal distance does most of a patient interview take place?
   a. Social space
   b. Public space
   c. Intimate space
   d. Personal space

_____ 5. Questions that give patients an opportunity to express their thoughts, feelings, and ideas are called
   a. direct questions.
   b. narrative questions.
   c. descriptive questions.
   d. open-ended questions.

_____ 6. When getting a SAMPLE history from bystanders at the scene, questions related to the M in SAMPLE include which of the following?
   a. Does the patient have a history of stroke, diabetes, or heart disease?
   b. Did she hit her head or fall?
   c. Is this the patient's first seizure?
   d. Does the patient take any seizure medications? What prescription and nonprescription medicines is she taking?

Short Answer

Answer each question in the space provided.

7. Discuss the basic elements of the communication process.

8. Should medical terminology be used when communicating with patients? Why or why not?

9. Give an example of how you should introduce yourself to a patient.

10. You are called to a private residence and find a 72-year-old man unresponsive. Describe how you will go about finding out information that may be useful in the care of this patient.

11. List five common patient responses to illness or injury.
1.
2.
3.
4.
5.

12. Your patient, an 85-year-old woman, has experienced a stroke. She is unable to speak but is able to understand your questions. Describe how you will communicate with this patient.

Answer Section

True/False

1. True

   Feedback is the response from the receiver (verbal or nonverbal) that allows the sender to know how her message is being received. In the feedback loop, the receiver becomes the sender and the sender becomes the receiver. The switch from sender to receiver and back again occurs often during the communication process.

   Objective: Discuss the basic elements of the communication process.

2. False

   SAMPLE is a memory aid used to standardize the approach to history taking. SAMPLE stands for Signs and symptoms, Allergies, Medications, Past medical history, Last oral intake, and Events leading to the injury or illness. If a patient is complaining of pain or discomfort, OPQRST is a memory aid that may help identify the type and location of the patient's present complaint.

   Objective: Explain the standardized approach to history taking using the OPQRST and SAMPLE acronyms.

3. True

   Questions that can be answered with yes or no or with one- or two-word responses are called closed or direct questions.

   Objective: Provide examples of open-ended and closed or direct questions.

Multiple Choice

4. a

   In the United States, social space is generally a distance of about 4½ to 12 feet. It is used for impersonal business transactions and much of a patient interview occurs at this distance.

Hearing and vision are the primary senses used in this space.

   Objective: Discuss the communication skills that should be used to interact with the patient.

5. d

   Questions that give patients an opportunity to express their thoughts, feelings, and ideas are called open-ended questions. Open-ended questions encourage patients to describe and explain what is wrong. An example of an open-ended question is "Can you tell me why you called us today?"

   Objective: Provide examples of open-ended and closed or direct questions.

6. d

   "M" stands for medications, which a bystander may or may not know about, but it is important to ask since a friend or family member may be present who knows about the patient's condition.

   Objective: Explain the standardized approach to history taking using the OPQRST and SAMPLE acronyms.

Short Answer

7. The communication process involves six basic elements: source, encoding, message, channel, receiver (decoder), and feedback. The source of verbal communication is spoken or written words. A message is the information to be communicated. The sender decides the message he wants to send and then encodes it. Encoding is the act of placing a message into words or images so that it is understood by the sender and receiver. The sender selects the path (channel) for transmitting the message to the receiver. The receiver is the person or group for whom the sender's message is intended. When a message is received, the receiver must interpret

(decode) the sender's message. Noise is anything that obscures, confuses, or interferes with the communication. Feedback is the response from the receiver (verbal or nonverbal) that allows the sender to know how the message is being received. Communication is successful if the sender and the receiver understand the same information because of the communication.

Objective: Discuss the basic elements of the communication process.

8. When communicating with your patients, do not use medical terms. Appropriate medical terminology should be used in your written reports and verbal communication with other healthcare professionals.

Objective: Discuss the communication skills that should be used to interact with the patient.

9. When communicating with a patient, begin by identifying yourself and establish your role by saying "My name is _____. I am an emergency medical responder trained to provide emergency care. I am here to help you." Address the patient by proper name, Mr. _____ or Mrs. _____. Ask the patient what he or she wishes to be called, and then ask for permission to use this name.

Objective: Discuss the communication skills that should be used to interact with the patient.

10. If the patient is unresponsive, gather as much information as possible by looking at the scene. Also look for medical identification tags and question family members, coworkers, or others at the scene.

Objective: Discuss the need to search for additional medical identification.

11. Common patient responses to illness or injury include:

- Fear
- Embarrassment
- Frustration
- Pain
- Regression
- Feeling of being powerless or helpless
- Anxiety
- Anger
- Sorrow
- Depression
- Guilt, shame, or blame

Objective: Discuss common patient responses to illness or injury.

12. You may be able to establish some other means of communication, such as a hand squeeze or even eyeblinks. If your patient appears to understand your questions but is unable to answer, stop asking the questions but continue to talk to the patient. Let her know that you understand she is unable to talk. It may be comforting to the patient to know that you are aware of her situation.

Objective: Discuss the communication skills that should be used to interact with the patient.

12 Patient Assessment

READING ASSIGNMENT Read Chapter 12, pages 249 to 300 in your textbook.

Sum It Up

- As an EMR, you must quickly look at the entire scene before approaching the patient. You must size up the scene to find out if there are any threats that may cause injury to you, other rescuers, or bystanders or that may cause additional injury to the patient.
- Scene size-up is the first phase of patient assessment and consists of five parts:
    1. Taking standard precautions
    2. Evaluating scene safety
    3. Determining the mechanism of injury (including considerations for stabilization of the spine) or the nature of the patient's illness
    4. Determining the total number of patients
    5. Determining the need for additional resources
- You must take appropriate standard precautions on every call. Consider the need for standard precautions before you approach the patient. Put on appropriate PPE on the basis of the information the dispatcher gives you and your initial survey of the scene. This equipment includes gloves, eye protection, mask, and gown, if necessary.
- The evaluation of scene safety is an assessment of the entire scene and surroundings to ensure your well-being and that of other rescuers, the patient(s), and bystanders.
- During the scene size-up, try to determine the nature of the illness or mechanism of injury.
- A medical patient is one whose condition is caused by an illness. The nature of the illness (NOI) describes the medical condition that resulted in the patient's call to 9-1-1. Examples include fever, difficulty breathing, chest pain, headache, and vomiting. You should try to find out the nature of the illness by talking to the patient, family, coworkers, and bystanders.
- Mechanism of injury (MOI) is the way in which an injury occurs as well as the forces involved in producing the injury. Kinetic energy is the energy of motion. The amount of kinetic energy an object has depends on the mass (weight) and speed (velocity) of the object. Kinematics is the science of analyzing the mechanism of injury and predicting injury patterns. The amount of injury is determined by the following three elements: (1) the type of energy applied, (2) how quickly the energy is applied, and (3) to what part of the body the energy is applied.

- A trauma patient is one who has experienced an injury from an external force. Traumatic situations include motor vehicle crashes, motor vehicle–pedestrian crashes, falls, bicycle crashes, motorcycle crashes, and penetrating traumas.
- Blunt trauma is any mechanism of injury that occurs without actual penetration of the body. Examples of mechanisms of injury causing blunt trauma include motor vehicle crashes, falls, sports injuries, and assaults with a blunt object. Blunt trauma produces injury first to the body surface and then to the body's contents.
- Penetrating trauma is any mechanism of injury that causes a cut or piercing of the skin. Examples of mechanisms of injury causing penetrating trauma include gunshot wounds, stab wounds, and blast injuries. Penetrating trauma usually affects organs and tissues in the direct path of the wounding object.
- A motor vehicle crash is classified by the type of impact. The five types of impact include head on (frontal), lateral, rear end, rotational, and rollover.
- In a frontal impact, such as a head-on collision, the vehicle stops and the occupants continue to move forward by one of two pathways: down and under or up and over.
  - In the down-and-under pathway, the victim's knees hit the vehicle's dashboard. The down-and-under pathway may be seen when the occupant is not wearing a lap and shoulder restraint system or when the occupant is wearing only the shoulder harness and not a lap belt.
  - In the up-and-over pathway, the victim's upper body strikes the steering wheel, resulting in injuries to the head, chest, abdomen, pelvis, and/or spine. The up-and-over pathway may be seen when the occupant is not wearing a lap and shoulder restraint system or when the occupant is wearing only a lap restraint (not the shoulder harness).
- Although mechanism of injury is important, it is not the only factor to consider when assessing a trauma patient and determining whether or not he is a priority patient. For some patients, the risk of significant injury is increased because of their age or a preexisting medical condition, despite what may appear to be a minor mechanism of injury. In some EMS systems, other factors for designating priority status are considered in addition to the mechanism of injury. These include anatomy, physiology, and patient factors.
- Adult pedestrians will typically turn away if they are about to be struck by an oncoming vehicle. This action results in injuries to the side or back of the body. A child will usually face an oncoming vehicle, which results in injuries to the front of the body.
- Falls are a common mechanism of injury. Factors to consider in a fall include the height from which the patient fell, the patient's weight, the surface the patient landed on, and the part of the patient's body that struck first.
- The ability to properly assess a patient is one of the most important skills you can master. As an EMR, you must learn to work quickly and efficiently in all types of situations. To work efficiently, you must approach patient assessment systematically. The emergency care you provide to your patient will be based on your assessment findings.
- While assessing your patient, you will discover her signs and symptoms. You must provide emergency medical care based on those signs and symptoms. Discovering the patient's signs and symptoms requires that you use your senses of sight (look), sound (listen), touch (feel), and smell.

- Patient assessment consists of the following components:
  1. Initial assessment
     - Scene size-up
       - Take standard precautions.
       - Evaluate scene safety.
       - Determine the MOI or the nature of the patient's illness.
       - Determine the total number of patients.
       - Determine the need for additional resources.
     - Primary survey
       - General impression
         a. Appearance
         b. Breathing (work of breathing)
         c. Circulation
       - **A**irway, level of responsiveness, cervical spine protection
       - **B**reathing (ventilation)
       - **C**irculation (perfusion)
       - **D**isability (neurological miniexam)
       - **E**xpose
       - Identify priority patients
     - Secondary survey
       - Vital signs
       - SAMPLE history, OPQRST
       - Head-to-toe or focused physical examination
  2. Reassessment
     - Repeat the primary survey.
     - Reassess vital signs.
     - Repeat the focused assessment regarding patient complaint or injuries.
     - Reevaluate emergency care.
- The primary survey is a rapid assessment to find and treat all immediate life-threatening conditions. It begins after the scene or situation has been found safe or made safe and you have gained access to the patient. During this phase of patient assessment, you will look for and treat life-threatening conditions as you discover them ("find and fix," "treat as you go") and decide if the patient needs immediate transport or additional on-scene assessment and treatment. You must perform a primary survey on every patient.
- The secondary survey is a physical examination performed to discover medical conditions and/or injuries that were not identified in the primary survey. During this phase of the patient assessment, you will also obtain vital signs, reassess changes in the patient's condition, and determine the patient's chief complaint, history of present illness, and significant past medical history. The secondary survey does not begin until the primary survey has been completed and treatment of life-threatening conditions has begun.
- A general impression (also called a first impression) is an across-the-room assessment. As you approach the patient, you will form a general impression without the patient's telling you what the complaint is. You can complete it in 60 seconds or less. The purpose of forming a general impression is to decide if the patient looks sick or not sick. If the patient looks sick, you must act quickly. As you gain experience, you will develop an instinct for quickly recognizing when a patient is sick. You will base your general impression of a patient on three main factors: (1) appearance, (2) breathing, and (3) circulation.
- After forming a general impression, begin the primary survey by assessing the patient's airway and level of responsiveness. Assessment of a patient's airway and assessment of the patient's level of responsiveness occur at the same time. Level of responsiveness is also called level of consciousness or mental status.

These terms refer to a patient's level of awareness. A patient's mental status is graded using a scale called the AVPU scale: A = **A**lert; V = responds to **V**erbal stimuli; P = responds to **P**ainful stimuli; U = **U**nresponsive.

- A patient who is oriented to person, place, time, and event is said to be alert and oriented × (times) 4 or A&O×4. Assessment of the mental status of a child older than 3 years of age is the same as that of an adult.

- For trauma patients or unresponsive patients with an unknown nature of illness, take spinal precautions. Spinal precautions are used to stabilize the head, neck, and back in a neutral position. This stabilization is done to minimize movement that could cause injury to the spinal cord.

- After making sure that the patient's airway is open, assess the patient's breathing to determine if breathing is adequate or inadequate. If the patient is unresponsive and breathing is inadequate or if the patient is not breathing, begin rescue breathing by using a pocket mask, mouth-to-barrier device, or BM device.

- Assessment of circulation involves evaluating for signs of obvious bleeding; central and peripheral pulses; skin color, temperature, and condition; and capillary refill (in children less than 6 years of age). Look from the patient's head to toes for signs of significant external bleeding. Control major bleeding, if present.

- During the disability phase of the primary survey, reassess the patient's mental status. Altered mental status means a change in a patient's level of awareness. Altered mental status is also called altered level of consciousness (ALOC). A patient who has an altered mental status is at risk of an airway obstruction.

- Expose pertinent areas of the patient's body for examination. Factors that you must consider when exposing the patient include protecting the patient's modesty, the presence of bystanders, and environmental and weather conditions.

- Determine if the patient requires on-scene stabilization or immediate transport ("load-and-go" situations) with additional emergency care en route to a hospital.

- The secondary survey is patient-, situation-, and time-dependent. For instance, a patient with an isolated injury, such as a painful ankle, would typically not require a head-to-toe physical examination. However, a secondary survey should be performed in the following situations:
  - Trauma patients with a significant MOI
  - Trauma patients with an unknown or unclear MOI
  - Trauma patients with an injury to more than one area of the body
  - All unresponsive patients
  - All patients with an altered mental status
  - Some responsive medical patients, as indicated by history and focused physical examination findings

- A quick secondary survey (head-to-toe assessment) of a trauma patient with a significant MOI is called a rapid trauma assessment. A significant MOI is one that is likely to produce serious injury. A quick secondary survey of a medical patient who is unresponsive or has an altered mental status is called a rapid medical assessment. A focused physical examination is an assessment of specific body areas that relate to the patient's illness or injury. The procedure for performing a secondary survey is the same for trauma and medical patients. However, the physical findings that you are looking for and discover may have a different meaning depending on whether the patient is a trauma or medical patient.

- When examining your patient, first look (inspect), listen (auscultate), and then feel (palpate) body areas to identify potential injuries.

- DCAP-BTLS is a helpful memory aid to remember what to look and feel for during the physical exam: **D**eformities, **C**ontusions (bruises), **A**brasions (scrapes), **P**unctures/penetrations, **B**urns, **T**enderness, **L**acerations (cuts), **S**welling.

- *Vital signs* are assessments of breathing, pulse, temperature, pupils, and blood pressure. Measuring vital signs is an important part of patient assessment. Vital signs are measured to:
  - —Detect changes in normal body function
  - —Recognize life-threatening situations
  - —Determine a patient's response to treatment
- Remember to take two or more sets of vital signs. Doing so will allow you to note changes (trends) in the patient's condition and response to treatment. Reassess and record vital signs at least every 5 minutes in an unstable patient and at least every 15 minutes in a stable patient.
- Reassessment consists of four main areas:
  - —Repeating the primary survey
  - —Reassessing vital signs
  - —Repeating the focused assessment
  - —Reevaluating emergency care
- Reassessment should be performed on every patient. It is performed after the secondary survey, if a secondary survey is performed. In some situations, the patient's condition may prevent performance of a secondary survey.
- Reassess at least every 15 minutes for a stable patient and every 5 minutes for an unstable patient. Continue to calm and reassure the patient.

▶ Tracking Your Progress

After reading this chapter, can you:	Page Reference	Objective Met?
• Define scene size-up and discuss its components?	251	☐
• Determine if the scene is safe to enter?	253	☐
• Describe common hazards and potential hazards found at the scene of a trauma patient and at the scene of a medical patient?	253	☐
• Differentiate between a trauma patient and a medical patient?	255	☐
• Define mechanism of injury and give examples of common mechanisms of injury?	255	☐
• Differentiate between blunt trauma and penetrating trauma?	255	☐
• Define nature of illness and give examples?	260	☐
• Discuss the reason for identifying the total number of patients at the scene?	261	☐
• Explain the reason for identifying the need for additional help or assistance?	261	☐
• Discuss the examination techniques used during patient assessment?	262	☐
• List and describe the components of patient assessment and the purpose of each component?	263	☐
• Summarize the reasons for forming a general impression of the patient?	264	☐
• Define chief complaint and give examples?	265	☐
• Discuss methods of assessing the airway in adult, child, and infant patients?	265	☐
• Discuss methods of assessing altered mental status in adult, child, and infant patients?	266	☐
• State reasons for management of the cervical spine once the patient has been determined to be a trauma patient?	268	☐
• Describe methods used for assessing if a patient is breathing?	268	☐

After reading this chapter, can you:

	Page Reference	Objective Met?
• State what care should be provided to adult, child, and infant patients with adequate breathing?	269	☐
• State what care should be provided to adult, child, and infant patients with inadequate breathing?	269	☐
• Discuss the need for assessing the patient for external bleeding?	270	☐
• Differentiate between central and peripheral pulses?	270	☐
• Differentiate obtaining a pulse in adult, child, and infant patients?	270	☐
• Describe normal and abnormal findings when assessing skin color?	271	☐
• Differentiate between pale, blue, red, and yellow skin colors?	271	☐
• Describe normal and abnormal findings when assessing skin temperature?	271	☐
• Differentiate between hot, cool, and cold skin temperatures?	271	☐
• Describe normal and abnormal findings when assessing skin moisture?	271	☐
• Describe normal and abnormal findings when assessing capillary refill in the infant or child patient?	271	☐
• Explain the reason for prioritizing a patient for care and transport?	274	☐
• Discuss the purpose and components of the secondary survey?	274	☐
• State the areas of the body that are evaluated during the secondary survey?	274	☐
• Recite examples of and explain why patients should receive a rapid trauma assessment?	274	☐
• Discuss the reason for performing a focused history and physical exam?	274	☐
• Distinguish between the secondary survey that is performed on a trauma patient and the one performed on a medical patient?	274	☐
• Identify the components of vital signs?	275	☐
• Explain baseline vital signs and describe trending of vital signs?	275	☐
• Describe the methods of obtaining a breathing rate?	275	☐
• Identify the attributes that should be obtained when assessing breathing?	276	☐
• Differentiate shallow, labored, and noisy breathing?	276	☐
• Describe the methods of obtaining a pulse rate?	277	☐
• Differentiate between strong, weak, regular, and irregular pulses?	277	☐
• Describe the methods of assessing blood pressure?	277	☐
• Define systolic pressure?	278	☐
• Define diastolic pressure?	278	☐
• Describe the methods of assessing the pupils?	282	☐
• Identify normal and abnormal pupil size?	282	☐
• Differentiate dilated (big) and constricted (small) pupil size?	282	☐
• Differentiate between reactive and nonreactive pupils and equal and unequal pupils?	282	☐
• Explain what additional care should be provided while you are performing the secondary survey?	283	☐
• Discuss the purpose of patient reassessment?	284	☐
• Describe the components of the reassessment?	294	☐
• Discuss the reasons for repeating the primary survey as part of reassessment?	294	☐
• Describe trending of assessment components?	294	☐

Chapter Quiz

True/False

Decide whether each statement is true or false. In the space provided, write T for true or F for false.

_____ **1.** The senses of sight, sound, touch, taste, and smell are used during patient assessment.

_____ **2.** *Sphygmomanometer* is the medical term for a blood pressure cuff.

_____ **3.** A head-to-toe physical examination is performed on every patient.

_____ **4.** A patient who appears "not sick" during the primary survey will most certainly remain stable until care is transferred to another healthcare professional.

_____ **5.** Methods used to assess the mental status of a child older than 3 years of age are the same as those used for adults.

Multiple Choice

In the space provided, identify the letter of the choice that best completes each statement or answers each question.

_____ **6.** When arriving at the scene of an emergency, you should first
  a. perform a scene size-up.
  b. perform a primary survey.
  c. find out who placed the call for help.
  d. provide emergency care to the most seriously injured person.

_____ **7.** You have been dispatched to a shopping mall for a possible shooting. The dispatcher said the caller indicated there are three victims. The suspect is believed to still be in the area. Your best plan of action is to
  a. drive to the scene, enter the mall, and quickly remove all patients.
  b. remain outside the entrance to the mall until law enforcement personnel tell you the scene is safe.
  c. park a safe distance from the scene and wait for law enforcement personnel to tell you that the scene is safe.
  d. enter the scene, quickly determine which patient is most seriously injured, and begin emergency care.

_____ **8.** The normal respiratory rate for an adult at rest is
  a. 6 to 12 breaths/min.   **c.** 20 to 30 breaths/min.
  b. 12 to 20 breaths/min.   **d.** 25 to 35 breaths/min.

_____ **9.** Which of the following represents a scale used to evaluate a patient's level of responsiveness?
  a. AVPU   **c.** OPQRST
  b. APGAR   **d.** SAMPLE

_____ **10.** While you are forming a general impression of a patient, which of the following would you consider a life-threatening condition?
  a. Vomiting   **c.** Major bleeding
  b. Dizziness   **d.** Abdominal pain

_____ **11.** After forming a general impression of the patient and evaluating mental status, you should next assess the patient's
  a. airway.
  c. circulation.
  b. breathing.
  d. upper and lower extremities.

_____ **12.** Vital signs are

    a. the reason EMS was called, usually in the patient's own words.

    b. assessments of breathing, pulse, skin, pupils, and blood pressure.

    c. the rhythmic contraction and expansion of the arteries with each beat of the heart.

    d. assessments of the entire scene and surroundings to ensure your well-being and that of other rescuers, the patient, and bystanders.

_____ **13.** You are called to a scene involving a possible toxic substance. You should park

    a. upwind from the incident.

    b. downhill from the incident.

    c. downwind from the incident.

    d. as far away as possible from the incident.

_____ **14.** Which of the following best describes the secondary survey?

    a. The secondary survey is a rapid assessment for life-threatening conditions.

    b. The secondary survey is limited to assessment of the patient's airway, breathing, and circulatory status.

    c. The secondary survey is a head-to-toe exam performed to identify additional injuries or other information.

    d. The secondary survey is a quick assessment of the scene, safety concerns, and resource requirements.

_____ **15.** You are called to the scene of a 39-year-old patient who fell from a ladder. On arrival, you find the patient unresponsive at the base of a 10-foot ladder. When assessing this patient's airway, you should

    a. perform the modified jaw-thrust maneuver.

    b. perform the head tilt–chin lift maneuver.

    c. perform the head tilt–chin lift maneuver only if head or neck trauma is observed.

    d. perform the modified jaw-thrust maneuver only if head or neck trauma is observed.

Short Answer

Answer each question in the space provided.

16. List three common hazards found at the scene of a trauma patient.

1.

2.

3.

17. Why is it important to identify the total number of patients at an emergency scene?

18. List four areas you should evaluate during the primary survey when assessing circulation and perfusion in a 5-year-old patient.

    1.

    2.

    3.

    4.

19. Explain what is meant by the phrase *spinal precautions.*

20. Differentiate between a central pulse and a peripheral pulse, and give examples of each.

21. Name three types of scenes that may require specially trained personnel to assist.

22. Explain the differences between blunt trauma and penetrating trauma.

23. List the five types of impacts that can occur in a motor vehicle crash.

    1.

    2.

    3.

    4.

    5.

Answer Section

True/False

1. False

The senses of smell, sight (look), sound (listen), and touch (feel) are all used to assess the patient. The sense of taste is not used during patient assessment.

2. True

Vital signs are assessments of breathing, pulse, temperature, pupils, and blood pressure. A sphygmomanometer (blood pressure cuff) is used to obtain the patient's blood pressure.

Objective: Identify the components of vital signs.

3. False

Depending on the severity of the patient's injury or illness, a head-to-toe physical exam may not be completed. This is because treatment of life-threatening conditions takes priority over performing this examination.

Objective: Discuss the purpose and components of the secondary survey.

4. False

Your patient's condition can change at any time. A patient who initially appears not sick may rapidly worsen and appear sick. Reassess your patient often.

Objective: Discuss the reasons for repeating the primary survey as part of reassessment.

5. True

Assessing the mental status of a child older than 3 years of age is the same as assessing the mental status of an adult.

Objective: Discuss methods of assessing altered mental status in adult, child, and infant patients.

Multiple Choice

6. a

Scene size-up begins as an EMR approaches the scene. During this phase, you will survey the scene to determine whether any threats may cause injury to you, other rescuers, the patient, or bystanders. This evaluation also allows you to determine the nature of the call and the need for additional resources as necessary.

Objective: Define scene size-up and discuss its components.

7. c

Do not enter a potentially violent scene until law enforcement personnel ensure that the scene is safe.

Objective: Determine if the scene is safe to enter.

8. b

The normal respiratory rate for an adult at rest is 12 to 20 breaths/minute.

9. a

A patient's mental status is "graded" using a scale called the AVPU scale as follows: A = *A*lert; V = Responds to *V*erbal stimuli; P = Responds to *P*ainful stimuli; U = *U*nresponsive.

Objective: Discuss methods of assessing altered mental status in adult, child, and infant patients.

10. c

Of the conditions listed, the presence of major bleeding is the condition that poses the greatest threat to life.

Objective: List and describe the components of patient assessment and the purpose of each component.

11. a

After forming a general impression, begin the primary survey by assessing the patient's airway and level of responsiveness. Assessment of a patient's airway and level of responsiveness occurs at the same time.

Objective: List and describe the components of patient assessment and the purpose of each component.

12. b

Vital signs are assessments of breathing, pulse, skin, pupils, and blood pressure.

Objective: Identify the components of vital signs.

13. a

When you arrive at a scene, park at a safe distance that is upwind or uphill from the incident. Contact your local hazardous material response team immediately. Do not enter the area unless you are trained to handle hazardous materials and are fully protected with proper equipment.

Objective: Determine if the scene is safe to enter.

14. c

The secondary survey is a head-to-toe exam performed to identify additional injuries or other information.

Objective: List and describe the components of patient assessment and the purpose of each component.

15. a

If a patient is unresponsive and you suspect trauma, open his airway by using the modified jaw-thrust maneuver.

Objective: Relate mechanism of injury to opening the airway.

Short Answer

16. Traffic, unstable vehicle, aircraft, or machinery; leaking fluids, downed power lines, fire, smoke, or potential fire hazards; entrapped victims.

Objective: Describe common hazards and potential hazards found at the scene of a trauma patient and at the scene of a medical patient.

17. It is important to quickly find out the number of patients on the scene in order to request additional resources if necessary.

Objective: Discuss the reason for identifying the total number of patients at the scene.

18. In the primary survey, assessment of circulation and perfusion in a patient less than 6 years of age includes:

1. Checking the patient's pulse
2. Looking for severe bleeding
3. Assessing skin temperature, color, and moisture
4. Assessing capillary refill

19. *Spinal precautions* means to stabilize the head, neck, and back in a neutral position. This is done to minimize movement that could cause injury to the spinal cord.

Objective: State reasons for management of the cervical spine once the patient has been determined to be a trauma patient.

20. A central pulse is a pulse found close to the trunk of the body. Examples of central pulses are the carotid pulse and femoral pulse. A peripheral pulse is located farther from the trunk of the body than a central pulse. Examples of peripheral pulses include the radial pulse, brachial pulse, posterior tibial pulse, and dorsalis pedis pulse.

Objective: Differentiate between central and peripheral pulses.

21. Scenes that may require the assistance of specially trained personnel include:

1. Toxic substances scenes
2. Low-oxygen areas
3. Crime scenes
4. Hostile situations
5. Unstable surfaces or slopes
6. Water and ice scenes

Objective: Explain the reason for identifying the need for additional help or assistance.

22. Blunt trauma is any mechanism of injury that occurs without actual penetration of the body. Examples of mechanisms of injury due to blunt trauma include motor vehicle crashes, falls, sports injuries, and assaults with a blunt object. Blunt trauma produces injury first to the body surface and then to the body's contents. This results in compression and/or stretching of the tissue beneath the skin. The amount of injury depends on how long the compression occurred, the force of the compression, and the area compressed.

Penetrating trauma is any mechanism of injury that causes a cut or piercing of the skin. Examples of mechanisms of injury due to penetrating trauma include gunshot wounds, stab wounds, and blast injuries. Penetrating trauma usually affects organs and tissues in the direct path of the wounding object.

Objective: Differentiate between blunt trauma and penetrating trauma.

23. A motor vehicle crash is classified by the type of impact. The five types of impact include head on (frontal), lateral, rear end, rotational, and rollover. The injuries that result depend on the type of collision, the position of the occupant inside the vehicle, and the use or nonuse of active or passive restraint systems.

Objective: Define mechanism of injury and give examples of common mechanisms of injury.

Medical Emergencies

► CHAPTER **13**

Medical Overview 100

► CHAPTER **14**

Neurological Disorders 103

► CHAPTER **15**

Endocrine Disorders 112

► CHAPTER **16**

Respiratory Disorders 118

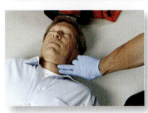

► CHAPTER **17**

Cardiovascular Disorders 127

▶ CHAPTER **18**

Abdominal Disorders   139

▶ CHAPTER **19**

Genitourinary and Renal Disorders   143

▶ CHAPTER **20**

Gynecologic Disorders   148

▶ CHAPTER **21**

Anaphylaxis   155

▶ CHAPTER **22**

Toxicology   163

▶ CHAPTER **23**

Psychiatric Disorders   170

▶ CHAPTER **24**

Diseases of the Nose   176

13 Medical Overview

READING ASSIGNMENT Read Chapter 13, pages 304 to 308 in your textbook.

Sum It Up

- A responsive medical patient can usually tell you what is wrong. After performing a scene size-up and primary survey, obtain the history of the present illness and a SAMPLE history. Then perform a focused physical exam that is guided by the patient's chief complaint and signs and symptoms. After the focused exam, take the patient's vital signs and provide appropriate emergency care based on your findings.

- After performing a scene size-up and primary survey, an unresponsive medical patient or a patient who has an altered mental status needs a rapid medical assessment. A rapid medical assessment is a quick head-to-toe exam that is performed using the same DCAP-BTLS approach used for trauma patients. Take the patient's vital signs, and try to find out what happened from family members or bystanders at the scene. Provide appropriate emergency care based on your findings.

▶ Tracking Your Progress

After reading this chapter, can you:	Page Reference	Objective Met?
• Describe the approach to the assessment of a responsive medical patient?	305	☐
• Describe the unique needs for assessing an individual who is unresponsive or has an altered mental status?	307	☐
• Recite examples of and explain why patients should receive a rapid medical assessment?	307	☐

Chapter Quiz

True/False

Decide whether each statement is true or false. In the space provided, write T for true or F for false.

_____ **1.** A patient is considered unresponsive if he does not respond to verbal or painful stimuli.

_____ **2.** Normally, a light shined into the pupil of one eye will cause pupil constriction of both eyes.

_____ **3.** A patient's blood pressure reading may be falsely low if the patient's arm is above the level of the heart.

Multiple Choice

In the space provided, identify the letter of the choice that best completes each statement or answers each question.

_____ **4.** A patient with a barrel-shaped chest may have
   a. kidney disease.   **c.** chronic lung disease.
   b. high blood pressure.   **d.** a bowel obstruction.

_____ **5.** Which of the following may decrease the respiratory rate?
   a. Fever   **c.** Exercise
   b. Anxiety   **d.** Narcotic use

Short Answer

Answer each question in the space provided.

6. A 78-year-old woman is complaining of difficulty breathing. At a minimum, what areas of the body should be assessed in this patient?

7. A 24-year-old man is complaining of nausea and vomiting. At a minimum, what areas of the body should be assessed in this patient?

8. A 48-year-old woman is found unresponsive. Family members state that the patient complained of weakness just prior to her collapse. At a minimum, what areas of the body should be assessed in this patient?

Answer Section

True/False

1. True

   Objective: Discuss methods of assessing altered mental status in adult, child, and infant patients.

2. True

   Objective: Differentiate between reactive and nonreactive pupils and equal and unequal pupils.

3. True

   Objective: Describe the methods of assessing blood pressure.

Multiple Choice

4. c

   A barrel chest is common in patients with a past medical history of chronic lung disease such as emphysema and bronchitis. Due to the chronic (long-term) nature of these diseases and the increased effort involved with breathing, it is not uncommon for the chest wall of these patients to change dimensions over time.

   Objective: Explain the standardized approach to history taking using the OPQRST and SAMPLE acronyms.

5. d

   The number of respirations per minute can be influenced by many factors. For example, exercise, stress, anxiety, pain, fever, and the use of stimulants can increase the respiratory rate. The use of narcotics or sedatives decreases the respiratory rate.

   Objective: Identify the attributes that should be obtained when assessing breathing.

Short Answer

6. A focused physical exam is usually performed for a responsive medical patient because she can usually tell you the problem that prompted the call for medical help. At a minimum, you should assess the patient's head, neck, chest, and lower extremities.

   Objective: Describe the approach to the assessment of a responsive medical patient.

7. At a minimum, you should assess the patient's chest and abdomen.

   Objective: Describe the approach to the assessment of a responsive medical patient.

8. An unresponsive patient (or a patient who has an altered mental status) requires a rapid head-to-toe exam to find out what is wrong.

   Objective: Describe the unique needs for assessing an individual who is unresponsive or has an altered mental status.

Neurological Disorders

READING ASSIGNMENT Read Chapter 14, pages 309 to 321 in your textbook.

Sum It Up

- A seizure is a temporary change in behavior or consciousness caused by abnormal electrical activity within one or more groups of brain cells. A seizure is a symptom of an underlying problem within the central nervous system. The most common cause of adult seizures in patients with a known seizure history is the failure to take antiseizure medication. The most common cause of seizures in infants and young children is a high fever. Epilepsy is a condition of recurring seizures; the cause is usually irreversible.

- The type of seizure that involves stiffening and jerking of the patient's body is called a tonic-clonic seizure (formerly called a grand mal seizure). This type of seizure typically has four phases:
  1. Aura: A peculiar sensation that comes before a seizure.
  2. Tonic phase: The body's muscles stiffen, the patient's breathing may be noisy, and the patient may turn blue.
  3. Clonic phase: Alternating jerking and relaxation of the body occur.
  4. Postictal phase: The period of recovery that follows a seizure; the patient often appears limp, has shallow breathing, and has an altered mental status.

- Status epilepticus is recurring seizures without an intervening period of consciousness. Status epilepticus is a medical emergency. It can cause brain damage or death if it is not treated.

- A stroke is caused by the blockage or rupture of an artery supplying the brain. There are two main forms of stroke: ischemic and hemorrhagic.
  1. Ischemic strokes are caused by a blood clot that decreases blood flow to the brain. Ischemic strokes can be further classified as either thrombotic or embolic. In a thrombotic stroke, a blood clot (thrombus) forms in a blood vessel of, or leading to, the brain. In an embolic stroke, a blood clot breaks up and travels through the circulatory system where it lodges in a vessel within or leading to the brain.
  2. Hemorrhagic strokes (also called cerebral hemorrhages) are caused by bleeding into the brain. Subarachnoid hemorrhage is caused by a ruptured blood vessel in the subarachnoid space, usually a result of an aneurysm (an abnormal bulging of a blood vessel). Intracerebral hemorrhage is caused by a ruptured blood vessel within the brain itself (usually a result of chronic high blood pressure).

- A transient ischemic attack (TIA) is a temporary interruption of the blood supply to the brain. Signs and symptoms typically last less than 1 hour, completely resolving within 24 hours, with no permanent damage.

- The FAST assessment is a useful tool that can be used to find out if a person who has an altered mental status might be having a stroke. The scale assesses four main areas:
  1. *Face.* Ask the patient to show his teeth. Both sides of the face should move equally. Does one side of the face droop?
  2. *Arms.* Ask the patient to raise his arms out in front of him (with eyes closed). Both arms should move the same, or both arms should not move at all. Does one arm drift downward?
  3. *Speech.* Ask the patient to repeat a simple sentence. The patient should be able to say the right words without slurring or forgetting or substituting words. Are the words slurred? Can he repeat the sentence correctly?
  4. *Time.* What time did the patient's symptoms begin?
- "Give Me 5 for Stroke" is a joint campaign of the American Academy of Neurology, the American College of Emergency Physicians, and the American Heart Association–American Stroke Association to encourage Americans to recognize stroke symptoms, call 9-1-1, and get to the emergency department.
  1. Walk: Is the person's balance off?
  2. Talk: Is her speech slurred or face droopy?
  3. Reach: Is one side weak or numb?
  4. See: Is her vision all or partly lost?
  5. Feel: Is her headache severe?
- The Cincinnati Prehospital Stroke Scale is another assessment tool that can be used to find out if the patient might be having a stroke. It tests three areas:
  1. Ask the patient to smile. Normal finding: Both sides of the face move equally. Abnormal finding: One side of the face does not move as well as the other side.
  2. Ask the patient to close his eyes, raise his arms out in front of him, and hold the position for 10 seconds. Normal finding: Both arms move equally or not at all. Abnormal finding: One arm drifts compared to the other.
  3. Ask the patient to say a simple sentence, for example, "You can't teach an old dog new tricks" or "The sky is blue in Cincinnati." Normal finding: The patient should be able to say the correct words with no slurring. Abnormal finding: The patient's words are slurred, inappropriate words are used, or the patient is unable to speak.
- If the patient's response is not normal in any area (with any stroke assessment tool used) and the patient's symptoms began within the last 3 hours, contact medical direction.
- Syncope (fainting) is a brief loss of responsiveness caused by a temporary decrease in blood flow to the brain. Syncope is sometimes called a blackout. Before fainting, a patient often has warning signs or symptoms. These warning signs and symptoms are called near syncope or presyncope. Syncope usually results within a few seconds of the onset of symptoms. The patient usually recovers shortly after lying down.

▶ Tracking Your Progress

After reading this chapter, can you:	Page Reference	Objective Met?
- Define altered mental status?	310	☐
- List and explain possible causes of altered mental status?	310	☐
- Establish the relationship between airway management and the patient with altered mental status?	311	☐

After reading this chapter, can you:	Page Reference	Objective Met?
• Define seizure and status epilepticus?	311	☐
• Discuss the pathophysiology of seizures?	311	☐
• Describe and differentiate the major types of seizures?	311	☐
• Describe the phases of a generalized seizure?	311	☐
• Discuss the assessment findings associated with seizures?	312	☐
• Describe the emergency medical care for the patient with seizures?	312	☐
• Define stroke and transient ischemic attack?	315	☐
• Describe and differentiate the types of strokes?	315	☐
• Discuss the pathophysiology of stroke?	317	☐
• Discuss the assessment findings associated with stroke?	317	☐
• Describe the emergency medical care for the patient experiencing a stroke?	318	☐
• Define syncope and near syncope?	318	☐
• Discuss the pathophysiology of syncope?	319	☐
• Discuss the assessment findings associated with syncope?	319	☐
• Discuss the emergency medical care for the patient with syncope or near syncope?	320	☐

Chapter Quiz

Multiple Choice

In the space provided, identify the letter of the choice that best completes each statement or answers each question.

Questions 1 to 4 pertain to the following scenario:

Your rescue crew is called to a local grocery store for a 27-year-old man experiencing a seizure. You arrive to find the patient on the ground at the checkout counter having an active, full-body seizure.

_____ 1. Which of the following would be an appropriate action?

    a. Move objects away from the patient to prevent injury.
    b. Lay on top of the patient to control his body movements.
    c. Restrain the patient by strapping him to a long backboard.
    d. Keep your distance from the patient until the seizure stops.

_____ 2. During the seizure, the patient repeatedly strikes his head on the tile floor. After the seizure is over, which of the following would be indicated?

    a. Give the patient something to drink.
    b. Fully immobilize the patient's spine.
    c. Begin cooling the patient's body with ice water.
    d. Place the patient in the recovery position to help clear his airway.

_____ 3. For about 2 minutes following the active seizure, the patient is slow to respond and confused. Suddenly, he begins seizing again. This condition is called

    a. a febrile seizure.
    b. status epilepticus.
    c. severe head trauma.
    d. a cerebrovascular accident.

_____ 4. Following the second seizure, the patient is not alert but moans when you call him by name. His vital signs are pulse 112 beats/min, blood pressure 118/90, and respirations 6/min with decreased tidal volume. His skin is warm, moist, and pale. To manage this patient's airway and breathing, you should

    a. insert an oral airway and deliver oxygen by nasal cannula at 10 to 15 L/min.

    b. insert an oral airway and deliver oxygen by nonrebreather mask at 10 to 15 L/min.

    c. provide continuous suctioning and give oxygen by nasal cannula at 4 to 6 L/min.

    d. insert a nasal airway and assist ventilations with a bag-mask device connected to oxygen at 10 to 15 L/min.

_____ 5. The type of seizure in which a patient appears to be staring blankly for short periods is called

    a. status epilepticus.

    b. aura-only seizure.

    c. tonic-clonic or generalized seizure.

    d. petit mal seizure or absence seizure.

Sentence Completion

In the blanks provided, write the words that best complete each sentence.

    6. A(n) _____ seizure is a type of generalized seizure in which the patient experiences a brief loss of consciousness (for 5 to 10 seconds) without a loss of muscle tone.

    7. A _____ _____ _____ is a type of partial seizure that involves motor or sensory symptoms with no change in mental status.

Matching

Match the key terms in the left column with the definitions in the right column by placing the letter of each correct answer in the space provided.

_____ 8. Aura

_____ 9. Hemorrhagic stroke

_____ 10. Ischemic stroke

_____ 11. Near syncope

_____ 12. Convulsions

_____ 13. Complex partial seizure

_____ 14. Altered mental status

_____ 15. Status epilepticus

_____ 16. Simple partial seizure

_____ 17. Epilepsy

A. A change in a patient's level of awareness

B. A condition of recurring seizures in which the cause is usually irreversible

C. Warning symptoms of an impending loss of consciousness

D. A type of partial seizure in which the patient's consciousness, responsiveness, or memory is impaired

E. A peculiar sensation that comes before a seizure

F. A stroke caused by bleeding into the brain

G. A type of partial seizure that involves motor or sensory symptoms with no change in mental status

H. The jerking movements during the clonic phase of a tonic-clonic seizure

I. A stroke caused by a thrombus or embolus

J. Recurring seizures without an intervening period of consciousness

Short Answer

Answer each question in the space provided.

18. List common causes of altered mental status using the memory aid AEIOU-TIPPS.

19. Why is aggressive airway management critical for a patient with an altered level of consciousness?

20. List the four phases of a tonic-clonic seizure.
1.
2.
3.
4.

21. What is a seizure?

22. Is status epilepticus a medical emergency? Why or why not?

23. Explain the difference between a thrombotic stroke and an embolic stroke.

24. Explain the differences between the tonic and clonic phases of a generalized seizure.

25. Describe a simple partial seizure.

26. List three factors that increase an individual's risk of having a stroke.
1.
2.
3.

Answer Section

Multiple Choice

1. a

While a patient is experiencing a seizure, attempt to limit the amount of harm the patient may do to himself. Move objects out of the patient's path, and put padding between the patient's head and the ground. Do not attempt to physically restrain the patient; restraining the patient may cause harm to you or the patient.

Objective: Define the role of the EMR relative to the responsibility for personal safety and the safety of the crew, the patient, and the bystanders.

2. b

This medical condition (a tonic-clonic seizure) now has a trauma element to it. Because the patient struck his head, protect his spine from further injury. Patients with an altered mental status should be placed in the recovery position only if trauma is not suspected.

Objective: State reasons for management of the cervical spine once the patient has been determined to be a trauma patient.

3. b

Status epilepticus is recurring seizures without an intervening period of consciousness. It is a medical emergency and can cause brain damage or death if it is not treated. Febrile seizures are due to a rapid rise in body temperature. Severe head trauma is also a cause of seizures. A cerebrovascular accident is another name for a stroke.

Objective: Define seizure and status epilepticus.

4. d

This patient is breathing well below the normal range for his age (12 to 20 breaths/min), and with the patient's decreased tidal volume (the amount of air moved in and out of the lungs with each breath) and pale skin condition, aggressive airway support is needed. A nasal airway may be tolerated by this patient. An oral airway would not be tolerated and may induce vomiting. The patient's ventilations should be assisted with a bag-mask device until his respiratory rate and tidal volume return to a normal range.

Objective: Establish the relationship between airway management and the patient with altered mental status.

5. d

Absence (petit mal) seizures are another type of generalized seizure. They usually occur in children older than 5 years of age and can occur in adults. An absence seizure is characterized by a brief loss of consciousness (for 5 to 10 seconds) without a loss of muscle tone. The patient may have a blank stare accompanied by slight head turning or eye blinking. This type of seizure does not cause muscle contractions and is not associated with an aura or postictal state.

Objective: Describe and differentiate the major types of seizures.

Sentence Completion

6. An **absence** seizure is a type of generalized seizure in which the patient experiences a brief loss of consciousness (for 5 to 10 seconds) without a loss of muscle tone.

Objective: Describe and differentiate the major types of seizures.

7. A **simple partial seizure** is a type of partial seizure that involves motor or sensory symptoms with no change in mental status.

Objective: Describe and differentiate the major types of seizures.

Matching

8. E	13. D
9. F	14. A
10. I	15. J
11. C	16. G
12. H	17. B

Short Answer

18.

- **A**lcohol, abuse
- **E**pilepsy (seizures)
- **I**nsulin (diabetic emergency)
- **O**verdose, (lack of) oxygen (hypoxia)
- **U**remia (kidney failure)
- **T**rauma (head injury), temperature (fever, heat- or cold-related emergency)
- **I**nfection
- **P**sychiatric conditions
- **P**oisoning (including drugs and alcohol)
- **S**hock, stroke

Objective: List and explain possible causes of altered mental status.

19. Any patient who has an altered mental status is at risk of not being able to manage her own airway. It is critical for you to aggressively assess the need for an oral or nasal airway and to continuously monitor and reassess the patient's airway. Suction as necessary.

Objective: Establish the relationship between airway management and the patient with altered mental status.

20. A tonic-clonic seizure usually has four phases:

   1. Aura
   2. Tonic phase
   3. Clonic phase
   4. Postictal phase

Objective: Describe the phases of a generalized seizure.

21. A seizure is a temporary change in behavior or consciousness caused by abnormal electrical activity within one or more groups of brain cells. A seizure is a symptom (not a disease) of an underlying problem within the central nervous system.

Objective: Define seizure and status epilepticus.

22. Status epilepticus is recurring seizures without an intervening period of consciousness. Status epilepticus is a medical emergency because brain damage (due to a lack of oxygen or a depletion of glucose) can occur in as little as 5 minutes of sustained seizure activity.

Objective: Define seizure and status epilepticus.

23. Ischemic strokes are classified as either thrombotic or embolic. In a thrombotic stroke, a blood clot (thrombus) forms in a blood vessel of, or leading to, the brain. The blood vessel may be partially or completely blocked by the blood clot.

   In an embolic stroke, a blood clot breaks up and travels through the circulatory system. The blood clot is now called an embolus. A cerebral embolus results from blockage of a vessel within the brain by a fragment of a foreign substance originating from outside the central nervous system, usually the heart or a carotid artery.

Objective: Describe and differentiate the types of strokes.

24. During the tonic phase of a generalized seizure, the body's muscles stiffen. The patient's breathing may be noisy, and he may turn blue. This phase usually lasts 15 to 20 seconds. During the clonic phase, alternating jerking and relaxation of the body occur. The jerking movements during the clonic phase are often called convulsions. This is the longest phase of the seizure. It may last several minutes. The patient's heart rate and blood pressure are increased. His skin is usually warm, flushed, and moist. He may lose control of his bowels and bladder. Bleeding may occur if the patient bites his tongue or cheek.

Objective: Describe the phases of a generalized seizure.

25. A simple partial seizure (also called focal seizure or focal motor seizure) involves motor or sensory symptoms with no change in mental status. This type of seizure usually lasts about 10 to 20 seconds. Examples of motor symptoms include stiffening or jerking of muscles in one part of the body. For instance, the patient's face or an extremity may begin to twitch or

jerk. Sensory symptoms may include pain, numbness, or tingling that is localized to a specific area.

Objective: Describe and differentiate the major types of seizures.

26. Risk factors for stroke include:

- Hypertension
- Cigarette smoking
- Cardiovascular diseases
  —Atherosclerosis
  —Myocardial infarction (heart attack)
  —Heart rhythm disorders (such as atrial fibrillation)
- Diabetes mellitus
- TIA
- Cocaine or amphetamine use

Objective: Discuss the pathophysiology of stroke.

15 Endocrine Disorders

▶ Read Chapter 15, pages 322 to 330 in your textbook.

Sum It Up

- Glucose, a sugar, is the basic fuel for body cells. The level of sugar in the blood (the blood sugar) must remain fairly constant to ensure proper functioning of the brain and body cells. Changes in glucose levels can result in changes in the patient's behavior.

- The body's blood glucose level is primarily regulated by the pancreas. Normal blood glucose levels generally range between 70 and 120 mg/dL.

- Insulin helps glucose enter the body's cells to be used for energy. As the blood glucose level drops toward normal, the release of insulin slows. Glucagon is a hormone that stimulates cells in the liver to break down stores of glycogen into glucose. This increases the blood glucose level.

- Diabetes mellitus is a disease involving the pancreas. There are three major types of diabetes mellitus.

  1. In type 1 diabetes mellitus, little or no insulin is produced by beta cells in the pancreas. This results in a buildup of glucose in the blood. Despite the buildup of glucose in the blood, the body's cells are starved for glucose because, without insulin, glucose is unable to enter most body cells. Although it may occur at any age, type 1 diabetes usually begins during childhood or young adulthood.

  2. Type 2 diabetes mellitus is the most common type of diabetes. It usually affects people older than 40 years of age, especially those who are over-weight. Type 2 diabetes is caused by a combination of insulin resistance and relative insulin shortage. Insulin resistance is a condition in which the pancreas releases insulin but the normal effect of insulin on the tissue cells of the body is diminished. In an attempt to counteract this resistance, the pancreas releases more insulin into the bloodstream. Insulin levels rise. In some cases, glucose builds up in the bloodstream despite the increased amount of insulin. This results in high blood glucose levels or type 2 diabetes.

  3. When a woman develops diabetes during pregnancy, it is called gestational diabetes. Gestational diabetes does not include previously diabetic pregnant patients. Hormones released during pregnancy can change the effectiveness of insulin. These changes usually begin in the fifth or sixth month of pregnancy. Diabetes develops if the pancreas cannot make enough insulin to control the level of glucose in the blood.

- Hypoglycemia is a lower-than-normal blood sugar level. In adults, hypoglycemia is a blood glucose level less than 70 mg/dL. Hypoglycemia is the most common diabetic emergency. The onset of hypoglycemia symptoms is sudden (minutes to hours). Prolonged hypoglycemia can lead to irreversible brain damage.
- Hyperglycemia is a higher-than-normal blood sugar level. The onset of hyperglycemia symptoms is gradual (hours to days). As hyperglycemia worsens, body cells become starved for sugar. Although sugar is present in the blood, it cannot be transported into the body's cells without insulin. The buildup of sugar causes the kidneys to increase urine output, which leads to dehydration. The body begins breaking down fats and proteins to provide energy. The breakdown of fats and proteins produces waste products, including acids. The patient begins breathing deeply and rapidly in an attempt to get rid of the excess acid by "blowing off" carbon dioxide. This breathing pattern is called Kussmaul respirations.
- Diabetic ketoacidosis (DKA) is severe, uncontrolled hyperglycemia (usually over 300 mg/dL). DKA usually occurs in people who have type 1 diabetes but may also occur in those who have type 2 diabetes. DKA is also called diabetic coma.
- Blood glucose testing is used to assist in the management of patients with specific signs and symptoms. The results obtained from the test help determine if the patient's glucose level is too high, too low, or within normal limits. The device used to measure the amount of glucose in a blood sample is called a blood glucose meter or glucometer.

▶ Tracking Your Progress

After reading this chapter, can you:	Page Reference	Objective Met?
• Discuss the role of glucose in the body?	323	☐
• Identify normal blood glucose levels and describe how blood glucose levels are regulated in the body?	323	☐
• Describe the relationship of insulin to blood glucose levels?	323	☐
• Discuss the hormones released from pancreatic cells and their function?	324	☐
• Describe the pathophysiology of each type of diabetes mellitus?	324	☐
• Discuss the possible complications of diabetes mellitus?	325	☐
• Discuss the pathophysiology of hypoglycemia?	326	☐
• Recognize the signs and symptoms of the patient with hypoglycemia?	326	☐
• Discuss the pathophysiology of hyperglycemia?	326	☐
• Recognize the signs and symptoms of the patient with hyperglycemia?	327	☐
• Describe the emergency care of the patient experiencing a diabetic emergency?	327	☐

Chapter Quiz

Multiple Choice

In the space provided, identify the letter of the choice that best completes each statement or answers each question.

_____ **1.** All the cells of the body require a constant supply of fuel and oxygen for normal functioning. The basic fuel for the body is

    a. insulin.   **c.** glucagon.

    b. glucose.   **d.** cholesterol.

_____ **2.** What role does insulin play in the delivery of sugar to the cells of the body?

    a. It helps sugar cross the cell membrane.

    b. It helps the kidneys remove excess sugar.

    c. It breaks down food into sugars that the body can use.

    d. It rids the body of the waste products produced when sugar is "burned" in the cells for energy.

_____ **3.** In adults, the normal blood glucose range is

    a. from 30 to 80 mg/dL.   **c.** from 70 to 120 mg/dL.

    b. from 40 to 90 mg/dL.   **d.** from 100 to 150 mg/dL.

_____ **4.** A lack of glucose can cause irreversible brain damage. Therefore, any diabetic patient with an altered mental status should be considered to have

    a. hypoglycemia and should be treated with insulin therapy in accordance with medical direction.

    b. hyperglycemia and should be treated with insulin therapy in accordance with medical direction.

    c. hypoglycemia and should be treated with oral glucose therapy in accordance with medical direction.

    d. hyperglycemia and should be treated with oral glucose therapy in accordance with medical direction.

_____ **5.** Which of the following scenarios would be consistent with hypoglycemia in a patient with a history of diabetes?

    a. The patient ran out of insulin 3 days ago.

    b. The patient has a bad stomach flu and threw up all morning.

    c. The patient cut her insulin dose in half to make it last longer.

    d. The patient had a huge breakfast and then ate some cake and ice cream.

_____ **6.** When dealing with patients with an altered mental status, which of the following must be done if trauma is suspected?

    a. Insert an oral airway.

    b. Maintain spinal stabilization.

    c. Immediately place the patient in the recovery position.

    d. Provide oxygen at 4 L/min by nonrebreather mask.

_____ **7.** The onset of hyperglycemia

    a. is rapid (minutes).   **c.** is chronic (weeks to years).

    b. is slow (hours to days)   **d.** follows no consistent time frame.

_____ **8.** The most common diabetic emergency is

    a. bradycardia.   **c.** hyperglycemia.

    b. hypoglycemia.   **d.** hyperventilation.

Questions 9-12 pertain to the following scenario:

Your rescue crew is called to the home of a 54-year-old woman. A neighbor called 9–1-1 when he found the patient wandering around the neighborhood confused and disoriented.

_____ **9.** On arrival, you find the patient standing on the sidewalk about two blocks from her home. She looks dazed and weak. You find no evidence of trauma but observe a medical identification bracelet that indicates the patient has diabetes. You should

    a. leave the patient in a standing position.

    b. have the patient lean against a tree if necessary.

    c. instruct the patient to walk home and lay on the couch.

    d. assist the patient to the ground or stretcher to assume the recovery position.

_____ **10.** During the focused history and physical examination, you note that the patient is confused, complains of weakness and hunger, and has cool, clammy skin. These finding are consistent with

   a. hypoglycemia.
   b. hyperglycemia.
   c. epilepsy.
   d. diabetic ketoacidosis.

_____ **11.** During questioning, the patient informs you she is an insulin-dependent diabetic. Which of the following statements by the patient would be consistent with your findings?

   a. "I ate too much food today."
   b. "I have exercised too much today."
   c. "I have not taken my insulin in 2 days."
   d. "I have a history of lower-back problems."

_____ **12.** Insulin-dependent diabetes is another name for

   a. adult-onset diabetes.
   b. type 1 diabetes.
   c. type 2 diabetes.
   d. gestational diabetes.

Short Answer

Answer each question in the space provided.

13. What is the most common type of diabetes?

14. List five signs or symptoms of hyperglycemia.

   1.
   2.
   3.
   4.
   5.

15. What is glucagon?

16. List three potential complications of uncontrolled diabetes.

   1.
   2.
   3.

Answer Section

Multiple Choice

1. b

Glucose is the form of sugar that the body burns for energy. Insulin is a hormone produced in the pancreas that helps move sugar into the cells. Glucagon is also a hormone produced in the pancreas. It stimulates the liver to release stored sugar. Cholesterol is a by-product of ingesting animal products.

Objective: Discuss the role of glucose in the body.

2. a

Sugar is a very large molecule, and without insulin it would not be able to enter the cells of the body. Insulin helps move sugar across the cell membrane.

Objective: Describe the relationship of insulin to blood glucose levels.

3. c

The values used for a normal blood glucose level vary. Some references state that the normal range is from 70 to 120 mg/dL. Others state that the normal range is from 80 to 120 mg/dL. Although both are acceptable, be aware that these norms may vary. In addition, it is important to note that when the tests are performed in a laboratory, the norms may vary by lab.

Objective: Identify normal blood glucose levels, and describe how blood glucose levels are regulated in the body.

4. c

Diabetic patients with an altered mental status should be considered hypoglycemic. If the patient is given oral glucose (by EMTs) and the patient is ultimately diagnosed as hyperglycemic rather than hypoglycemic, the extra sugar given will not adversely affect the patient. Basic life support personnel are not authorized to assist in the administration of insulin.

Objective: Discuss the pathophysiology of hypoglycemia.

5. b

The blood sugar level may become too low if the diabetic patient:

- Has taken too much insulin
- Has not eaten enough food
- Has overexercised and burned off sugar faster than normal
- Experiences significant physical stress (such as an infection) or emotional stress

Remember that the brain cannot store glucose. If hypoglycemia is not corrected, signs and symptoms reflecting the brain's lack of an adequate glucose supply will quickly follow. These signs and symptoms may include tiredness, irritability, visual disturbances, difficulty concentrating, confusion, combativeness, fainting, seizures, and loss of consciousness. Prolonged hypoglycemia can lead to irreversible brain damage. Taking too little insulin or eating too much would lead to the reverse disorder, hyperglycemia.

Objective: Recognize the signs and symptoms of the patient with hypoglycemia.

6. b

Remember to stabilize the spine as soon as possible for patients with an altered mental status if trauma is suspected. Spinal stabilization should be initiated early during the primary survey. Inserting an oral airway would be indicated if the patient were unconscious without a gag reflex. The recovery position (lateral recumbent) is used for patients with an altered mental status of nontraumatic origin. Finally, the use of a nonrebreather mask for these patients is indicated; however, oxygen must be flowed at a higher rate (generally 15 L/min).

Objective: State reasons for management of the cervical spine once the patient has been determined to be a trauma patient.

7. b

While hyperglycemia may take hours or days to develop, hypoglycemia has a rapid onset. For this reason, it is important to be thorough when obtaining information pertaining to the history surrounding the patient's present illness.

Objective: Discuss the pathophysiology of hyperglycemia.

8. b

Hypoglycemia is the most common diabetic emergency.

Objective: Discuss the pathophysiology of hypoglycemia.

9. d

Assist the patient to the ground or stretcher and place her in the recovery position. Do not allow a patient with an altered mental status to remain standing, to walk unassisted, or to sit on an object from which she may fall.

Objective: Describe the emergency care of the patient experiencing a diabetic emergency.

10. a

Early signs and symptoms of hypoglycemia (low blood sugar level) include headache, hunger, nausea, and weakness. As this condition progresses, the patient may experience tremors and tachycardia (increased heart rate) and the skin will be cool and pale. Epilepsy is a disease associated with seizures. Diabetic ketoacidosis (DKA) is severe, uncontrolled hyperglycemia (usually over 300 mg/dL).

Objective: Recognize the signs and symptoms of the patient with hypoglycemia.

11. b

This patient has signs and symptoms of hypoglycemia. A patient response consistent with hypoglycemia would be "I have exercised too much today." By overexerting herself, the patient burned off most of her sugar, resulting in hypoglycemia. Overeating and a failure to take prescribed insulin would lead to hyperglycemia. Lower-back pain would not be a factor.

Objective: Describe the pathophysiology of each type of diabetes mellitus.

12. b

Insulin-dependent diabetes is also called type 1 diabetes. Although it may occur at any age, type 1 diabetes usually begins during childhood or young adulthood. Type 2 diabetes is also called noninsulin-dependent diabetes mellitus (NIDDM) or adult-onset diabetes. Gestational diabetes is diabetes during pregnancy.

Objective: Describe the pathophysiology of each type of diabetes mellitus.

Short Answer

13. Type 2 diabetes mellitus is the most common type of diabetes. It usually affects people older than 40 years of age, especially those who are overweight.

Objective: Describe the pathophysiology of each type of diabetes mellitus.

14. Signs or symptoms of hyperglycemia include:

- Altered mental status (varies from drowsiness to coma)
- Rapid, deep breathing (Kussmaul respirations)
- Sweet or fruity (acetone) breath odor
- Loss of appetite
- Thirst
- Dry skin
- Abdominal pain
- Nausea and/or vomiting
- Increased heart rate
- Normal or slightly decreased blood pressure
- Weakness

Objective: Recognize the signs and symptoms of the patient with hyperglycemia.

15. Glucagon is a hormone released from alpha cells in the pancreas. It stimulates cells in the liver to break down stores of glycogen into glucose to increase the blood glucose level.

Objective: Discuss the hormones released from pancreatic cells and their function.

16. Potential complications of uncontrolled diabetes include:

- Changes in the retina that can lead to blindness
- Kidney damage
- Nerve damage that can lead to loss of sensation, numbness, and pain.
- Circulatory disorders (heart attack, stroke, blood vessel damage, slow wound healing)

Objective: Discuss the possible complications of diabetes mellitus.

Respiratory Disorders

READING ASSIGNMENT Read Chapter 16, pages 331 to 347 in your textbook.

Sum It Up

- After making sure that the scene is safe, form a general impression before approaching the patient with a respiratory emergency. If the patient looks agitated or limp or appears to be asleep, approach him immediately and begin the primary survey. Approach the patient immediately and begin the primary survey if the patient looks as if he is struggling (laboring) to breathe, has noisy breathing, is breathing faster or more slowly than normal, or looks as if his chest is not moving normally. Approach the patient immediately and begin your primary survey if the patient's skin looks flushed, pale, gray, or cyanotic.

- Patients with dyspnea often sit or stand to inhale adequate air. In a tripod position, the patient prefers to sit up and lean forward, with the weight of her upper body supported by her hands on her thighs or knees. Orthopnea is breathlessness when lying flat that is relieved or lessened when the patient sits or stands. Paroxysmal nocturnal dyspnea is a sudden onset of difficulty breathing that occurs at night. It occurs because of a buildup of fluid in the alveoli or pooling of secretions during sleep.

- The normal respiratory rate for an adult at rest is 12 to 20 breaths/minute. If the rate is below 12, it is called bradypnea. If the rate is above 20, it is called tachypnea.

- Retractions are a "sinking in" of the soft tissues between and around the ribs or above the collarbones. Indentations of the skin above the collarbones (clavicles) are called supraclavicular retractions. Indentations of the skin between the ribs are called intercostal retractions. Indentations of the skin below the rib cage are called subcostal retractions.

- Head bobbing is an indicator of increased work of breathing in infants. When the baby breathes out, the head falls forward. The baby's head comes up when the baby breathes in and his chest expands.

- When determining the patient's level of respiratory distress, find out as much patient information as possible and apply the most appropriate interventions and treatments. This needs to be done rapidly and accurately. The patient should be placed in one of four categories: (1) no breathing difficulty or shortness of breath, (2) mild breathing difficulty, (3) moderate breathing difficulty, or (4) severe breathing difficulty.

- Croup is an infection, usually caused by one of the same viruses responsible for common colds. The virus affects the larynx and the area just below it. It is spread from person to person by droplets from coughing and sneezing.

Viral croup most commonly occurs in children between the ages of 6 months and 3 years, although it can occur in older children.

- Epiglottitis is a bacterial infection of the epiglottis. When epiglottitis occurs in children, it typically affects children between 3 and 7 years of age. Since there is now a vaccine for epiglottitis, it is uncommon in children and more commonly seen in adults. The onset of symptoms is usually sudden, developing over a few hours. Respiratory arrest may occur because of a complete airway obstruction or a combination of partial airway obstruction and fatigue. Do not attempt to look into the patient's mouth or throat. This may agitate the patient and worsen respiratory distress.

- Pertussis, also called whooping cough, is a highly contagious bacterial infection of the respiratory tract. The bacterium that causes pertussis is found in the mouth, nose, and throat of an infected person. The disease is spread from person to person by droplets from coughing and sneezing. Pertussis can affect persons of any age.

- Cystic fibrosis is an inherited disease that appears in childhood. A defective gene inherited from each parent results in an abnormality in the glands that produce or secrete sweat and mucus. In CF, mucus in the lining of the bronchi becomes very thick and sticky, making it difficult to remove with coughing. The mucus builds up in the lungs, blocking the airways, and leading to repeated respiratory infections and breathing difficulty.

- Asthma (also known as reactive airway disease, or RAD) is widespread, temporary narrowing of the air passages that transport air from the nose and mouth to the lungs. After exposure to a trigger, the smooth muscles surrounding the bronchioles spasmodically contract and swell, and mucus secretion increases. Airway passages are narrowed because of smooth muscle contraction, excessive mucus secretion, or a combination of both. This results in the trapping of air in the bronchioles. Exhalation becomes prolonged as the patient tries to exhale the trapped air.

- Chronic bronchitis is defined as sputum production for 3 months of a year for at least 2 consecutive years. The major cause of chronic bronchitis is cigarette smoking. Excessive mucus production in the bronchi causes a chronic or recurrent productive cough. Because the size of the airway opening is decreased, some secretions are trapped in the alveoli and smaller air passages.

- Emphysema is an irreversible enlargement of the air spaces distal to the terminal bronchioles. This disease leads to destruction of the walls of the alveoli, distention of the alveolar sacs, and loss of lung elasticity.

- Pneumonia is an infection that often affects gas exchange in the lung. It may involve the lower airways and alveoli, part of a lobe, or an entire lobe of the lung. Pneumonia is most often caused by bacteria and viruses, although it may also be caused by fungi and parasites.

- A pulmonary embolus is usually the result of a clot that forms in the deep veins in the leg and then travels through the veins to the heart and then to the pulmonary circulation. The clot becomes trapped in the smaller branches of the pulmonary arteries, causing partial or complete blood flow obstruction. As a result, a portion of the lung is ventilated but not perfused.

- Pulmonary edema is most commonly caused by failure of the left ventricle of the heart. When the left ventricle fails, fluid is forced into the lung tissue as the right ventricle continues to pump blood into the pulmonary circulation. The alveoli fill with fluid, limiting their ability to effectively exchange oxygen and carbon dioxide.

- A spontaneous pneumothorax is a type of pneumothorax that does not involve trauma to the lung. A primary spontaneous pneumothorax occurs in people with no history of lung disease. This condition most commonly occurs in tall, thin men between the ages of 20 and 40. It rarely occurs in persons older than 40 years. A secondary spontaneous pneumothorax most often occurs as a complication of lung disease.

► Tracking Your Progress

After reading this chapter, can you:	Page Reference	Objective Met?
• Describe assessment of the patient with breathing difficulty?	332	☐
• Explain orthopnea and paroxysmal nocturnal dyspnea?	332	☐
• Explain possible questions to ask a patient with breathing difficulty?	334	☐
• Describe a method of categorizing a patient's level of respiratory distress?	335	☐
• List examples of trauma and medical conditions that may cause breathing difficulty?	337	☐
• Identify the pathophysiology, assessment findings, and emergency care for croup?	337	☐
• Identify the pathophysiology, assessment findings, and emergency care for epiglottitis?	338	☐
• Identify the pathophysiology, assessment findings, and emergency care for pertussis?	340	☐
• Identify the pathophysiology, assessment findings, and emergency care for cystic fibrosis?	340	☐
• Identify the pathophysiology, assessment findings, and emergency care for asthma?	341	☐
• Identify the pathophysiology, assessment findings, and emergency care for chronic bronchitis?	342	☐
• Identify the pathophysiology, assessment findings, and emergency care for emphysema?	344	☐
• Identify the pathophysiology, assessment findings, and emergency care for pneumonia?	344	☐
• Identify the pathophysiology, assessment findings, and emergency care for acute pulmonary embolism?	345	☐
• Identify the pathophysiology, assessment findings, and emergency care for acute pulmonary edema?	345	☐
• Identify the pathophysiology, assessment findings, and emergency care for spontaneous pneumothorax?	346	☐

Chapter Quiz

Multiple Choice

In the space provided, identify the letter of the choice that best completes each statement or answers each question.

_____ 1. For most patients, the main stimulus for breathing is derived from the level of _____ in the bloodstream. However, chronic respiratory disease may change the stimulus for breathing to the level of _____ in the bloodstream.

    a. carbon dioxide, oxygen   **c.** oxygen, carbon monoxide

    b. oxygen, carbon dioxide   **d.** carbon dioxide, hemoglobin

_____ 2. Apnea means

    a. difficulty breathing.   **c.** breathlessness when lying flat.

    b. absent breathing.   **d.** difficulty breathing that occurs at night.

_____ 3. An early sign of nontraumatic respiratory distress is
    a. facial droop.
    c. agonal respirations.
    b. unconsciousness.
    d. increased respiratory rate.

_____ 4. You are called to an adult-care facility for a 78-year-old woman complaining of difficulty breathing that has worsened over the past 2 days. Which of the following comments by the patient would _not_ be consistent with the typical signs and symptoms of pneumonia?
    a. "My chest hurts when I take a deep breath."
    b. "My feet are much more swollen than normal."
    c. "I have had a fever and the chills for the past week."
    d. "I keep coughing up yellow stuff from my lungs."

_____ 5. You respond to the home of a 34-year-old man complaining of difficulty breathing and chest pain. He states that his chest pain worsens with deep inspiration and coughing. He denies any recent trauma and denies any past medical history. The term given to this complaint is
    a. hemothorax.
    c. tracheal deviation.
    b. flail segment.
    d. pleuritic chest pain.

_____ 6. You are called to the home of a 5-year-old female. Her parents tell you that she started developing a high fever several hours ago and now is acting "funny." The patient is found sitting up in bed. She is drooling and does not answer your questions although she appears to be responsive. When treating this patient,
    a. you should attempt to visualize the back of her throat for an obstruction.
    b. allow the patient to continue sitting up and administer blow-by oxygen.
    c. you should insist on laying the patient down to increase perfusion to the brain.
    d. lay the patient down gently, insert an oral airway, and begin positive-pressure ventilations with a bag-mask device.

_____ 7. You respond to the home of a 22-month-old male patient with difficulty breathing and a nonproductive cough. His father tells you that the child has had a fever for the last several days. While assessing the patient, you observe a harsh, barklike cough and stridor. He is conscious and responds appropriately for his age. These findings are consistent with _____. Appropriate emergency care for this patient should consist of _____, _____, _____.
    a. Croup; blow-by oxygen therapy, position of comfort, and transport to the hospital for further evaluation
    b. Croup; blow-by oxygen therapy, insertion of a nasal airway, and transport in the recovery position to the hospital for further evaluation
    c. Epiglottitis; blow-by oxygen therapy, close inspection of the mouth and throat, and transport to the hospital for further evaluation
    d. Epiglottitis; oxygen by nonrebreather mask, position of comfort, and transport for further evaluation

Sentence Completion

Complete each statement.

8. _____ is breathlessness when lying flat that is relieved or lessened when the patient sits or stands.

9. _____ is an irreversible disease that leads to the destruction of the walls of the alveoli, distention of the alveolar sacs, and a loss of lung elasticity.

10. _____ _____ is a buildup of fluid in the alveoli, most commonly due to failure of the left ventricle of the heart.

11. _____ is a respiratory infection that may involve the lower airways and alveoli, part of a lobe, or an entire lobe of the lung.

12. _____ _____ _____ is a sudden onset of difficulty breathing that occurs at night because of a buildup of fluid in the alveoli or pooling of secretions during sleep.

Matching

Match the key terms in the right column with the definitions in the left column by placing the letter of each correct answer in the space provided.

_____ 13. A clot that travels through the circulatory system, eventually becoming trapped in the smaller branches of the pulmonary arteries, causing partial or complete blood flow obstruction

_____ 14. Windpipe

_____ 15. Indentations of the skin above the collarbones (clavicles)

_____ 16. A respiratory infection that may involve the lower airways and alveoli, part of a lobe, or an entire lobe of the lung

_____ 17. Sitting up and leaning forward with the weight of the upper body supported by the hands on the thighs or knees

_____ 18. Asthma that is triggered by factors not related to allergies

_____ 19. Low levels of oxygen in the blood stimulate breathing instead of an increase in carbon dioxide levels

_____ 20. Breastbone

_____ 21. Indentations of the skin between the ribs

_____ 22. The exchange of gases between a living organism and its environment

_____ 23. A faster-than-normal respiratory rate for a person's age

_____ 24. A buildup of fluid in the alveoli, most commonly due to failure of the left ventricle of the heart

_____ 25. A sudden onset of difficulty breathing that occurs at night because of a buildup of fluid in the alveoli or pooling of secretions during sleep

_____ 26. A lack of oxygen

_____ 27. The amount of air moved into or out of the lungs during a normal breath

_____ 28. Abnormal breathing in which the abdominal muscles move in a direction opposite the chest wall

_____ 29. Widening of the nostrils when a patient breathes in

_____ 30. Indentations of the skin below the rib cage

_____ 31. Breathlessness when lying flat that is relieved or lessened when the patient sits or stands

_____ 32. A slower-than-normal respiratory rate for a person's age

A. Sternum

B. Tidal volume

C. Seesaw breathing

D. Pulmonary edema

E. Bradypnea

F. Hypoxia

G. Croup

H. Subcostal retractions

I. Trachea

J. Nasal flaring

K. Supraclavicular retractions

L. Pulmonary embolus

M. Orthopnea

N. Head bobbing

O. Tripod position

P. Nonallergic asthma

Q. Respiration

R. Hypoxic drive

S. Tachypnea

T. Pneumonia

U. Paroxysmal nocturnal dyspnea

V. Intercostal retractions

Continued

_____ **33.** An infection that affects the larynx and the area just below it

_____ **34.** An indicator of increased work of breathing in infants—when the baby breathes out, the head falls forward; the baby's head comes up when the baby breathes in and his chest expands

Short Answer

Answer each question in the space provided.

35. List five signs or symptoms of acute pulmonary edema.

1.
2.
3.
4.
5.

36. List four possible triggers for an asthma attack.

1.
2.
3.
4.

37. List five signs and symptoms associated with asthma.

1.
2.
3.
4.
5.

38. List five factors that increase a person's risk for pulmonary embolism.

1.
2.
3.
4.
5.

39. Describe the emergency care for a patient with chronic bronchitis.

40. List five signs and symptoms associated with emphysema.

1.
2.
3.
4.
5.

Answer Section

Multiple Choice

1. a

The main stimulus for breathing is the level of carbon dioxide in the blood. A buildup of carbon dioxide in the blood causes an increase in the rate and depth of ventilation. An unusually low level of carbon dioxide in the blood results in a decrease in the rate and depth of ventilation.

Chronic respiratory diseases may alter the normal respiratory drive over time because of the prolonged high levels of carbon dioxide. Instead of an increase in carbon dioxide levels stimulating breathing, low levels of oxygen in the blood become the breathing stimulus. This kind of breathing stimulus is called *hypoxic drive.* In such patients, giving high-concentration oxygen for prolonged periods may depress respirations and result in respiratory arrest.

Objective: Differentiate between ventilation and respiration.

2. b

Apnea means an absence of breathing (*a–* = "without"; *-pnea* = "breathing"). Dyspnea is difficulty breathing. Orthopnea is breathlessness when lying flat that is relieved or lessened when the patient sits or stands. Paroxysmal nocturnal dyspnea is a sudden onset of difficulty breathing that occurs at night. It occurs because of a buildup of fluid in the alveoli or pooling of secretions during sleep.

Objective: Describe assessment of the patient with breathing difficulty.

3. d

When in distress (respiratory or otherwise), one of the body's first lines of defense is to increase the respiratory rate to increase the oxygen content in the blood. A facial droop is most commonly associated with a patient who has experienced a cerebrovascular accident (stroke). Unconsciousness, if caused by respiratory distress, is a very late sign of disease progression. Patients in respiratory distress generally progress from anxious and agitated, to confused, to a sleepy or tired appearance, to unconsciousness. Agonal respirations are slow, gasping respirations associated with a critical patient who is about to become completely apneic. Such patients must be quickly and aggressively managed with a bag-mask device and supplemental oxygen.

Objective: Describe assessment of the patient with breathing difficulty.

4. b

Pedal edema (pooling of fluid in the lower extremities) is not commonly associated with pneumonia. It is more commonly associated with congestive heart failure. Pleuritic chest pain, fever and chills, and a productive cough with yellow or green sputum are commonly associated with pneumonia. Other signs and symptoms may include an increased respiratory rate, increased heart rate, and abnormal lung sounds in the area of the lung affected by the infection.

Objective: Identify the pathophysiology, assessment findings, and emergency care for pneumonia.

5. d

Chest pain may be described as pleuritic if the pain increases with movement, palpation, or deep inspiration. True pleuritic chest pain is caused by an infection of the pleura (the double-walled sac that surrounds the lungs). Hemothorax (blood in the pleural space) and a flail segment (multiple rib fractures creating a free-floating section of the chest wall) may also present with this type of chest pain however, these conditions are a result of trauma. Tracheal deviation, discovered on palpation of the trachea, is a late sign of a tension pneumothorax.

Objective: Describe assessment of the patient with breathing difficulty.

6. b

This patient is exhibiting signs and symptoms of epiglottitis. Do not attempt to visualize the airway, and do not upset the patient. Allow the patient to assume a position of comfort, allow the parent to stay with the patient if removal makes the patient agitated, maximize oxygen delivery without upsetting the patient, and provide prompt transport to an appropriate facility. You may not be able to perform a physical examination on this patient if your efforts upset her.

Objective: Identify the pathophysiology, assessment findings, and emergency care for epiglottitis.

7. a

The gradual onset, the age of the patient, the presence of stridor, and the harsh, barking cough are signs and symptoms suggestive of croup. Your treatment should focus on keeping the patient calm and providing supplemental oxygen. Epiglottitis generally has a more rapid onset, affects older children (age 3 to 7 years), and presents with difficulty swallowing, talking, and breathing. Epiglottitis may progress to the extent that the swollen epiglottis completely blocks the airway. Such patients should be treated carefully and rapidly. Make sure the patient is comfortable (generally sitting up and next to a parent), give high-flow oxygen (blow-by if a nonrebreather mask agitates the child), and arrange for transport as quickly and safely as possible to the closest appropriate medical facility.

Objective: Identify the pathophysiology, assessment findings, and emergency care for croup.

Sentence Completion

8. **Orthopnea** is breathlessness when lying flat that is relieved or lessened when the patient sits or stands.

Objective: Explain orthopnea and paroxysmal nocturnal dyspnea.

9. **Emphysema** is an irreversible disease that leads to the destruction of the walls of the alveoli, distention of the alveolar sacs, and a loss of lung elasticity.

Objective: Identify the pathophysiology, assessment findings, and emergency care for emphysema.

10. **Pulmonary edema** is a buildup of fluid in the alveoli, most commonly due to failure of the left ventricle of the heart.

Objective: Identify the pathophysiology, assessment findings, and emergency care for acute pulmonary edema.

11. **Pneumonia** is a respiratory infection that may involve the lower airways and alveoli, part of a lobe, or an entire lobe of the lung.

Objective: Identify the pathophysiology, assessment findings, and emergency care for pneumonia.

12. **Paroxysmal nocturnal dyspnea** is a sudden onset of difficulty breathing that occurs at night because of a buildup of fluid in the alveoli or pooling of secretions during sleep.

Objective: Explain orthopnea and paroxysmal nocturnal dyspnea.

Matching

13.	L	24.	D
14.	I	25.	U
15.	K	26.	F
16.	T	27.	B
17.	O	28.	C
18.	P	29.	J
19.	R	30.	H
20.	A	31.	M
21.	V	32.	E
22.	Q	33.	G
23.	S	34.	N

Short Answer

35. Signs and symptoms of acute pulmonary edema include the following:

- Restlessness, anxiety
- Dyspnea on exertion
- Orthopnea
- Paroxysmal nocturnal dyspnea
- Frothy, blood-tinged sputum
- Cool, moist skin
- Use of accessory muscles
- Jugular venous distention
- Wheezing
- Rapid, labored breathing

- Increased heart rate
- Increased or decreased blood pressure (depending on severity of edema)

Objective: Identify the pathophysiology, assessment findings, and emergency care for acute pulmonary edema.

36. Possible asthma triggers include:

   - Allergens such as dust mites, cockroaches, pollens, molds, pet dander, dust, shellfish, some medications
   - Environmental irritants such as smoke, dust, paint fumes, smog, aerosol sprays, perfumes
   - Weather factors such as extremes of heat, cold, humidity
   - Exercise
   - Colds, flu, sore throat, sinus infection
   - Emotional stress

   Objective: Identify the pathophysiology, assessment findings, and emergency care for asthma.

37. Signs and symptoms associated with asthma include:

   - Wheezing
   - Restlessness
   - Dry cough
   - Dyspnea
   - Chest tightness
   - Rapid breathing
   - Increased heart rate
   - Retractions
   - Use of accessory muscles

   Objective: Identify the pathophysiology, assessment findings, and emergency care for asthma.

38. Factors that increase the risk for pulmonary embolism include the following:

   - Obesity
   - Prolonged bed rest or immobilization
   - Recent surgery, particularly of the legs, pelvis, abdomen, or chest

   - Leg or pelvic fractures or injuries
   - Use of high-estrogen oral contraceptives
   - Pregnancy
   - Chronic atrial fibrillation (a heart rhythm disorder)

   Objective: Identify the pathophysiology, assessment findings, and emergency care for acute pulmonary embolism.

39. Allow the patient to assume a position of comfort. If signs of breathing difficulty are present, give oxygen by nonrebreather mask at 15 L/min or as ordered by medical direction. If no signs of respiratory distress are evident, give oxygen by nasal cannula at 2 L/min or as ordered by medical direction. Monitor the patient closely, reassessing every 5 minutes, and be prepared to assist ventilations as necessary. Provide calm reassurance to help reduce the patient's anxiety. Encourage the patient to cough and breathe deeply to help in the removal of secretions.

   Objective: Identify the pathophysiology, assessment findings, and emergency care for chronic bronchitis.

40. Signs and symptoms associated with emphysema include:

   - Barrel chest
   - Use of accessory muscles
   - Pursed-lip breathing
   - Chronic cough
   - Prolonged exhalation
   - Increased respiratory rate
   - Dyspnea with exertion

   Objective: Identify the pathophysiology, assessment findings, and emergency care for emphysema.

17 Cardiovascular Disorders

READING ASSIGNMENT ▶ Read Chapter 17, pages 348 to 367 in your textbook.

Sum It Up

- Acute coronary syndromes (ACS) are conditions caused by temporary or permanent blockage of a coronary artery as a result of coronary artery disease (CAD). ACSs include unstable angina pectoris and myocardial infarction.
- Arteriosclerosis means "hardening of the walls of the arteries." As the walls of the arteries become hardened, they lose their elasticity. In atherosclerosis, the inner lining (endothelium) of the walls of large- and medium-size arteries become narrowed and thicken.
- Conditions that may increase a person's chance of developing a disease are called risk factors. While some risk factors can be changed, others cannot. Risk factors that can be changed are called modifiable risk factors. Risk factors that cannot be changed are called nonmodifiable risk factors. Factors that can be part of the cause of a person's risk of heart disease are called contributing risk factors.
- Ischemia is decreased blood flow to an organ or tissue. Ischemia can result from narrowing or blockage of an artery or spasm of an artery. Atherosclerosis is a common reason for narrowing of a coronary artery.
- Angina pectoris (literally, "choking in the chest") is a symptom of CAD that occurs when the heart's need for oxygen exceeds its supply. A person is said to have stable angina pectoris when the symptoms are relatively constant and predictable in terms of severity, signs and symptoms, precipitating events, and response to therapy. A person who has unstable angina pectoris has angina that is progressively worsening, occurs at rest, or is brought on by minimal physical exertion.
- An acute myocardial infarction (acute MI, or heart attack) occurs when a coronary artery becomes severely narrowed or is completely blocked, usually by a blood clot (thrombus). When the affected portion of the heart muscle (myocardium) is deprived of oxygen long enough, the area dies (infarcts). If too much of the heart muscle dies, shock (hypoperfusion) and cardiac arrest will result.
- The risk of death from a heart attack is related to the time elapsed between the onset of symptoms and the start of treatment. The earlier the patient can receive emergency care, the greater the chances of preventing ischemic heart tissue from becoming dead heart tissue.

- Signs and symptoms of a heart attack vary. Although chest discomfort is the most common symptom of a heart attack, some patients never have chest pain. Older adults, diabetic individuals, and women who have a heart attack are more likely to present with signs and symptoms that differ from those of a "typical" patient. This is called an atypical presentation or atypical signs and symptoms.

- If the heart stops beating, no blood will flow. If no blood flows, oxygen cannot be delivered to the body's cells. When the heart stops, the patient is said to be in cardiac arrest. The signs of cardiac arrest include sudden unresponsiveness, absent breathing, and no signs of circulation. Chest compressions are used to circulate blood any time that the heart is not beating. Chest compressions are combined with rescue breathing to oxygenate the blood. The combination of rescue breathing and external chest compressions is called cardiopulmonary resuscitation (CPR).

- Sudden cardiac death (SCD) is the unexpected death from cardiac causes early after symptom onset (immediately or within 1 hour) or without the onset of symptoms. Survival of cardiac arrest depends on a series of critical actions called the chain of survival. The chain of survival is the ideal series of events that should take place immediately after recognizing an injury or the onset of sudden illness. The chain consists of four steps:
    1. Early access
    2. Early CPR
    3. Early defibrillation
    4. Early advanced care

- An automated external defibrillator (AED) contains a computer programmed to recognize heart rhythms that should be shocked (defibrillated), such as ventricular fibrillation (VF or VFib). A standard AED is used for a patient who is unresponsive, not breathing, pulseless, and 8 years of age or older (about 55 pounds, or more than 25 kg). A special key or pad-cable system is available for some AEDs so that the machine can be used on children between 1 and 8 years of age. The key or pad-cable system decreases the amount of energy delivered to a dose appropriate for a child. If a child is in cardiac arrest and a key or pad-cable system is not available, use a standard AED.

- When an adult experiences a cardiac arrest as a result of VF, prompt defibrillation is the most important treatment you can provide from the time of the arrest to about 5 minutes following the arrest. If you witness a cardiac arrest, assess the patient's airway, breathing, and circulation and then quickly apply an AED. Perform CPR until the AED is ready.

- To ensure delivery of the best-quality patient care possible, the medical director (or designated representative) carefully reviews every call in which an AED is used. Each call is reviewed to determine if the patient was treated according to professional standards and local standing orders.

- If the patient has a pacemaker or implantable cardioverter-defibrillator (ICD) in place, place the AED pads at least 1 inch from the device.

- Before using an AED, familiarize yourself with the manufacturer's recommendations regarding the use of the device around water. If a medication patch is present on the patient's chest, make sure you are wearing gloves and then remove the patch.

- To operate an AED, place the AED next to the rescuer who will be operating it. Turn on the power. Connect the AED pads to the AED cables (if not preconnected). Then apply the pads to the patient's bare chest in the locations indicated on the pads. Connect the cable to the AED. Analyze the patient's heart rhythm. If the AED advises that a shock is indicated, check the patient from head to toe to make sure no one is touching the patient (including you) before pressing the shock control. Make sure oxygen is not flowing over the patient's chest. Shout, "Stand clear!" Press the shock control once it is illuminated and the machine indicates it is ready to deliver the shock. Resume CPR, beginning with chest compressions, immediately after delivery of the shock unless the patient regains consciousness or begins spontaneous movement.

- Maintenance procedures for an AED should be performed according to the manufacturer's recommendations. Failure of an AED is most often related to improper device maintenance, commonly battery failure.

▶ Tracking Your Progress

After reading this chapter, can you:	Page Reference	Objective Met?
• Define cardiovascular disease, coronary heart disease (CHD), and coronary artery disease (CAD)?	350	☐
• Define acute coronary syndromes (ACSs)?	350	☐
• Describe the pathophysiology of coronary artery disease and the processes of atherosclerosis and arteriosclerosis?	350	☐
• Define peripheral artery disease (PAD)?	350	☐
• Define and give examples of modifiable, nonmodifiable, and contributing risk factors for heart disease?	350	☐
• Define and differentiate stable and unstable angina pectoris?	351	☐
• Define acute myocardial infarction (MI) and describe possible assessment findings and symptoms associated with this condition?	351	☐
• Describe atypical assessment findings and symptoms associated with acute coronary syndromes?	352	☐
• Explain the importance of advanced life support intervention, if it is available, when caring for a patient with a cardiovascular emergency?	353	☐
• Describe the emergency medical care of the patient experiencing a cardiovascular emergency?	355	☐
• Discuss the position of comfort for patients with various cardiac emergencies?	355	☐
• Define cardiac arrest and explain its possible causes?	355	☐
• Define sudden cardiac death?	356	☐
• Describe the links in the chain of survival?	356	☐
• Discuss the EMR's role in the chain of survival?	356	☐
• Define defibrillation?	356	☐
• Differentiate between the fully automated defibrillator and the semiautomated defibrillator?	356	☐
• Differentiate among a manual defibrillator, an implantable cardioverter-defibrillator, and an automated external defibrillator (AED)?	358	☐
• Describe AED use on adults and children?	359	☐
• List the indications for automated external defibrillation?	361	☐
• Explain the fact that not all patients with chest pain will experience cardiac arrest, nor do all patients with chest pain need to be attached to an AED?	361	☐
• Discuss the advantages of AEDs?	361	☐

After reading this chapter, can you:	Page Reference	Objective Met?
• Discuss the use of remote defibrillation through adhesive pads?	361	☐
• Discuss the goal of quality management in automated external defibrillation?	362	☐
• Discuss the procedures that must be taken into consideration for standard operation of the various types of AEDs?	362	☐
• Explain the role medical direction plays in the use of automated external defibrillation?	362	☐
• List the steps in the operation of the AED?	363	☐
• Discuss the circumstances that may result in inappropriate shocks?	363	☐
• Explain the considerations for interruption of cardiopulmonary resuscitation when you are using an AED?	363	☐
• Discuss the importance of postresuscitation care?	365	☐
• List the components of postresuscitation care?	365	☐

Chapter Quiz

Multiple Choice

In the space provided, identify the letter of the choice that best completes each statement or answers each question.

_____ 1. Which of the following correctly reflects the main components of the cardiovascular system?
   a. The heart, blood, and blood vessels
   b. The lungs, the heart, and the capillaries
   c. Lymph and the lymph system
   d. The lung and the alveoli

_____ 2. Blood pressure is best defined as
   a. adequate circulation of blood through an organ or part of the body.
   b. the force exerted by the blood on the inner walls of the heart and blood vessels.
   c. the pressure exerted against the walls of the arteries when the left ventricle contracts.
   d. the pressure exerted against the walls of the arteries when the left ventricle is relaxed.

_____ 3. To assist in lowering body temperature, blood vessels may
   a. dilate, thus giving the patient a red or flushed appearance.
   b. dilate, thus giving the patient a pale or cyanotic appearance.
   c. constrict, thus giving the patient a red or flushed appearance.
   d. constrict, thus giving the patient a pale or cyanotic appearance.

_____ 4. Which chamber of the heart is responsible for pumping blood to the lungs?
   a. Right atrium   c. Left atrium
   b. Right ventricle   d. Left ventricle

_____ 5. Blood is carried back to the heart in vessels of relative low pressure. Many of these vessels contain valves to prevent the backflow of blood as it returns to the heart. These vessels are called
   a. aortas.   c. arteries.
   b. veins.   d. capillaries.

_____ 6. The heart muscle (myocardium) requires a constant supply of fresh blood for proper functioning. The arteries that supply the heart with blood are the
   a. carotid arteries.   c. femoral arteries.
   b. coronary arteries.   d. pulmonary arteries.

_____ **7.** The term given to the death (necrosis) of heart muscle is
    a. angina pectoris.   **c.** acute myocardial infarction (AMI).
    b. cardiac tamponade.   **d.** congestive heart failure (CHF).

_____ **8.** The most common symptom associated with cardiac compromise and the lack of oxygenation of the heart is
    a. nausea.   **c.** chest pain or discomfort.
    b. pulmonary edema.   **d.** swelling of the feet or lower back.

_____ **9.** When you are performing a focused history and physical examination on a patient with chest pain, your physical examination
    a. should precede the primary survey.
    b. should be limited to a rapid assessment of the chest.
    c. should be limited to a thorough assessment of the upper torso.
    d. should evaluate all areas of the body that may be affected by cardiac compromise.

_____ **10.** Nitroglycerin may relieve chest pain associated with coronary artery disease. It does so by
    a. numbing the heart muscle.
    b. dilating the coronary arteries, thus increasing blood flow to the heart.
    c. constricting the coronary arteries, thus increasing blood pressure and perfusion.
    d. constricting the veins of the body, thus increasing blood pressure and blood flow to the heart.

_____ **11.** What differentiates angina pectoris from an acute myocardial infarction (AMI)?
    a. The sensation of pain is less for patients experiencing angina pectoris.
    b. Shortness of breath is absent for patients experiencing angina pectoris.
    c. Angina pectoris does not result in death of a portion of the heart muscle.
    d. An acute myocardial infarction always results in sudden death, whereas angina pectoris can be reversed.

_____ **12.** Which of the following is most commonly associated with failure of or damage to the left ventricle?
    a. Pulmonary edema   **c.** Swelling in the lower back
    b. Swelling in the feet   **d.** Jugular venous distention (JVD)

Matching

Match the key terms in the right column with the definitions in the left column by placing the letter of each correct answer in the space provided.

_____ **13.** Disease of the coronary arteries and the complications that result, such as angina pectoris or a heart attack

_____ **14.** Unexpected death from cardiac causes early after symptom onset (immediately or within 1 hour) or without the onset of symptoms

_____ **15.** Decreased blood flow to an organ or tissue

_____ **16.** The delivery of an electric shock to a patient's heart to end an abnormal heart rhythm

_____ **17.** An abnormal awareness of one's heartbeat

_____ **18.** Narrowing and thickening of the inner lining (endothelium) of the walls of large and medium-size arteries because of a buildup of plaque

_____ **19.** Death of heart tissue that occurs when a coronary artery becomes severely narrowed or is completely blocked, usually by a blood clot (thrombus)

A. Peripheral artery disease

B. Acute myocardial infarction

C. Pulmonic valve

D. Ventricular fibrillation

E. Coronary artery bypass graft

F. Manual defibrillator

G. Congestive heart failure

H. Systolic blood pressure

I. Fainting

J. Coronary artery disease

K. Implantable cardioverter-defibrillator

L. Acute coronary syndromes

M. Stent

N. Coronary heart disease

Continued

_____ 20. An atrioventricular valve located between the left atrium and left ventricle

_____ 21. A term used for diseases that slow or stop blood flow through the arteries that supply the heart muscle with blood

_____ 22. A semilunar valve located at the junction of the right ventricle and pulmonary artery

_____ 23. A surgical procedure in which a graft is created from a healthy blood vessel from another part of the patient's body to reroute blood flow around a diseased coronary artery

_____ 24. The pressure exerted against the walls of the arteries when the left ventricle is at rest

_____ 25. Atherosclerosis that affects the arteries that supply the arms, legs, and feet

_____ 26. An atrioventricular valve located between the right atrium and right ventricle

_____ 27. The pressure exerted against the walls of the arteries when the left ventricle contracts

_____ 28. A surgically implanted device programmed to recognize heart rhythms that are too fast or life-threatening and deliver a shock to reset the rhythm

_____ 29. A small plastic or metal tube that is inserted into a vessel or duct to help keep it open and maintain fluid flow through it

_____ 30. A sudden, temporary loss of consciousness

_____ 31. A machine that requires that the rescuer analyze and interpret the patient's cardiac rhythm

_____ 32. An abnormal heart rhythm in which the heart's electrical impulses are completely disorganized and the heart cannot pump blood effectively

_____ 33. A condition in which one or both sides of the heart fail to pump efficiently

_____ 34. The ideal series of events that should take place immediately after recognizing an injury or the onset of sudden illness

_____ 35. A procedure in which a balloon-tipped catheter is inserted into a partially blocked coronary artery; when the balloon is inflated, plaque is pressed against the walls of the artery, improving blood flow to the heart muscle

_____ 36. Conditions caused by temporary or permanent blockage of a coronary artery due to coronary artery disease

O. Sudden cardiac death

P. Angioplasty

Q. Atherosclerosis

R. Defibrillation

S. Tricuspid valve

T. Diastolic blood pressure

U. Chain of survival

V. Ischemia

W. Mitral valve

X. Palpitations

Short Answer

Answer each question in the space provided.

37. List five possible causes of cardiac arrest.

1.

2.

3.

4.

5.

38. Explain the purpose of the chain of survival, and list each component of the chain.

39. Explain why it is important to make sure that oxygen is not flowing over the patient's chest before you deliver a shock with an AED.

40. Briefly describe the steps in the operation of an automated external defibrillator.

41. List six "typical" signs or symptoms of a heart attack.

1.

2.

3.

4.

5.

6.

42. Explain why a patient with a heart or breathing-related complaint should not be permitted to walk to the stretcher.

43. Complete the following table:

	Adult	Child	Infant
Rescue breaths			
Location of pulse check			
Depth of chest compressions			
Rate of chest compressions			
Ratio of chest compressions to rescue breaths (one cycle)	1 rescuer: 2 rescuers:	1 rescuer: 2 rescuers:	1 rescuer: 2 rescuers:

44. When should a pediatric-capable automated external defibrillator be used?

45. You are on the scene of a cardiac arrest. As you prepare to apply the AED pads, you note the patient has an excessive amount of chest hair. Describe the appropriate actions that should be taken in this situation.

46. List three groups of patients who are more likely to have a heart attack and present with signs and symptoms that differ from those of a "typical" patient.

1.

2.

3.

Answer Section

Multiple Choice

1. a

The circulatory system is made up of the cardiovascular and lymphatic systems. The cardiovascular system is made up of three main parts: a pump (the heart), fluid (blood), and a container (the blood vessels).

Objective: Describe the structure and function of the cardiovascular system.

2. b

Blood pressure takes into account the pressure during contraction and relaxation of the heart muscle. A reading of 120/80, for example, indicates that during contraction of the heart a force of 120 mm Hg is exerted on the walls of the arteries while during relaxation this force drops to 80 mm Hg. A blood pressure taken by palpation (i.e., 120/P) is an approximation of the systolic blood pressure. Adequate circulation of blood through an organ or the body refers to perfusion. Adequate blood pressure supports perfusion.

Objective: Define blood pressure, systolic blood pressure, and diastolic blood pressure.

3. a

By dilating the peripheral vessels, the circulatory system sends more blood to the surface of the body. This blood is cooled and returns to the body's core. Imagine yourself playing basketball on a hot day. Your skin may become red or flushed due to increased blood flow to the skin. Sweating allows the skin to cool down. This cooler temperature is transmitted to the blood supply. Some medications may interfere with this process.

Objective: Describe the structure and function of each of the blood vessels: arteries, arterioles, capillaries, venules, and veins.

4. b

The right ventricle pumps blood to the lungs. The left ventricle pumps blood to the body.

The atria are thin-walled chambers that receive blood from the systemic circulation and lungs.

Objective: Name the chambers of the heart and their function.

5. b

Veins always carry blood toward the heart. Deoxygenated blood returns from the capillary beds of the body through veins to the heart. Reoxygenated blood returns from the capillary beds through the two pulmonary veins from each lung to the left atrium.

Objective: Describe the structure and function of each of the blood vessels: arteries, arterioles, capillaries, venules, and veins.

6. b

The right and left coronary arteries are the first arteries that branch off the aorta as blood flows from the left ventricle. The carotid arteries are located in the neck just lateral to the trachea (windpipe). The femoral arteries are located in the crease between the abdomen and the thigh. The pulmonary arteries are responsible for delivering deoxygenated blood from the right ventricle to the lungs.

Objective: Name the major arteries, and describe their location and the parts of the body they nourish.

7. c

Coronary artery disease results in the reduced flow of blood through the coronary arteries. If the flow of blood to the heart is reduced too much, heart muscle cells will die. *Infarction* refers to death. Myocardium is the medical term for the heart muscle; therefore, an acute myocardial infarction (AMI) is a heart attack. While a heart attack and angina pectoris both present in much the same way and both may be attributed to coronary artery disease, a heart attack differs from angina pectoris. In angina, death of heart cells does not occur. Since EMRs are not physicians, patients presenting with cardiac-type chest pain should be assumed to be having an acute myocardial infarction.

Objective: Define acute myocardial infarction (AMI) and describe possible assessment findings and symptoms associated with this condition.

8. c

When the heart is deprived of oxygen, the result is chest pain or discomfort. Any patient complaining of chest pain or discomfort should be immediately treated with high-flow oxygen by nonrebreather mask. The pain associated with cardiac compromise may be described in many ways: a dull ache, indigestion, a heavy weight on the chest, or a sharp pain that radiates to another body area. Pulmonary edema, nausea, and pedal or sacral edema (swelling of the feet or lower back) may accompany chest pain; however, chest pain is the most common complaint.

Objective: Describe the emergency medical care of the patient experiencing a cardiovascular emergency.

9. d

Do not be confused by the term *focused history* and physical examination. The emphasis of the physical examination is determined by the conscious patient's chief complaint. However, the physical findings for a particular complaint may be seen in body regions away from the area of distress. For example, a patient complaining of chest pain may have swelling of the feet (pedal edema) from failure of the right ventricle. This sign is an important and pertinent finding. Do not merely examine the area of discomfort, or you may miss additional signs relevant to the patient's distress.

Objective: Describe the emergency medical care of the patient experiencing a cardiovascular emergency.

10. b

NTG causes relaxation (dilation) of the smooth muscle of blood vessel walls. Relaxation of the veins results in pooling of blood in the dependent portions of the body, due to gravity. This effect reduces the amount of blood returning to the heart, decreasing the heart's workload. NTG causes some relaxation of the walls of arteries, including the coronary arteries. This helps reduce the resistance the heart must overcome to pump blood out to the body, thus decreasing the heart's workload. NTG relaxes normal and atherosclerotic coronary arteries on

the outer surface of the heart. This helps to improve blood flow and the delivery of oxygen to the heart, thus improving blood flow to the heart muscle that was previously deprived of oxygen (ischemia). Relief of ischemia reduces chest pain and discomfort.

Objective: Describe the emergency medical care of the patient experiencing a cardiovascular emergency.

11. c

The clinical difference between angina pectoris and an acute myocardial infarction (AMI) is the presence of dead tissue that results following an AMI. Both angina and an AMI present similarly. This is not surprising since the discomfort felt during angina and that felt during an AMI are of the same origin, ischemic heart tissue. Sudden death does not always result from an AMI, or there would be no such thing as a patient with a history of previous heart attacks.

Objective: Define acute coronary syndromes.

12. a

Because the left ventricle pumps oxygenated blood away from the lungs toward the body, a backup of this flow would result in an increase in the amount of blood in the lungs. More blood in the lungs causes the capillary beds to leak fluid into the lung's air sacs (alveoli). Fluid in the lungs is called *pulmonary edema*. If the right ventricle fails, deoxygenated blood will back up as it returns from the body to the heart. This backup may result in jugular venous distention (JVD) and swelling in the feet and lower back.

Objective: Define acute pulmonary edema, and describe its relationship to left ventricular failure.

Matching

13.	N	21.	J
14.	O	22.	C
15.	V	23.	E
16.	R	24.	T
17.	X	25.	A
18.	Q	26.	S
19.	B	27.	H
20.	W	28.	K

29.	M	33.	G
30.	I	34.	U
31.	F	35.	P
32.	D	36.	L

Short Answer

37. Possible causes of cardiac arrest include:

    - Heart and blood vessel diseases, such as heart attack and stroke
    - Choking or respiratory arrest
    - Seizures
    - Diabetic emergency
    - Severe allergic reaction
    - Severe electric shock
    - Poisoning or drug overdose
    - Drowning
    - Suffocation
    - Trauma
    - Severe bleeding
    - Abnormalities present at birth

    Objective: Define cardiac arrest, and explain its possible causes.

38. Survival of cardiac arrest depends on a series of critical actions called the *chain of survival*. The chain of survival is the ideal series of events that should take place immediately after recognizing an injury or the onset of sudden illness. The chain consists of four crucial steps:

    1. Early access (recognition of an emergency and calling 9-1-1)
    2. Early CPR
    3. Early defibrillation
    4. Early advanced care

    A break in any of the links in the chain can reduce the patient's chance of survival, despite excellence in the rest of the chain.

    Objective: Describe the links in the chain of survival.

39. Before delivering a shock with an AED, make sure that oxygen is not flowing over the patient's chest. Fire can be ignited by sparks from poorly applied AED pads in an oxygen-enriched atmosphere.

    Objective: Discuss the procedures that must be taken into consideration for standard operation of the various types of AEDs.

40. Follow these steps to operate an AED:

    1. *Power:* Be sure the patient is lying face-up, on a firm, flat surface. Start CPR if the AED is not immediately available. Place the AED next to the rescuer who will be operating it. Turn on the power. Depending on the brand of AED, this is done by either pressing the "on" button or lifting up the AED screen or lid.

    2. *Pads:* Open the package containing the AED pads. Connect the pads to the AED cables (if not preconnected). Then apply the pads to the patient's bare chest. The correct position for the pads is usually shown on the package containing the pads. Alternately, it may be shown in a diagram on the AED itself. If the patient's chest is wet, quickly dry it before applying the pads. Briefly stop CPR to allow pad placement on the patient's chest. Connect the cable to the AED.

    3. *Analyze:* Analyze the patient's heart rhythm. Some AEDs require that you press an "analyze" button. Other defibrillators automatically start to analyze when the pads are attached to the patient's chest. Do not touch the patient while the AED is analyzing the rhythm.

    4. *Shock:* If the AED advises that a shock is indicated, check the patient from head to toe to make sure no one (including you) is touching the patient before pressing the shock control. Make sure oxygen is not flowing over the patient's chest. Remove oxygen delivery devices, such as a bag-valve mask, from around the patient and stretcher. Shout, "Stand clear!" Press the shock control once it is illuminated and the machine indicates it is ready to deliver the shock. Resume CPR, beginning with chest compressions, immediately after delivery of the shock unless the patient regains consciousness or begins spontaneous movement. After five cycles of CPR, reanalyze the rhythm. Continue this sequence until the patient regains a pulse, the patient regains consciousness or begins spontaneous movement, or advanced life support personnel take over patient care. The decision to remain on scene for ALS personnel, transport to a rendezvous with ALS, or transport directly to a medical facility depends on local protocol, transport time, and medical direction.

    Objective: List the steps in the operation of the automated external defibrillator.

41. Typical heart attack signs and symptoms include:

    - Uncomfortable squeezing, ache, dull pressure, or pain in the center of the chest lasting more than a few minutes
    - Discomfort in one or both arms, the back, neck, jaw, or stomach
    - Anxiety, dizziness, irritability
    - Abnormal pulse rate (may be irregular)

- Abnormal blood pressure
- Nausea, vomiting
- Lightheadedness
- Fainting or near fainting
- Breaking out in a cold sweat
- Weakness
- Difficulty breathing (dyspnea)
- Palpitations
- Feeling of impending doom

Objective: Define acute myocardial infarction (AMI), and describe possible assessment findings and symptoms associated with this condition.

42. Do not allow any patient who has a heart or breathing-related complaint to perform activities that require exertion, such as walking to the stretcher. Asking the patient to walk to a stretcher or ambulance *increases* the heart's need for oxygen. When providing emergency care to such patients, your goal is to *decrease* oxygen demand. Bring the stretcher to the patient—not the patient to the stretcher.

Objective: Describe the emergency medical care of the patient experiencing a cardiovascular emergency.

43. See table below.

can be used on children between 1 and 8 years of age. The key or pad-cable system decreases the amount of energy delivered to a dose appropriate for a child. If a child is in cardiac arrest and a key or pad-cable system is not available, use a standard AED.

Objective: Describe AED use in adults and children.

45. If the patient has a hairy chest, the AED pads may not stick to the patient's chest. The AED will be unable to analyze the patient's heart rhythm and will give a "check electrodes" message. Try pressing down firmly on each AED pad and see if that corrects the problem. If the "check electrodes" message from the AED persists (and you have a second set of AED pads available), quickly remove the AED pads. This will remove some of the patient's chest hair. Quickly look at the patient's chest. If a lot of chest hair remains, quickly shave the areas of the chest where the AED pads will be placed. Put on a second set of AED pads. Follow the prompts by the AED.

Objective: Discuss the use of remote defibrillation through adhesive pads.

	Adult	**Child**	**Infant**
Rescue breaths	About 10 to 12 breaths/min 1 breath every 5 to 6 sec	About 12 to 20 breaths/min 1 breath every 3 to 5 sec	About 12 to 20 breaths/min 1 breath every 3 to 5 sec
Location of pulse check	Carotid	Carotid	Brachial
Depth of chest Compressions	1½ to 2 inches	⅓ to ½ the chest depth	⅓ to ½ the chest depth
Rate of chest compressions	About 100/min	About 100/min	About 100/min
Ratio of chest compressions to rescue breaths (one cycle)	*1 or 2 rescuers:* 30 compressions to 2 breaths (30:2)	*1 rescuer:* 30 compressions to 2 breaths (30:2) *2 rescuers:* 15 compressions to 2 breaths (15:2)	*1 rescuer:* 30 compressions to 2 breaths (30:2) *2 rescuers:* 15 compressions to 2 breaths (15:2)

Objective: Describe the emergency medical care of the patient experiencing a cardiovascular emergency.

44. A standard AED is used for a patient who is unresponsive, not breathing, pulseless, and 8 years of age or older (about 55 pounds or >25 kg). A special key or pad-cable system is available for some AEDs so that the machine

46. Older adults, diabetic individuals, and women are more likely to have a heart attack and present with signs and symptoms that differ from a "typical" patient. This is called an *atypical presentation* or *atypical signs and symptoms.*

Objective: Describe atypical assessment findings and symptoms associated with acute coronary syndromes.

18 Abdominal Disorders

READING ASSIGNMENT Read Chapter 18, pages 368 to 375 in your textbook.

Sum It Up

- The abdominal cavity is bordered superiorly by the diaphragm, inferiorly by the pelvis, posteriorly by the spine, and anteriorly by the abdominal wall. The major blood vessels of the abdomen are the aorta and inferior vena cava.
- The abdominal cavity is lined by a smooth membrane called the peritoneum. The area behind the peritoneal cavity is called the retroperitoneum or retroperitoneal space. The kidneys, ureters, and rectum are examples of structures located in the retroperitoneal space.
- The abdominal cavity is divided into four quadrants. The right upper quadrant (RUQ) contains the liver, the gallbladder, portions of the stomach, the large and small intestine, part of the pancreas, and the major blood vessels. The left upper quadrant (LUQ) contains the stomach, spleen, pancreas, and large and small intestines. The right lower quadrant (RLQ) contains the cecum, appendix, and large and small intestines. The left lower quadrant (LLQ) contains the intestines.
- Acute abdomen is a sudden onset of abdominal pain.
- Abdominal pain may or may not be the result of a problem involving an organ within the abdominal cavity. Pain that is felt in a part of the body that is away from the tissues or organ that causes the pain is called referred pain.
- Gastritis is an inflammation of the stomach lining. Assessment findings and symptoms include belching, nausea and vomiting, and indigestion. The patient may complain of a burning sensation in the upper abdomen.
- A peptic ulcer is an open sore in the lining of the stomach (gastric ulcer), duodenum (duodenal ulcer), or esophagus (esophageal ulcer).
- Bleeding may occur from any part of the GI tract. GI bleeding is a medical emergency.
- Upper GI bleeding is bleeding from the esophagus, stomach, or duodenum. Assessment findings and symptoms include hematemesis (vomiting blood). Vomited blood may be bright red if it is recent or if bleeding is forceful. The patient may also present with syncope, fatigue, and shortness of breath.
- Lower gastrointestinal bleeding can originate in the small intestine, colon, or rectum. Assessment findings and symptoms include rectal bleeding, increased frequency of stools, and cramping pain.

- Assess the patient. Form a general impression and perform a primary survey. If you have not already done so, establish patient priorities, determine the need for additional resources, and make a transport decision. Once you have made a transport decision, obtain a SAMPLE history from the patient if he is responsive. Remember to use the OPQRST tool if he is complaining of pain or discomfort.
- If the patient is responsive, perform a focused physical examination. Observe the patient's position. Assess the patient's pulse, respirations, and blood pressure. Assess the abdomen for DCAP-BTLS. Look to see if abdominal distention is present. Palpate the abdomen and determine if the abdomen feels soft or hard (rigid).
- If the patient is unresponsive or has an altered mental status, quickly size up the scene, form a general impression, perform a primary survey, and then proceed to the rapid medical assessment. Provide all information obtained to the EMS personnel who arrive on the scene.
- Prehospital care for a patient experiencing abdominal discomfort is supportive. Allow the patient to assume a position of comfort and provide calm reassurance. Administer oxygen. Be alert for signs and symptoms of shock. Reassess as often as indicated.

▶ Tracking Your Progress

After reading this chapter, can you:	Page Reference	Objective Met?
• Describe the borders of the abdominal cavity?	369	☐
• Name the two major blood vessels in the abdomen?	369	☐
• Define peritoneum and retroperitoneal space?	369	☐
• Name the organs located in the right upper quadrant, left upper quadrant, right lower quadrant, and left lower quadrant?	369	☐
• Define acute abdomen and referred pain?	370	☐
• Define hematemesis and melena?	372	☐
• Describe assessment findings and symptoms of upper GI bleeding and lower GI bleeding?	372	☐
• Discuss assessment of the patient with abdominal pain?	372	☐
• Discuss the specific questions to ask to obtain a history of a patient with abdominal pain?	372	☐
• Discuss emergency care for the patient with abdominal pain?	373	☐

Chapter Quiz

True/False

Decide whether each statement is true or false. In the space provided, write T for true or F for false.

_____ **1.** Vomited blood is always bright red in color.

_____ **2.** Lower GI bleeding is bleeding from the esophagus, stomach, or duodenum.

_____ **3.** Although it is unnecessary for prehospital personnel to determine the specific cause of abdominal pain, it is important to understand the possible causes of the complaint.

Multiple Choice

In the space provided, identify the letter of the choice that best completes each statement or answers each question.

_____ 4. The abdominal cavity is lined by a smooth membrane called the
   a. peristalsis.
   b. peritoneum.
   c. pericardium.
   d. visceral pleura.

_____ 5. The two major blood vessels of the abdomen are the
   a. aorta and iliac vessels.
   b. aorta and inferior vena cava.
   c. aorta and superior vena cava.
   d. superior and inferior venae cavae.

_____ 6. Referred pain
   a. is felt in the skin, joint, and muscles.
   b. is felt directly over the injured or diseased organ.
   c. is felt in the body cavity next to the injured or diseased organ.
   d. is felt in a part of the body that is away from the tissues or organ that causes the pain.

_____ 7. The primary cause of peptic ulcer disease is
   a. reflux of stomach acid.
   b. excessive consumption of alcohol.
   c. a stomach infection caused by _H. pylori_ bacteria.
   d. excess secretion of digestive juices, such as hydrochloric acid, by stomach cells.

_____ 8. Hematemesis means
   a. vomiting blood.
   b. black, tarry stools.
   c. clay-colored stools.
   d. coughing up blood.

Answer Section

True/False

1. False

   Vomited blood may be bright red if it is recent or if bleeding is forceful. If blood accumulates in the stomach and is partially digested and then vomited, the vomited material may resemble coffee grounds.

   Objective: Discuss hemorrhagic causes of acute abdominal pain.

2. False

   Lower gastrointestinal bleeding can originate in the small intestine, colon, or rectum. Upper GI bleeding is bleeding from the esophagus, stomach, or duodenum.

   Objective: Discuss hemorrhagic causes of acute abdominal pain.

3. True

   Prehospital care for a patient experiencing abdominal discomfort is supportive.

   Objective: Discuss assessment of the patient with abdominal pain.

Multiple Choice

4. b

   Because the abdominal cavity is lined by a smooth membrane called the *peritoneum,* the abdominal cavity is sometimes called the *peritoneal cavity.*

   Objective: Define peritoneum and retroperitoneal space.

5. b

   The major blood vessels of the abdomen are the aorta and inferior vena cava.

   Objective: Name the two major blood vessels in the abdomen.

6. d

   Pain that is felt in a part of the body that is away from the tissues or organ that causes the pain is called *referred pain.*

   Objective: Define acute abdomen and referred pain.

7. c

   The primary cause of peptic ulcer disease is a stomach infection caused by *H. pylori* bacteria. A contributing cause is excess secretion of digestive juices. Over time, the protective mucous lining of the stomach, duodenum, or esophagus is worn away by excess secretion of digestive juices, such as hydrochloric acid, by stomach cells. The lining of the stomach, duodenum, or esophagus can also be disrupted by prolonged use of medications (such as NSAIDs) or alcohol. Esophageal ulcers are typically associated with the reflux of stomach acid.

   Objective: Discuss hemorrhagic causes of acute abdominal pain.

8. a

   Assessment findings and symptoms of upper GI bleeding include hematemesis (vomiting blood). Vomited blood may be bright red if it is recent or if bleeding is forceful. Forceful and repeated vomiting may cause hematemesis by tearing small blood vessels lining the stomach and esophagus. Coughing up blood is called *hemoptysis.* Black, tarry stools are called *melena.*

   Objective: Define hematemesis and melena.

Genitourinary and Renal Disorders

READING ASSIGNMENT ▶ Read Chapter 19, pages 376 to 384 in your textbook.

Sum It Up

- The urinary system consists of the kidneys, ureters, urinary bladder, and urethra. The kidneys' main roles are to filter water-soluble waste products from the blood, reabsorb water, electrolytes (such as sodium, potassium, and calcium), and nutrients, and excrete what is not needed into the urine. The ureters are tubes about 10 inches long that drain urine from the kidneys to the urinary bladder. The urinary bladder serves as a temporary storage site for urine. Urine released from the bladder travels through a muscular tube called the urethra to the outside of the body. In males, the urethra also transports semen from the body.

- The urinary system is responsible for the following functions:
  - Maintaining a balance of salts and other substances in the blood
  - Excreting waste products and foreign chemicals
  - Assisting in regulating arterial blood pressure
  - Producing a hormone that aids the formation of red blood cells

- Kidney stones, also called renal calculi, are one of the most common genitourinary disorders. A kidney stone is a hard mass that forms from crystallization of excreted substances in the urine. A stone that lodges in a ureter can cause urine to back up behind it and into the kidney, which continues to produce urine. The backup of urine causes the kidney to stretch, which increases pressure and causes severe pain. Assessment findings and symptoms can include excruciating pain that is usually located in the flank, radiating to the groin. Nausea, vomiting, and sweating are common. Irritation of the ureter by the stone can cause hematuria (blood in the urine). The patient may experience dysuria (painful or burning urination) as the stone nears the bladder.

- A urinary tract infection is an infection that affects any part of the urinary tract. Inflammation or infection limited to the urethra is called urethritis and of the bladder is called cystitis. Inflammation or infection of the kidneys is called pyelonephritis.

- A urinary catheter is a tube that is inserted into the bladder to empty it of urine. It may be inserted before some surgical procedures, for some diagnostic tests, or as a means of urinary drainage for patients who have a chronic illness or are confined to bed.

- Pyelonephritis is often the result of a bacterial bladder infection and a backflow of urine from the bladder into the ureters or kidney. Severe or recurring infections can cause permanent kidney damage.

- Renal failure, also called kidney failure, is a condition in which the kidneys fail to remove wastes adequately, concentrate urine, and conserve electrolytes to meet the demands of the body. Acute renal failure, also called acute kidney injury, is a sudden deterioration of kidney function that is potentially reversible. Chronic renal failure develops over months and years and is usually irreversible. End-stage renal disease exists when kidney failure is permanent.

- Patients who have acute or chronic renal failure or who have ESRD may undergo dialysis. Dialysis is a procedure, normally performed by the kidneys, that removes waste products from the blood.

- Hemodialysis involves the transfer of a large volume of blood between the patient and the dialysis machine. The patient's AV shunt, fistula, or graft is connected by needles and tubing to the machine. A specialized chemical solution (dialysate) is used in the dialyzer to draw excess water, minerals, and waste products from the blood through a semipermeable membrane. The dialysate also balances the other electrolytes in the body. Possible complications of hemodialysis include muscle cramps, nausea and vomiting, hypotension from too-rapid fluid removal, dehydration, blood loss, and sepsis. Infection and hemorrhage can occur at the vascular access site.

- In peritoneal dialysis, a catheter is inserted into the patient's peritoneal cavity through a small abdominal incision below the umbilicus. During the dialysis process, dialysate is instilled into the patient's peritoneal cavity through the catheter and left in the abdomen for a designated period determined by the patient's physician. The patient's peritoneum serves as a semipermeable membrane across which wastes and excess fluids are exchanged. The fluid is then drained from the abdomen, measured, and discarded. Possible complications of peritoneal dialysis include peritonitis from bacteria entering the peritoneal cavity through or around the catheter, blockage of the catheter from clots, kinking of the catheter, hypotension, and hypovolemia.

- Prehospital care for a patient experiencing a genitourinary emergency is supportive. Administer oxygen. If signs and symptoms of pulmonary edema are present, place the patient in a sitting position. If the patient has an AV shunt or fistula and is bleeding from the vascular access site, control bleeding with direct pressure. Be alert for signs and symptoms of shock and if present, keep the patient in a supine position. The patient experiencing a genitourinary emergency needs to be transported for physician evaluation. Reassess as often as indicated until patient care is turned over to EMS personnel.

▶ Tracking Your Progress

After reading this chapter, can you:	Page Reference	Objective Met?
• Discuss the anatomy and physiology of the genitourinary system?	377	☐
• Discuss the functions of the genitourinary system?	378	☐
• Identify the pathophysiology, assessment findings, and symptoms associated with kidney stones?	378	☐
• Identify the pathophysiology, assessment findings, and symptoms associated with a urinary tract infection?	378	☐

After reading this chapter, can you:	Page Reference	Objective Met?
• Discuss types of urinary catheters?	379	☐
• Identify the pathophysiology, assessment findings, and symptoms associated with pyelonephritis?	379	☐
• Identify the pathophysiology, assessment findings, and symptoms associated with renal failure?	379	☐
• Discuss types of dialysis?	380	☐
• Discuss complications related to dialysis?	380	☐
• Discuss assessment of the patient with a genitourinary disorder?	381	☐
• Discuss the specific questions to ask to obtain a history of a patient with a genitourinary disorder?	382	☐
• Describe the emergency care for a patient experiencing a kidney stone, urinary tract infection, pyelonephritis, or renal failure?	383	☐

Chapter Quiz

Multiple Choice

In the space provided, identify the letter of the choice that best completes each statement or answers each question.

_____ 1. The functional units of the kidney are called

    a. ureters.
    b. urethra.
    c. nephrons.
    d. tubules.

_____ 2. Which of the following reflects appropriate emergency care for bleeding from an arteriovenous fistula?

    a. Apply an air splint.
    b. Apply a tourniquet.
    c. Apply pressure at the brachial artery.
    d. Apply direct pressure to the bleeding site.

_____ 3. The renal veins return blood to the

    a. Thoracic aorta.
    b. abdominal aorta.

Matching

Match the key terms in the left column with the definitions in the right column by placing the letter of each correct answer in the space provided.

_____ **4.** Pyelonephritis

_____ **5.** Hematuria

_____ **6.** Urethra

_____ **7.** Acute renal failure

_____ **8.** Urinary hesitancy

_____ **9.** Renal calculi

_____ **10.** Hemodialysis

_____ **11.** Urea

_____ **12.** Urinary catheter

_____ **13.** Dysuria

_____ **14.** Chronic renal failure

_____ **15.** Cystitis

_____ **16.** End-stage renal disease

_____ **17.** Peritoneal dialysis

A. Painful or burning urination

B. A sudden deterioration of kidney function that is potentially reversible

C. A waste product removed from the blood by the kidneys

D. Difficulty in starting urination

E. Inflammation or infection of the urinary bladder

F. Removal of waste products and excess water and salt from the blood using the lining of the abdomen as the filter

G. Blood in the urine

H. A gradual deterioration of kidney function that develops over months and years and is usually irreversible

I. Urine released from the bladder travels through this structure

J. Inflammation or infection of the kidneys

K. A tube that is inserted into the bladder to empty it of urine

L. Kidney stones

M. Removal of waste products and excess water and salt from the blood using an external machine as the filter

N. Permanent kidney failure

Short Answer

Answer each question in the space provided.

18. List two possible complications of peritoneal dialysis.

1.

2.

19. List three functions of the urinary system.

1.

2.

3.

20. List six possible assessment findings and symptoms of pyelonephritis.

1.

2.

3.

4.

5.

6.

Answer Section

Multiple Choice

1. c

Each kidney contains about 1 million filters called *nephrons*, which are the functional units of the kidney. Each nephron is made up of a network of capillaries and tubules through which the blood is filtered and nutrients are reabsorbed.

Objective: Discuss the anatomy and physiology of the genitourinary system.

2. d

If the patient has an AV shunt or fistula and is bleeding from the vascular access site, control bleeding with direct pressure. Be alert for signs and symptoms of shock, and if present, keep the patient in a supine position.

Objective: Describe the emergency care for a patient experiencing a kidney stone, urinary tract infection, pyelonephritis, or renal failure.

3. c

The kidneys receive their blood supply from the renal arteries, which are branches of the abdominal aorta. Blood is returned to the inferior vena cava via the renal veins.

Objective: Discuss the anatomy and physiology of the genitourinary system.

Matching

4.	J	**11.**	C
5.	G	**12.**	K
6.	I	**13.**	A
7.	B	**14.**	H
8.	D	**15.**	E
9.	L	**16.**	N
10.	M	**17.**	F

Short Answer

18. Possible complications of peritoneal dialysis include peritonitis from bacteria entering the peritoneal cavity through or around the catheter, blockage of the catheter from clots, kinking of the catheter, hypotension, and hypovolemia.

Objective: Discuss complications related to dialysis.

19. The urinary system is responsible for the following functions:

- Maintaining a balance of salts and other substances in the blood
- Excreting waste products and foreign chemicals
- Assisting in regulating arterial blood pressure
- Producing a hormone that aids the formation of red blood cells

Objective: Discuss the functions of the genitourinary system.

20. Assessment findings and symptoms of pyelonephritis often include the following:

- Fever, chills
- Fatigue
- Nausea, vomiting
- Dysuria
- Hematuria
- Cloudy or abnormal urine color
- Foul or strong urine odor
- Flank pain or lower-back pain
- Warm, moist skin
- Increased urinary frequency

Objective: Identify the pathophysiology, assessment findings, and symptoms associated with pyelonephritis.

READING ASSIGNMENT ▶ Read Chapter 20, pages 385 to 393 in your textbook.

Sum It Up

- Gynecology is the study of the female reproductive system. Gynecologic emergencies are conditions that affect the female reproductive organs. Patients experiencing a gynecologic emergency most often present with either abdominal pain or vaginal bleeding.

- Assessment of the patient experiencing a gynecologic emergency includes careful history-taking skills.

- When performing a physical exam, keep in mind that your patient may be anxious about having her clothing removed and having an examination performed by a stranger. Be certain to explain what you are about to do and why it must be done. Remember to properly drape or shield an unclothed patient from the stares of others. Conduct the examination professionally and efficiently, and talk with your patient throughout the procedure.

- As an EMR, you must not visually inspect the vaginal area unless major bleeding is present or you anticipate that childbirth is about to occur. In these situations, it is best to have another healthcare professional or law enforcement officer present. If possible, include a female attendant or rescuer in your examination. The vaginal area is touched only during delivery and (ideally) when another healthcare professional or law enforcement officer is present.

- Pelvic inflammatory disease (PID) is an infection of the uterus, fallopian tubes, and other female reproductive organs. It is usually caused by sexually transmitted bacteria, such as chlamydia and gonorrhea. PID occurs when bacteria enter a woman's vagina and spread upward into her cervix, uterus, fallopian tubes, and other reproductive organs. An untreated infection can lead to septic shock and infertility.

- Chlamydia is a sexually transmitted disease that can be transmitted during vaginal, anal, or oral sex. It can also be passed from an infected mother to her baby during vaginal childbirth. Chlamydia can be easily treated and cured with antibiotics.

- Gonorrhea is an STD that multiplies in warm, moist areas of the reproductive tract such as the cervix, uterus, and fallopian tubes in women and in the urethra in men and women. Several antibiotics are available that can successfully cure gonorrhea; however, the number of strains of gonorrhea that are resistant to drug therapy are increasing, making treatment more difficult.

- Syphilis is an STD transmitted through direct contact with a syphilis sore (called a chancre) during vaginal, anal, or oral sex. Syphilis can also be spread from mother to baby during pregnancy. Syphilis is diagnosed by means of a blood test and, if caught in its early stages, can be successfully treated with antibiotics.

- Genital human papillomavirus (HPV) is a sexually transmitted infection that is transmitted through genital contact, usually during vaginal or anal sex. According to the Centers for Disease Control and Prevention, there is no treatment for HPV itself, but there are treatments for the diseases that HPV can cause.

- An ectopic pregnancy occurs when a fertilized egg implants outside the uterus. An ectopic pregnancy is a medical emergency. The most common site where this occurs is inside a fallopian tube. An ectopic pregnancy that occurs in a fallopian tube is called a *tubal pregnancy*. Severe bleeding can occur as a result of ruptured blood vessels. The patient may complain of mild cramping on one side of the pelvis, nausea, lower-back pain, and lower abdominal or pelvic pain. If rupture occurs, the patient often complains of a sudden onset of severe pain on one side of the lower abdomen. Vaginal bleeding may or may not be present. Severe internal bleeding may be present. The patient may have signs of shock, such as decreasing blood pressure, an increased heart rate, and cool, clammy skin.

- Although there are many causes of abdominal pain, you must consider lower abdominal pain in any woman of childbearing age to be caused by an ectopic pregnancy until proved otherwise.

- An ovarian cyst is a fluid-filled sac that develops on or within an ovary. The most common type of ovarian cyst forms during the menstrual cycle and goes away on its own in 1 to 3 months. Although most ovarian cysts do not cause symptoms, others can cause symptoms if the cyst pushes on nearby structures, ruptures, or bleeds.

- Vaginitis, an inflammation of the vagina, may be caused by an infection due to bacteria or yeast or by reduced estrogen levels after menopause. Vaginitis usually responds well to appropriate medication therapy.

- Cervicitis, an inflammation of the cervix, is often caused by infection with sexually transmitted diseases, including gonorrhea and chlamydia. Treatment for cervicitis usually includes antibiotics to treat the underlying infection.

- Cervical cancer is one of the most common cancers that affect a woman's reproductive organs. Treatment for cervical cancer varies depending on the number of layers of the cervix that are affected.

- Uterine fibroids are growths that often cause no symptoms and seldom require treatment. When uterine fibroids do cause symptoms, they can include back or leg pain, heavy menstrual bleeding, pelvic pressure or pain, prolonged menstrual periods, or bleeding between periods.

- Trauma to the external genitalia may occur from bicycle injuries, blows, foreign body insertion, childbirth lacerations, or sexual assault. Trauma to the external genitalia should be treated as are other bleeding soft tissue injuries. Control bleeding with local pressure to the area, using trauma dressings or sanitary napkins. Do not pack or place dressings inside the vagina. Monitor the patient's vital signs closely and treat for shock if indicated.

- Criminal assault situations require initial and ongoing assessment and management, as well as psychological care. When possible, have an EMR of the same gender assess the sexual assault victim. Maintain a nonjudgmental attitude during the SAMPLE history and focused assessment. Protect the crime scene and document any pertinent findings. Discourage the patient from bathing, douching, urinating, or cleaning wounds until after transport and evaluation at the receiving facility. The patient should not be allowed to eat or drink because doing so washes away evidence. Handle the patient's clothing as little as possible. Bag all items separately in paper bags, and seal with evidence tape (if available). Examine the genitalia only if profuse bleeding is present. Transport to an appropriate medical facility for further care.

After reading this chapter, can you:	Page Reference	Objective Met?
• Identify the following structures: ovaries, uterus, cervix, labia, fallopian tubes, vagina, perineum, and endometrium?	386	☐
• Identify specific details of the medical history that should be obtained with the gynecologic patient?	387	☐
• Identify specific physical findings that should be assessed in the gynecologic patient?	387	☐
• Describe the typical assessment findings, symptoms, and emergency care for pelvic inflammatory disease?	388	☐
• Describe the typical assessment findings, symptoms, and emergency care for a suspected ectopic pregnancy?	390	☐
• Identify potential sources of trauma to the external genitalia and explain management of injuries?	391	☐
• Discuss the assessment of a sexual assault victim and identify the ways in which it differs from usual assessment?	391	☐
• Identify principles of management for the sexual assault victim?	392	☐

Chapter Quiz

Multiple Choice

In the space provided, identify the letter of the choice that best completes each statement or answers each question.

_____ 1. The ovaries are responsible for
    a. stretching to adapt to the increasing size of a fetus.
    b. contracting to expel an infant from the mother's body.
    c. receiving and transporting the egg to the uterus.
    d. producing eggs and secreting hormones.

_____ 2. In a normal pregnancy, the egg will travel to the uterus through the
    a. cervix.
    b. vagina.
    c. urethra.
    d. fallopian tubes.

_____ 3. Your rescue crew has been dispatched to transport an assault patient from a crime scene. Local law enforcement personnel have secured the scene. Your patient is a 24-year-old woman complaining of head pain. She states she was jumped while jogging in the park and was hit in the head with a small bat. A police officer informs you the patient told her that she was raped. Appropriate interventions should include
    a. having the police officer transport the patient to the hospital to complete a "rape kit" examination.
    b. full spinal stabilization, oxygen therapy, focused history and physical examination, and transport.
    c. full spinal stabilization, oxygen therapy, focused history and physical examination to determine if a rape occurred, and transport.
    d. allowing the patient to bathe quickly, full spinal stabilization, focused history and physical examination, and transport.

Sentence Completion

In the blanks provided, write the words that best complete each sentence.

4. Patients experiencing a gynecologic emergency most often present with either _____ _____ or _____ _____.

5. The _____ is a pear-shaped, hollow, muscular organ located in the pelvic cavity that prepares for pregnancy each month of a woman's reproductive life.

6. The _____ is the narrow opening at the distal end of the uterus that connects the uterus to the vagina.

Short Answer

Answer each question in the space provided.

7. List three signs or symptoms of an ectopic pregnancy.
   1.
   2.
   3.

8. Discuss the emergency medical care for a patient experiencing vaginal bleeding (with no history of trauma).

9. In addition to the SAMPLE history, what questions should be asked of the patient who has vaginal bleeding?

10. List seven common assessment findings and symptoms of gynecologic emergencies.
    1.
    2.
    3.
    4.
    5.
    6.
    7.

11. List six possible assessment findings and symptoms of an ovarian cyst.

    1.

    2.

    3.

    4.

    5.

    6.

12. When caring for a victim of alleged sexual assault, how should the patient's clothing be handled?

Answer Section

Multiple Choice

1. d

   The ovaries are paired, almond-shaped organs located on either side of the uterus. The ovaries perform two main functions: producing eggs and secreting hormones, such as estrogen and progesterone.

   Objective: Identify the following structures: ovaries, uterus, cervix, labia, fallopian tubes, vagina, perineum, and endometrium.

2. d

   The fallopian tubes receive and transport the egg to the uterus after ovulation. If fertilization occurs, the developing fetus (unborn infant) implants itself in the uterine wall and develops there.

   Objective: Identify the following structures: ovaries, uterus, cervix, labia, fallopian tubes, vagina, perineum, and endometrium.

3. b

   Spinal stabilization is indicated due to the trauma to the head. Here are some guidelines for dealing with alleged sexual assault: It is not your job to determine the truth of the patient's statements. It is also not your job to be judgmental or critical of the patient. You are dealing with a patient who has multiple injuries: an injured head, possible injuries to the pelvic area, and the very real injury to her psyche. Rape is a traumatic event, both physically and emotionally. Be professional and supportive. Be thorough in your history taking but not intrusive. Be supportive, but not chatty. Have a crew member of the same gender, if available, interact with the patient. Be gentle and brief in conducting a physical examination. Examination of the patient's genitalia should be done only if profuse bleeding is present. If the suspected injury is not so significant that you would need to treat it, observing the area only makes the patient more uncomfortable and may result in the damage of important evidence. Make sure that your documentation is accurate and complete.

   Objective: Identify principles of management for the sexual assault victim.

Sentence Completion

4. Patients experiencing a gynecologic emergency most often present with either **abdominal pain** or **vaginal bleeding.**

   Objective: Identify specific physical findings that should be assessed in the gynecologic patient.

5. The **uterus** (womb) is a pear-shaped, hollow, muscular organ located in the pelvic cavity that prepares for pregnancy each month of a woman's reproductive life.

   Objective: Identify the following structures: ovaries, uterus, cervix, labia, fallopian tubes, vagina, perineum, and endometrium.

6. The **cervix** is the narrow opening at the distal end of the uterus that connects the uterus to the vagina.

   Objective: Identify the following structures: ovaries, uterus, cervix, labia, fallopian tubes, vagina, perineum, and endometrium.

Short Answer

7. Signs or symptoms of an ectopic pregnancy may include:

   - Missed menstrual period or intermittent spotting over 6 to 8 weeks
   - Vaginal bleeding ranging from spotting to hemorrhage
   - Sudden onset of severe pain on one side of the lower abdomen
   - Severe pain in the back of the shoulder
   - Abdominal tenderness

Signs of shock (such as cool, clammy skin, decreasing blood pressure, increased heart rate)

Objective: Describe the typical assessment findings, symptoms, and emergency care for a suspected ectopic pregnancy.

8. For a patient experiencing vaginal bleeding (with no history of trauma), emergency care includes doing the following:

   - Take appropriate standard precautions.
   - Provide specific treatment based on the patient's signs and symptoms.
   - Establish and maintain an open airway. Administer oxygen.
   - Treat for shock, if indicated
   - Maintain body temperature
   - Apply external vaginal pads as necessary. As the pad becomes blood-soaked, replace it with a new one. All blood-soaked garments and pads should accompany the patient to the hospital. Transport. If the patient is stable, reassess every 15 minutes. If the patient is unstable, reassess every 5 minutes.

   Objective: Identify specific physical findings that should be assessed in the gynecologic patient.

9. If the patient is having vaginal bleeding, ask the following questions:

   - How long have you been bleeding?
   - Is the blood dark red (like menstrual blood) or bright red?
   - Is the bleeding heavier or lighter than that in a normal menstrual period? How many sanitary napkins or tampons have you used (in pads or tampons per hour)?
   - Have you passed any clots?
   - Do you feel dizzy when standing?

   Objective: Identify specific details of the medical history that should be obtained with the gynecologic patient.

10. Common assessment findings and symptoms of gynecologic emergencies include:

    - Abdominal pain of sudden or gradual onset
    - Abdominal tenderness
    - Vaginal discharge
    - Abnormal vaginal bleeding
    - Fever, chills
    - Fainting
    - Sweating
    - Increased heart rate
    - Nausea, vomiting
    - Pain during intercourse
    - Pain that worsens with coughing or urination
    - Pain in the tip of the shoulder (may occur in ectopic pregnancy)

    Objective: Identify specific physical findings that should be assessed in the gynecologic patient.

11. Although most ovarian cysts do not cause symptoms, others can cause symptoms if the cyst pushes on nearby structures, ruptures, or bleeds. Possible assessment findings and symptoms include the following:

    - Lower abdominal or pelvic pain that may be severe, sudden, and sharp
    - Irregular menstrual periods
    - Dull ache in the lower back and thighs
    - Faintness, dizziness, or weakness
    - Feeling of lower abdominal or pelvic pressure or fullness
    - Pelvic pain after strenuous exercise or sexual intercourse
    - Weight gain
    - Pain or pressure with urination or bowel movements
    - Difficulty passing urine completely
    - Nausea and vomiting

12. Handle the patient's clothing as little as possible. Bag all items separately in paper bags, and seal with evidence tape (if available). Do not use plastic bags for bloodstained articles. Plastic holds in moisture, which can promote the growth of bacteria. Bacterial growth can contaminate evidence.

    Objective: Identify principles of management for the sexual assault victim.

CHAPTER

21 Anaphylaxis

READING ASSIGNMENT ▶ Read Chapter 21, pages 394 to 405 in your textbook.

Sum It Up

- An allergic reaction is an exaggerated immune response to any substance. The substance that causes an allergic reaction can enter the body in four ways: ingestion, injection, inhalation, or absorption through the skin or mucous membranes. Possible causes include insect bites or stings, food, plants, and medications, among others.

- An antigen is any substance that is foreign to an individual and causes antibody production. An antibody is a substance produced by white blood cells to defend the body against bacteria, viruses, or other antigens. The antibodies attach to mast cells, which are found in connective tissue. This process, called sensitization, occurs with the body's first exposure to the antigen. When an antigen causes signs and symptoms of an allergic reaction, the antigen is called an allergen. When an allergic reaction is severe and affects multiple body systems, it is called anaphylaxis. Anaphylaxis is a life-threatening emergency.

- Assessment findings pertaining to the respiratory system may include tightness in the throat ("lump in the throat") or chest, coughing, rapid breathing, labored breathing, noisy breathing, hoarseness, stridor, difficulty talking, and wheezing. Assessment findings pertaining to the cardiovascular system may include an increased heart rate, lightheadedness, fainting, weakness, irregular heart rhythm, decreased blood pressure, and circulatory collapse. Assessment findings pertaining to the nervous system may include restlessness, fear, panic or a feeling of impending doom, headache, an altered mental status, unresponsiveness, and seizures. Assessment findings pertaining to the skin may include itching (pruritus), hives (urticaria), red skin (flushing), and swelling to the face, neck, hands, feet, and/or tongue. The patient may state that he has a warm tingling feeling in the face, mouth, chest, feet, and hands. Assessment findings pertaining to the gastrointestinal system may include nausea, vomiting, abdominal cramps or pain, an urgency to urinate, and diarrhea. Generalized findings may include itchy, watery eyes and a runny nose.

- Assessment findings that reveal shock (hypoperfusion) or respiratory distress indicate the presence of a severe allergic reaction.

- If the patient has come in contact with a substance that caused a past allergic reaction and complains of respiratory distress or shows signs and symptoms of shock, form a general impression, perform an initial assessment, and perform a focused history and physical exam. Assess the patient's baseline vital signs and SAMPLE history. Give oxygen if not already done in the initial assessment. Find out if the patient has a prescribed epinephrine autoinjector available. With approval from medical direction, help the patient with administration of the epinephrine autoinjector. Reassess in 2 minutes. Record reassessment findings.
- If the patient had contact with a substance that causes an allergic reaction without signs of respiratory distress or shock, continue with a focused assessment. A patient without wheezing or signs of respiratory compromise or hypotension should not receive epinephrine.
- A patient experiencing an allergic reaction may initially present with airway or respiratory compromise, or airway or respiratory compromise may develop as the allergic reaction progresses.
- If the patient's condition improves, provide supportive care. Continue to give oxygen and treat for shock. Signs that indicate the patient's condition is worsening include decreasing mental status, increasing breathing difficulty, and decreasing blood pressure. Treat for shock. Be prepared to begin CPR and use the AED, if necessary.

▶ Tracking Your Progress

After reading this chapter, can you:	Page Reference	Objective Met?
• Define allergic reaction?	395	☐
• Discuss the routes by which a substance that causes an allergic reaction can enter the body?	395	☐
• List common causes of allergic reactions?	396	☐
• Discuss latex allergy among patients and healthcare professionals?	396	☐
• Define antigen, antibody, sensitization, and allergen?	396	☐
• Discuss the inflammatory process?	397	☐
• Define anaphylaxis?	398	☐
• Differentiate signs and symptoms of a mild allergic reaction from those of a moderate or severe allergic reaction?	398	☐
• Discuss assessment of the patient with an allergic reaction?	399	☐
• Identify specific details of the medical history that should be obtained form the patient with an allergic reaction?	400	☐
• Describe the emergency medical care for the patient with an allergic reaction?	401	☐
• State the generic and trade names, medication form, dose, administration, action, indications, contraindications, and adverse effects of the epinephrine autoinjector?	402	☐

Chapter Quiz

Multiple Choice

In the space provided, identify the letter of the choice that best completes each statement or answers each question.

_____ 1. Any substance that is foreign to an individual and causes antibody production is known as an
  a. antigen.
  b. antibody.
  c. allergen.
  d. antihistamine.

_____ 2. Which of the following is considered a sign or symptom of a moderate or severe allergic reaction?
  a. Anxiety, runny nose
  b. Stridor, wheezing
  c. Rash, itching
  d. Coughing, tingling of the hands and/or feet

_____ 3. Which of the following foods have a high association with latex allergy?
  a. Hazelnut and mango
  b. Fig and walnut
  c. Kiwi and papaya
  d. Avocado and banana

_____ 4. What is the appropriate site for administration of the epinephrine autoinjector?
  a. The back of the hand
  b. Under the tongue (sublingual)
  c. The center of a buttock
  d. The lateral aspect of the midthigh

_____ 5. When administering an epinephrine autoinjector, it is important to
  a. hold the applicator at a 45- to 60-degree angle to the skin.
  b. hold the injector in place until all the medication has been delivered.
  c. remove the injector from the skin immediately after the needle springs forward.
  d. make the needle spring forward before applying the device to the patient's skin.

Questions 6–9 pertain to the following scenario:

Your ambulance crew is called to the scene of a one-car vehicle collision. You arrive at the scene and find that a pickup truck has hit a tree. There is only one occupant in the vehicle, and his seat belt is still on. The damage to the vehicle is minimal. Your scene size-up indicates that the patient's car is not leaking any fluids and there do not appear to be any hazards other than oncoming traffic. Local law enforcement has diverted traffic away from the scene. You are wearing a reflective traffic vest and appropriate personal protective equipment.

_____ 6. Following the scene size-up, you should immediately
  a. remove the patient from the vehicle.
  b. form a general impression and begin the primary survey.
  c. attempt to pry the vehicle away from the tree.
  d. provide supplemental oxygen by nonrebreather mask at 10 to 15 L/min.

_____ 7. The patient is unconscious. His respiratory rate is 30 breaths/min. His pulse rate is 96 beats/min, with moderate strength at the radial artery. Which of the following signs would lead you to believe that this patient may be experiencing an anaphylactic reaction?
  a. The patient's abdomen is rigid to palpation.
  b. The patient's face is swollen and blotchy red.
  c. The patient's blood pressure is 150/84 and rising.
  d. The patient's pupils are unequal and do not react to light.

8. During the physical exam, you find that the patient has a stinger embedded in his neck. The area around the sting is swollen and white surrounded by a red, rashlike appearance. The patient is wearing a bracelet that indicates he is allergic to bee stings. While the police are attempting to gather information about the patient, they find several epinephrine autoinjectors in the vehicle's glove compartment. Use of an epinephrine autoinjector

  a. is contraindicated because the patient is unconscious.
  b. is contraindicated because the patient has suffered trauma.
  c. is appropriate if authorization is given by medical direction.
  d. is appropriate regardless of authorization from medical direction because this patient is near death.

9. If the patient's breathing is adequate, which of the following regarding airway and breathing support for this patient is correct?

  a. The patient's airway should be maintained with an oral airway, and oxygen should be given by nonrebreather mask at 10 to 15 L/min.
  b. The patient's airway should be maintained with the head tilt–chin lift maneuver. Oxygen therapy should be delivered by nonrebreather mask at 10 to 15 L/min.
  c. The patient's airway should be maintained with the headtilt–chin lift maneuver and a nasal airway. Oxygen should be delivered by nasal cannula at 4 to 6 L/min.
  d. The patient's airway should be maintained with a jaw-thrust maneuver and a nasal airway. Oxygen should be administered by nonrebreather mask at 10 to 15 L/min.

Matching

Match the key terms in the right column with the definitions in the left column by placing the letter of each correct answer in the space provided.

_____ **10.** Hives

_____ **11.** Any substance that is foreign to an individual and causes antibody production

_____ **12.** An exaggerated response by the body's immune system to a substance

_____ **13.** An antigen that causes signs and symptoms of an allergic reaction

_____ **14.** A severe allergic reaction; a life-threatening emergency

_____ **15.** A substance produced by white blood cells to defend the body against bacteria, viruses, or other antigens

_____ **16.** Itching

_____ **17.** The production of antibodies in response to the body's first exposure to an antigen

A. Pruritus

B. Anaphylaxis

C. Sensitization

D. Allergen

E. Antibody

F. Urticaria

G. Allergic reaction

H. Antigen

Short Answer

Answer each question in the space provided.

18. List the four routes by which a substance that causes an allergic reaction can enter the body.

  1.
  2.
  3.
  4.

19. List three cardiac-related signs or symptoms of an allergic reaction.

1.

2.

3.

20. List five respiratory-related signs or symptoms of an allergic reaction.

1.

2.

3.

4.

5.

21. Differentiate between patients having an allergic reaction and patients having an allergic reaction who require immediate medical care, including immediate use of an epinephrine autoinjector.

22. List four skin-related signs or symptoms of an allergic reaction.

1.

2.

3.

4.

23. Describe the difference in dosages of an epinephrine autoinjector for an adult and one for a child.

24. List three gastrointestinal system–related signs or symptoms of an allergic reaction.

1.

2.

3.

25. List three signs or symptoms in a patient experiencing an allergic reaction that suggest an impending airway obstruction.

1.

2.

3.

Answer Section

Multiple Choice

1. a

An antigen is any substance that is foreign to an individual and causes antibody production. When the body's immune system detects an antigen, white blood cells respond by producing antibodies specific to that antigen. An antibody is a substance produced by white blood cells to defend the body against bacteria, viruses, or other antigens. When an antigen causes signs and symptoms of an allergic reaction, the antigen is called an *allergen*. An antihistamine is a substance (such as Benadryl) that is used to counteract the effects of histamine in the body and treat allergic reactions.

Objective: Define antigen, antibody, sensitization, and allergen.

2. b

Hoarseness, difficulty swallowing or talking, stridor, difficulty breathing, coughing, and wheezing are all examples of moderate or severe allergic reaction signs and symptoms.

Objective: Differentiate signs and symptoms of a mild allergic reaction from those of a moderate or severe allergic reaction.

3. d

Association with Latex Allergy	Food
High	Banana, avocado, chestnut
Moderate	Apple, celery, kiwi, papaya, potato, tomato
Low or uncertain	Cherry, fig, hazelnut, mango, nectarine, peach, peanut, pear, pineapple, walnut

Objective: Discuss latex allergy among patients and healthcare professionals.

4. d

Epinephrine is injected into the large muscle of the thigh. The correct placement of the autoinjector is the lateral (outside) aspect of the thigh, midway between the waist and the knee.

Objective: State the generic and trade names, medication form, dose, administration, action, indications, contraindications, and adverse effects of the epinephrine autoinjector.

5. b

When the autoinjector is pressed flush against the skin, the spring-loaded needle is released to pierce the skin. The medication is then injected. You must keep the device flush with the skin until all the medication is delivered. If the needle is not flush (at a 90-degree angle) with the skin, the medication may not be delivered deep enough for proper absorption. Do not release the spring-loaded needle before applying the device to the skin. Autoinjector devices are designed for use by nonmedical personnel and should be complete with instructions. When in doubt, read the instructions and consult medical direction.

Objective: State the generic and trade names, medication form, dose, administration, action, indications, contraindications, and adverse effects of the epinephrine autoinjector.

6. b

The scene size-up indicates the patient is in no danger in his current position; therefore, you should turn your attention to forming a general impression and then performing a primary survey to determine the presence of any life-threatening conditions. Freeing the vehicle from the tree does not appear to be at all necessary and may result only in disturbing the patient's spinal alignment. Any such actions should be carried out only by properly trained personnel when access to the patient is denied due to obstruction. The method of maintaining the patient's airway and delivering oxygen should be decided on after evaluating the mechanism of injury and the patient's presentation, status, and past medical history.

Objective: List and describe the components of patient assessment and the purpose of each component.

7. b

Red, swollen skin with hives suggests an allergic reaction. A rigid abdomen should lead you to suspect that the patient has damaged an abdominal organ and may be bleeding internally. Generally, in anaphylactic reactions, the patient's blood pressure will decrease. An increasing blood pressure in a trauma patient may indicate closed head trauma. Deviation from a normal pupil response may also suggest closed head injury.

Objective: Differentiate signs and symptoms of a mild allergic reaction from those of a moderate or severe allergic reaction.

8. c

Specific criteria must be met before administration of a drug. First, the patient must be showing the signs and symptoms associated with the indication of giving the medication. Second, the patient must have been prescribed the medication. Finally, the EMR must have specific authorization from medical direction to administer the medication (either on-line or off-line medical direction).

Objective: Differentiate signs and symptoms of a mild allergic reaction from those of a moderate or severe allergic reaction.

9. d

You are dealing with a patient with two main problems. First, he has been involved in a vehicle collision, and, second, he is possibly having a severe allergic reaction. Both problems must be addressed. Opening and maintaining the patient's airway must be accomplished with the jaw-thrust maneuver, and the patient's spine must be fully stabilized. If the patient has no gag reflex, either an oral or a nasal airway may be used. However, if the patient is semiresponsive, a nasal airway may be tolerated, whereas an oral airway will not be tolerated. High-flow oxygen should be administered by nonrebreather mask because the patient's breathing is adequate but his condition is unstable.

Objective: State what care should be provided to the adult, child, and infant patient with adequate breathing.

Matching

10.	F	**14.**	B
11.	H	**15.**	E
12.	G	**16.**	A
13.	D	**17.**	C

Short Answer

18. The substance that causes an allergic reaction can enter the body in four ways: ingestion, injection, inhalation, or absorption through the skin or mucous membranes.

    Objective: Discuss the routes by which a substance that causes an allergic reaction can enter the body.

19. Cardiac-related signs or symptoms of an allergic reaction include:

    - Increased heart rate
    - Decreased blood pressure
    - Lightheadedness
      Weakness

    Objective: Differentiate signs and symptoms of a mild allergic reaction from those of a moderate or severe allergic reaction.

20. Respiratory-related signs or symptoms of an allergic reaction include:

    - Tightness in throat or chest
    - Coughing
    - Rapid breathing
    - Labored breathing
    - Noisy breathing
    - Hoarseness (losing the voice)
    - Stridor
    - Wheezing (audible without a stethoscope)
      Difficulty talking

    Objective: Differentiate signs and symptoms of a mild allergic reaction from those of a moderate or severe allergic reaction.

21. Not all patients experiencing an allergic reaction require epinephrine. Epinephrine is administered to patients who have signs and symptoms of a severe allergic reaction, including respiratory distress and/or signs and symptoms of shock.

    Objective: Differentiate signs and symptoms of a mild allergic reaction from those of a moderate or severe allergic reaction.

22. Skin-related signs or symptoms of an allergic reaction include:

- Warm tingling feeling in face, mouth, chest, feet, and hands
- Itching
- Red skin (flushing)
- Swelling of face, neck, hands, feet, and/or tongue
- Hives

Objective: Differentiate signs and symptoms of a mild allergic reaction from those of a moderate or severe allergic reaction.

23. Dosage for an adult is one adult autoinjector (0.3 mg), and dosage for a child is one infant or child autoinjector (0.15 mg).

Objective: State the generic and trade names, medication form, dose, administration, action, indications, contraindications, and adverse effects of the epinephrine autoinjector.

24. Gastrointestinal system–related signs or symptoms of an allergic reaction include:

- Nausea
- Vomiting
- Abdominal cramps
- Diarrhea

Objective: Differentiate signs and symptoms of a mild allergic reaction from those of a moderate or severe allergic reaction.

25. The presence of stridor, hoarseness, difficulty swallowing, or swelling of the tongue suggests an impending airway obstruction. If any of these signs are present, request advanced life support assistance as soon as possible. If ALS personnel are not available, complete your primary survey and then prepare the patient for prompt transport to the closest appropriate facility.

Objective: Differentiate signs and symptoms of a mild allergic reaction from those of a moderate or severe allergic reaction.

CHAPTER

22 Toxicology

READING ASSIGNMENT ▶ Read Chapter 22, pages 406 to 420 in your textbook.

Sum It Up

- A poison is any substance taken into the body that interferes with normal body function. Poisoning is exposure to a substance that is harmful in any dosage. A toxin is a poisonous substance. An antidote is a substance that neutralizes a poison.

- A poison control center (PCC) is a medical facility that provides free telephone advice to the public and medical professionals about exposure to poisonous substances. Medical professionals at a PCC can help determine the toxicity of a substance and give advice about the emergency care the patient should receive.

- A poison may be a solid, liquid, spray, or gas. Toxins enter the body in four ways: ingestion, inhalation, injection, or absorption. Exposure to a toxin may be accidental or intentional.

- Signs and symptoms of a toxic exposure can vary depending on the substance involved; the route of entry; the amount ingested, inhaled, injected, or absorbed; and the length of the exposure.

- Signs, symptoms, and characteristics that often occur together in toxic exposures are called toxidromes. When the cause of a toxic exposure is unknown, knowing the typical signs and symptoms of certain toxic exposures can help you identify the poison and give appropriate care. Toxic exposures that involve more than one substance (such as alcohol and recreational drugs) are often difficult to recognize and treat. In these situations, the patient will most likely not have signs and symptoms specific to only one toxidrome.

- A thorough scene size-up on arrival at the scene of a toxic exposure is essential. Resist the temptation to immediately enter the scene and begin patient care. Without some knowledge of the substance involved, you could place yourself and your crew at an unnecessary risk of exposure. Assess the situation for potential or actual danger. Contact dispatch for additional resources as necessary.

- Finding out as much information as you can about the circumstances surrounding a toxic exposure is important. In cases involving an intentional exposure, keep in mind that the history obtained from the patient may not be reliable. Relay all information you obtained when transferring care to ALS personnel.

- When caring for a patient exposed to a toxin, try to find out (and document) the exact name of the substance. If applicable, send all containers, bottles, labels, and other evidence of poison agents to the receiving facility.

▶ Tracking Your Progress

	Page Reference	Objective Met?
After reading this chapter, can you:		
• Define poison, poisoning, toxin, antidote, and poison control center?	407	☐
• Discuss the role of the poison control center in the United States?	407	☐
• Describe the routes of entry of toxic substances into the body?	408	☐
• Define toxidrome and discuss the assessment findings associated with various toxidromes?	408	☐
• Define substance abuse, substance misuse, tolerance, addiction, withdrawal, and overdose?	408	☐
• Give examples of stimulants and signs and symptoms of stimulant misuse or abuse?	409	☐
• Give examples of depressants and signs and symptoms of depressant misuse or abuse?	410	☐
• Give examples of signs and symptoms of alcohol misuse or abuse?	411	☐
• Define alcohol withdrawal syndrome and delirium tremens?	411	☐
• Give examples of hallucinogens and signs and symptoms of hallucinogen misuse or abuse?	412	☐
• Give examples of designer drugs and signs and symptoms of designer drug misuse or abuse?	412	☐
• Discuss assessment of the patient with a toxicological emergency?	413	☐
• Identify specific details of the medical history that should be obtained in the patient with a toxicological emergency?	414	☐
• Describe the emergency medical care for the patient with a toxicological emergency?	415	☐
• List common poisonings by ingestion and the signs and symptoms related to common poisonings by this route?	415	☐
• Discuss the emergency medical care for poisoning by ingestion?	416	☐
• List common poisonings by inhalation and the signs and symptoms related to common poisonings by this route?	416	☐
• Discuss the emergency medical care for poisoning by inhalation?	417	☐
• List common poisonings by injection and the signs and symptoms related to common poisonings by this route?	418	☐
• Discuss the emergency medical care for poisoning by injection?	418	☐
• List common poisonings by surface absorption and the signs and symptoms related to common poisonings by this route?	418	☐
• Discuss the emergency medical care for poisoning by surface absorption?	419	☐

Chapter Quiz

Multiple Choice

In the space provided, identify the letter of the choice that best completes each statement or answers each question.

_____ 1. Alcohol withdrawal syndrome occurs after a decline in or cessation of alcohol consumption. The signs and symptoms associated with this syndrome include tremors, anxiety, gastrointestinal distress, hallucinations, disorientation, and seizures. These signs and symptoms generally appear within ___ after the last ingestion of alcohol.

    a. 30 to 60 minutes   **c.** 6 to 48 hours
    b. 1 to 2 hours   **d.** 1 to 2 weeks

Questions 2–6 pertain to the following scenario.

Your rescue crew responds for an "unknown" medical problem at a local apartment complex. Your scene size-up reveals a woman found lying in bed. There are pill and alcohol bottles on the nightstand. There do not appear to be any weapons in the immediate area.

_____ 2. Before making contact with this patient, you should

    a. look for a suicide note.
    b. inspect the labels of the pill bottles.
    c. check the fluid level in the alcohol bottles.
    d. ensure that standard precautions have been taken.

_____ 3. Which of the following should be performed first?

    a. SAMPLE history
    b. Primary survey
    c. Baseline vital signs
    d. Head-to-toe physical examination

_____ 4. The patient is conscious and crying. She will not answer any of your questions but appears to be alert. While assessing her airway, you note there are pill fragments in her mouth. You should

    a. instruct the patient to spit out all the fragments.
    b. give the patient a glass of water to rinse the fragments down.
    c. probe the patient's mouth with your finger to get all the fragments.
    d. leave the fragments in place for further examination at the receiving facility.

_____ 5. You are preparing to transport this patient. What should you do with the pill bottles?

    a. Send them in a bag to the hospital for further examination.
    b. Throw them away in an approved biohazard waste container.
    c. Leave them where found for a subsequent police investigation.
    d. Leave them on the nightstand, but write down the names of the medications for further examination at the hospital.

_____ 6. Which of the following is true about the presence of alcohol at this scene?

    a. It is not important since alcohol is a legal substance.
    b. It is important only if the patient is under legal drinking age.
    c. It is important only if the substance is distilled spirits rather than beer or wine.
    d. It is important because alcohol may enhance, hasten, or otherwise change the nature of the drug overdose.

Questions 7–9 pertain to the following scenario.

Your ambulance is called to a local park for a 24-year-old man with an altered mental status. You arrive to find your patient standing on a park bench yelling gibberish and laughing hysterically. His face is flushed and red. As you approach, he begins crying uncontrollably. He attempts to get away from you by digging a hole in the cement.

_____ 7. Which of the following substances would most commonly be associated with this reaction?

    a. Alcohol   **c.** Hallucinogens
    b. Barbiturates   **d.** Benzodiazepines

_____ 8. When treating this patient, you should anticipate what type of behavior?

    a. Joyful and funny

    b. Slow to respond and sleepy

    c. Calm and thoughtful

    d. Disruptive, possibly violent, and dangerous

_____ 9. Your physical examination of this patient fails to reveal any findings other than his altered mental status. If physically possible, this patient should be transported in what position?

    a. Fully immobilized and restrained if appropriate (according to local protocol and patient's signs and symptoms)

    b. Recovery position (lateral recumbent) and restrained if appropriate (according to local protocol and patient's signs and symptoms)

    c. Prone with a backboard secured over the patient to prevent any patient movement

    d. Supine between two secured backboards (one on top and one on the bottom) to prevent any patient movement

Sentence Completion

In the blanks provided, write the words that best complete each sentence.

10. A(n) _____ is a substance that neutralizes a poison.

11. A(n) _____ is a poisonous substance.

12. A(n) _____ is any substance taken into the body that interferes with normal body function.

13. Signs, symptoms, and characteristics that often occur together in toxic exposures are called _____.

Matching

Match the key terms in the right column with the definitions in the left column by placing the letter of each correct answer in the space provided.

_____ 14. Any substance taken into the body that interferes with normal body function

_____ 15. An intentional or unintentional overmedication or ingestion of a toxic substance

_____ 16. Signs, symptoms, and characteristics that often occur together in toxic exposures

_____ 17. The self-administration of a substance for unintended purposes, or for appropriate purposes but in improper amounts or doses, or without a prescription for the person receiving the medication

_____ 18. Exposure to a substance that is harmful in any dosage

_____ 19. A series of signs and symptoms that occur 6 to 48 hours after a chronic alcoholic reduces his or her intake or stops consuming alcohol

_____ 20. Requiring progressively larger doses of a drug to achieve the desired effect

A. Toxin

B. Poisoning

C. Substance abuse

D. Poison control center

E. Withdrawal

F. Sudden sniffing death syndrome

G. Antidote

H. Addiction

I. Overdose

J. Toxidrome

K. Substance misuse

L. Poison

M. Delirium tremens

N. Tolerance

O. Alcohol withdrawal syndrome

P. Inhalants

Continued

_____ **21.** A psychological and physical dependence on a substance that has gone beyond voluntary control

_____ **22.** Household and commercial products that can be abused by intentionally breathing the product's gas or vapors for its mind-altering effects

_____ **23.** A poisonous substance

_____ **24.** The deliberate, persistent, and excessive self-administration of a substance in a way that is not medically or socially approved

_____ **25.** A substance that neutralizes a poison

_____ **26.** Signs and symptoms associated with alcohol withdrawal that have progressed beyond the usual symptoms of withdrawal and are potentially fatal

_____ **27.** A medical facility that provides free telephone advice to the public and medical professionals about exposure to poisonous substances

_____ **28.** A condition that can occur when a person sniffs highly concentrated amounts of the chemicals in solvents or aerosol sprays

_____ **29.** The condition produced when an individual stops using or abusing a drug to which he or she is physically or psychologically addicted

Short Answer

Answer each question in the space provided.

30. List three examples of medical conditions that signs and symptoms of alcohol misuse or abuse can mimic.

1.

2.

3.

31. List five common signs or symptoms of poisoning.

1.

2.

3.

4.

5.

32. Give five examples of signs or symptoms that you should anticipate in a patient experiencing an opioid (narcotic) exposure.

1.

2.

3.

4.

5.

Answer Section

Multiple Choice

1. c

Typically, the signs and symptoms associated with alcohol withdrawal syndrome will occur within 6 to 48 hours after the last ingestion of alcohol. The onset of these symptoms does not necessarily mean that all the alcohol has left the patient's body. Rather, it means that the blood alcohol level has fallen below the patient's physical dependency level. In other words, a patient may begin to exhibit the signs and symptoms of withdrawal while still legally intoxicated. Such patients should be considered unstable, and advanced life support care should be requested immediately.

Objective: Define alcohol withdrawal syndrome and delirium tremens.

2. d

After a rapid scene size-up, you need to turn your attention to assessing the patient. There will be adequate time later to gather specific information about the medications and the alcohol; they are potentially important "pieces of the puzzle." The most important piece is your patient's condition. You cannot (should not) address the patient's condition before taking proper standard precautions.

Objective: List and describe the components of patient assessment and the purpose of each component.

3. b

Performing a primary survey to assess the patient's mental status, airway, breathing, circulation status, and potentially life-threatening conditions must take precedence over any other activity. If the patient is conscious, a focused history and physical exam should follow the primary survey. If unconscious, a rapid head-to-toe physical examination should follow.

Objective: List and describe the components of patient assessment and the purpose of each component.

4. a

Do not stick your fingers in the mouth of a conscious patient with a possible altered mental status. The patient may follow your instructions and spit the pill fragments out. If not, you may attempt to remove the fragments with a suction catheter or other appropriate device. Do not have the patient wash the fragments down or leave the fragments in the patient's mouth. Swallowing the fragments may further complicate the incident and the patient's outcome. If the fragments are left in the patient's mouth, they will dissolve in the mouth and be ingested.

Objective: Discuss the emergency medical care for poisoning by ingestion.

5. a

Whenever possible, send the medication bottles to the hospital. The name of the medication is important but is only one part of the total picture. Sending the bottles enables the hospital to compare the date of purchase of the medication to the daily dose prescribed and the amount of medications in the bottle. This comparison allows the facility to better appreciate the total ingestion dose. The pill bottle labels may also contain other information valuable to the receiving facility staff.

Objective: Discuss the emergency medical care for poisoning by ingestion.

6. d

Alcohol is a drug and a toxin (a poisonous substance). Alcohol may affect the reaction to the pill overdose. This information is important and should be passed on to the receiving facility.

Objective: Discuss the emergency medical care for poisoning by ingestion.

7. c

While alcohol can cause erratic behavior, the presence of the irrational behavior and quick mood swings are suggestive of hallucinogens. The other choices (alcohol, barbiturates, and benzodiazepines) are depressants and are not typically associated with the behavior described in this scenario.

Objective: Give examples of hallucinogens and assessment findings and symptoms of hallucinogen misuse or abuse.

8. d

Use extreme caution when handling this patient. He may go from being calm to being violent very quickly. Make sure that local law enforcement personnel are available to help you control this patient.

Objective: Give examples of hallucinogens and assessment findings and symptoms of hallucinogen misuse or abuse.

9. b

The ideal position would be the recovery position, since no factors are present that indicate the need for spinal immobilization. Do *not* "sandwich" the patient between backboards or between a backboard and the stretcher. Continuous assessments and treatment are hampered by this unnecessary and unprofessional technique of controlling the patient. Patients placed in these positions have died from unwitnessed aspiration of vomitus. Contact medical direction and follow local protocol if restraints are necessary to protect you and the patient from harm.

Objective: Describe how to restrain a patient safely.

Sentence Completion

10. An **antidote** is a substance that neutralizes a poison.

    Objective: Define poison, poisoning, toxin, antidote, and poison control center.

11. A **toxin** is a poisonous substance.

    Objective: Define poison, poisoning, toxin, antidote, and poison control center.

12. A **poison** is any substance taken into the body that interferes with normal body function.

    Objective: Define poison, poisoning, toxin, antidote, and poison control center.

13. Signs, symptoms, and characteristics that often occur together in toxic exposures are called **toxidromes**.

Objective: Define toxidrome, and discuss the assessment findings associated with various toxidromes.

Matching

14.	L	22.	P
15.	I	23.	A
16.	J	24.	C
17.	K	25.	G
18.	B	26.	M
19.	O	27.	D
20.	N	28.	F
21.	H	29.	E

Short Answer

30. Signs and symptoms of alcohol misuse or abuse can mimic those of other medical conditions (such as a diabetic emergency, head injury, epilepsy, drug reaction, or CNS infection).

    Objective: Give examples of signs and symptoms of alcohol misuse or abuse.

31. Common signs and symptoms of poisoning include:

    - Altered mental status
    - Difficulty breathing
    - Headache
    - Nausea
    - Vomiting
    - Diarrhea
    - Chest or abdominal pain
    - Sweating
    - Seizures
    - Burns around the mouth
    - Burns on the skin

    Objective: Discuss assessment of the patient with a toxicological emergency.

32. Signs or symptoms that you should anticipate in a patient experiencing an exposure to opioids (narcotics) include altered mental status, coma, slow or absent breathing, slow heart rate, low blood pressure, and constricted pupils. *Note:* Meperidine, propoxyphene, and diphenoxylate may cause *dilated* pupils.

    Objective: Define toxidrome, and discuss the assessment findings associated with various toxidromes.

READING ASSIGNMENT ▶ Read Chapter 23, pages 421 to 430 in your textbook.

Sum It Up

- Behavior is the way in which a person acts or performs. It includes any or all of a person's activities, including physical and mental activity. Abnormal behavior is an individual's way of acting or conducting himself that is not consistent with society's norms and expectations, interferes with the individual's well-being and ability to function, or may be harmful to the individual or others. A psychiatric disorder is a disorder of behavior or personality without obvious brain damage.

- As an EMR, you will likely encounter various behavioral emergencies. A behavioral emergency is a situation in which a patient displays abnormal behavior that is unacceptable to the patient, family members, or community. A behavioral emergency can be caused by extremes of emotion or by psychological or physical conditions. A number of factors can result in such emergencies, including mental illness, a lack of oxygen, low blood sugar, alcohol or drugs, situational stressors, medical illnesses, or psychological crises.

- Anxiety is a state of worry and agitation that is usually triggered by a real or imagined situation. An anxiety disorder is more intense than normal anxiety.

- A panic attack is an intense fear that occurs for no apparent reason.

- Obsessive-compulsive disorder (OCD) is a type of anxiety disorder. Obsessions are recurring thoughts, impulses, or images that cause the person anxiety. Compulsions are recurring behaviors or rituals that are performed with the hope of preventing obsessive thoughts or making them go away.

- A phobia is an irrational and constant fear of a specific activity, object, or situation (other than a social situation). A social phobia is an extreme anxiety response in situations in which the individual may be seen by others. A phobic reaction resembles a panic attack.

- Depression is a state of mind characterized by feelings of sadness, worthlessness, and discouragement. It often occurs in response to a loss, such as the loss of a job, the death of a loved one, or the end of a relationship.

- Bipolar disorder is a brain disorder that causes unusual shifts in a person's mood, energy, and ability to function. A person with bipolar disorder has alternating episodes of mood elevation (mania) and depression. The person's mood is often normal between the periods of mania and depression.

- Paranoia is a mental disorder characterized by excessive suspiciousness or delusions. Paranoid patients are suspicious, distrustful, and prone to argument. They are excitable and unpredictable, with outbursts of bizarre or aggressive behavior.
  - Delusions are false beliefs that the patient believes are true, despite facts to the contrary.
  - Hallucinations are false sensory perceptions. The patient sees, hears, or feels things that others cannot.
- Schizophrenia is a group of mental disorders. Symptoms include hallucinations, delusions, disordered thinking, rambling speech, and bizarre or disorganized behavior. Schizophrenic patients can become combative and are at high risk for suicidal and homicidal behavior.
- A suicide gesture is self-destructive behavior that is unlikely to have any possibility of being fatal. A suicide attempt is self-destructive behavior for the purpose of ending one's life that, for unanticipated reasons, fails. A completed suicide is death by a self-inflicted, consciously intended action.
- Most people who commit suicide express their intentions beforehand. You should take every expression of suicide seriously and arrange for patient transport for evaluation.
- Excited delirium, also called agitated delirium, is abnormal behavior characterized by elevated temperature, agitation, aggression, and "superhuman" strength, especially during attempts to restrain the patient. Possible underlying causes include manic-depressive psychosis, schizophrenia, stimulant abuse, cocaine intoxication, alcohol withdrawal, and head trauma.
- When called to a scene that involves a behavioral emergency, remember that the scene may be unpredictable. Take steps to ensure your safety and that of other healthcare professionals responding to the scene. Complete a scene size-up before beginning emergency medical care. Carefully assess the scene for possible dangers. Start by visually locating the patient. Visually scan the area for possible weapons. Be prepared to spend time at the scene. Limit the number of people around the patient. Take time to calm the patient.
- Avoid restraining a patient unless the patient is a danger to you, herself, or others. When using restraints, have police present, if possible, and get approval from medical direction. If you must use restraints, apply them with the help of law enforcement and other EMS personnel.

▶ Tracking Your Progress

After reading this chapter, can you:	Page Reference	Objective Met?
- Define behavior, abnormal behavior, psychiatric disorder, behavioral emergencies, delusions, and hallucinations?	422	☐
- Discuss the general factors that may cause an alteration in a patient's behavior?	422	☐
- Give examples of psychological crises?	423	☐
- Briefly discuss anxiety disorders, panic attacks, obsessive-compulsive disorder, phobias, depression, bipolar disorder, paranoia, and schizophrenia.	423	☐

After reading this chapter, can you:

After reading this chapter, can you:	Page Reference	Objective Met?
• Define suicide gesture, suicide attempt, and completed suicide and discuss the characteristics of an individual's behavior that suggest that the patient is at risk for suicide?	426	☐
• Discuss the special considerations for assessing a patient with a psychiatric disorder?	427	☐
• Discuss the general principles of an individual's behavior that suggest that the person is at risk for violence?	428	☐
• Discuss methods of calming a patient who has a psychiatric disorder?	428	☐
• Discuss special medical and legal considerations for managing behavioral emergencies?	429	☐

Chapter Quiz

Matching

Match the key terms in the right column with the definitions in the left column by placing the letter of each correct answer in the space provided.

_____ 1. The amount of force necessary to keep a patient from injuring you, himself, or others

_____ 2. A situation in which a patient displays abnormal behavior that is unacceptable to the patient, family members, or community

_____ 3. False sensory perceptions seen, heard, or felt by a person that others cannot

_____ 4. A state of worry and agitation that is usually triggered by a real or imagined situation

_____ 5. Recurring thoughts, impulses, or images that cause the person anxiety

_____ 6. A state of mind characterized by feelings of sadness, worthlessness, and discouragement

_____ 7. Self-destructive behavior that is unlikely to have any possibility of being fatal

_____ 8. Conditions that involve excessive anxiety ranging from uneasiness to terror

_____ 9. A type of anxiety disorder in which the individual performs recurring behaviors or rituals with the hope of preventing obsessive thoughts or making them go away

_____ 10. Recurring behaviors or rituals performed with the hope of preventing obsessive thoughts or making them go away

_____ 11. An extreme anxiety response in situations in which the individual may be seen by others and fears that she will act in an embarrassing or shameful manner

A. Obsessions

B. Completed suicide

C. Abnormal behavior

D. Hallucinations

E. Bipolar disorder

F. Compulsions

G. Panic attack

H. Phobia

I. Suicide attempt

J. Anxiety disorder

K. Suicide gesture

L. Delusions

M. Behavior

N. Obsessive-compulsive disorder

O. Reasonable force

P. Anxiety

Q. Depression

R. Schizophrenia

S. Behavioral emergency

T. Social phobia

U. Paranoia

Continued

_____ 12. A group of mental disorders characterized by hallucinations, delusions, disordered thinking, and bizarre or disorganized behavior

_____ 13. A brain disorder that causes alternating episodes of mood elevation (mania) and depression

_____ 14. False beliefs that the patient believes are true, despite facts to the contrary

_____ 15. Death by a self-inflicted, consciously intended action

_____ 16. A mental disorder characterized by excessive suspiciousness or delusions

_____ 17. Self-destructive behavior for the purpose of ending one's life but, for unanticipated reasons, failing

_____ 18. A way of acting or conducting oneself that is not consistent with society's norms and expectations

_____ 19. An irrational and constant fear of a specific activity, object, or situation (other than a social situation)

_____ 20. The way in which a person acts or performs

_____ 21. An intense fear that occurs for no apparent reason

Short Answer

Answer each question in the space provided.

22. List five examples of medical conditions that may cause changes in behavior.

    1.

    2.

    3.

    4.

    5.

23. Explain the difference(s) between a suicide gesture, suicide attempt, and completed suicide.

24. List six situational stressors that may cause changes in behavior.

    1.

    2.

    3.

    4.

    5.

    6.

25. Discuss methods you should use to calm a patient who has a psychiatric disorder.

Answer Section

Matching

1. O
2. S
3. D
4. P
5. A
6. Q
7. K
8. J
9. N
10. F
11. T
12. R
13. E
14. L
15. B
16. U
17. I
18. C
19. H
20. M
21. G

Short Answer

22. Medical conditions that may cause changes in behavior include:

    - Poisoning
    - Central nervous system infection
    - Head trauma
    - Seizure disorder
    - Lack of oxygen (hypoxia)
    - Low blood sugar
    - Inadequate blood flow to the brain Extremes of temperature (excessive cold or heat)

    Objective: Discuss the general factors that may cause an alteration in a patient's behavior.

23. A suicide gesture is self-destructive behavior that is unlikely to have any possibility of being fatal. For instance, threatening to kill oneself and then taking 10 aspirin tablets. A suicide gesture is a conscious or subconscious attempt to get attention, rather than end life. A suicide attempt is self-destructive behavior for the purpose of ending one's life but, for unanticipated reasons, the attempt fails. For instance, an individual may take a sufficient number of aspirin tablets to cause death but be found by a family member before death occurs. A completed suicide is death by a self-inflicted, consciously intended action.

    Objective: Define suicide gesture, suicide attempt, and completed suicide, and discuss the characteristics of an individual's behavior that suggest that the patient is at risk for suicide.

24. Examples of situational stressors that may cause changes in behavior include:

    - Rape
    - Loss of a job
    - Career change
    - Death of a loved one
    - Marital stress or divorce
    - Physical or psychological abuse
    - Natural disasters (tornado, flood, earthquake, hurricane)
    - Human-made disasters (war, explosion)

    Objective: Discuss the general factors that may cause an alteration in a patient's behavior.

25. Methods of calming a patient who has a psychiatric disorder include:

    - Approach the patient slowly and purposefully—do not make any quick movements.
    - Maintain good eye contact.
    - Be calm, direct, courteous, and respectful.
    - Allow the patient to tell his story without being judgmental.
    - Provide honest reassurance.
    - Have a definite plan of action.
    - Do not threaten, challenge, or argue with the patient.
    - Involve trusted family members or friends.
    - Avoid unnecessary physical contact.

    Do not assume that you cannot talk with the patient; try talking with him.

    Objective: Discuss methods of calming a patient who has a psychiatric disorder.

24 Diseases of the Nose

Sum It Up

- The nasal mucosa is supplied with many blood vessels that lie close to the surface where they can be injured and bleed. A nosebleed, also called epistaxis, can be caused by trauma or medical conditions.
- Typical assessment findings and symptoms associated with epistaxis include bleeding from the nose, which can range from a trickle to a strong flow of blood.
- An anterior nosebleed is usually easy to control. If there is no risk of spinal injury, have the patient lean his head forward. Tell the patient to breathe through his mouth. Pinch the fleshy part of the patient's nostrils together with your thumb and two fingers for 15 minutes.
- A posterior nosebleed is difficult to control, and the patient can develop shock. A patient with a posterior nosebleed needs rapid transport to the hospital. Treat for shock if present.

▶ Tracking Your Progress

After reading this chapter, can you:	Page Reference	Objective Met?
• Define epistaxis and describe common causes of this condition?	432	☐
• Identify common assessment findings and symptoms associated with epistaxis?	432	☐
• Discuss the emergency care for epistaxis?	433	☐

Chapter Quiz

True/False

Decide whether each statement is true or false. In the space provided, write T for true or F for false.

_____ 1. Hypertension is the most common cause of epistaxis.

_____ 2. Blood that is swallowed often makes a person feel nauseous, increasing the chance of vomiting.

Short Answer

Answer each question in the space provided.

3. You are called to the local courthouse for "a woman bleeding." You find the patient in the women's restroom. On entry into the restroom, you see a significant amount of blood in the sink and on the wall behind the sink and many large drops of blood on the floor. The patient, a 35-year-old woman, is crying and appears anxious. She says that her nosebleed started about 20 minutes ago and she can't get it to stop. Describe your management of this patient.

4. Why is it important to instruct the patient with epistaxis not to blow her nose or sniffle?

Answer Section

True/False

1. F

   The most common cause of epistaxis is nose picking.

   Objective: Define epistaxis and describe common causes of this condition.

2. T

   Blood that is swallowed often makes a person feel nauseous, increasing the chance of vomiting. Thus, if possible, a patient with a nosebleed should sit up and lean her head forward, as opposed to leaning it back (a common misconception).

   Objective: Discuss the emergency care for epistaxis.

Short Answer

3. Take standard precautions, and instruct the patient not to blow her nose or sniffle. Have her lean her head forward to keep blood from draining into the back of her throat. Tell the patient to breathe through her mouth. Pinch the fleshy part of the patient's nostrils together with your thumb and two fingers for 15 minutes. On the basis of the description of the amount of blood lost, transport for physician evaluation is recommended.

   Objective: Discuss the emergency care for epistaxis.

4. Telling the patient with a nosebleed not to blow her nose or sniffle can prevent clots from forming or can break clots that have already developed.

   Objective: Discuss the emergency care for epistaxis.

Module 7

Shock

► CHAPTER **25**

Shock   180

CHAPTER
25 Shock

READING ASSIGNMENT Read Chapter 25, pages 434 to 440 in your textbook.

Sum It Up

- Perfusion is the circulation of blood through an organ or a part of the body. Shock is the inadequate flow of blood through an organ or a part of the body.
- Cardiogenic shock can result if the heart beats too quickly or too slowly or if the heart muscle does not have enough force to pump blood effectively to all parts of the body.
- Shock caused by severe bleeding is called hemorrhagic shock. The bleeding may be internal, external, or both. Shock caused by a loss of blood, plasma, or other body fluid is called hypovolemic shock.
- Obstructive shock occurs when blood flow is slowed or stopped by a mechanical or physical obstruction. This type of shock may occur when blood collects in the sac surrounding the heart, preventing efficient cardiac contraction, or when air is present in the chest due to a lung injury, putting pressure on the great vessels in the chest and limiting blood flow.
- When shock caused by container failure occurs (distributive shock), the blood vessels lose their ability to adjust the flow of blood. Instead of expanding and constricting as needed, the blood vessels remain enlarged. The amount of fluid in the body remains constant (there is no actual loss of fluid), but blood pools in the outer areas of the body. As a result, there is an inadequate amount of blood to fill the enlarged vessels, and the vital organs are not perfused. The four major causes of this type of shock are injury to the spinal cord (neurogenic shock), severe infection (septic shock), severe allergic reaction (anaphylactic shock), and psychological causes (psychogenic shock).
- Early (compensated) shock is often difficult to recognize. Remember to look for it and to consider the patient's mechanism of injury or the nature of the illness when assessing your patient. Early shock is usually reversible if it is recognized and the patient receives emergency care to correct the cause of the shock.
- Late (decompensated) shock results when the patient's systolic blood pressure drops to less than 90 mm Hg. In this phase of shock, the body's defense mechanisms lose their ability to make up for the lack of oxygenated blood. The signs of late shock are more obvious than those of early shock, but late shock is more difficult to treat.

- Irreversible shock is also called terminal shock. You will feel an irregular pulse as the patient's heart becomes irritable and begins to beat irregularly. Permanent damage occurs to the vital organs because the cells and organs have been without oxygenated blood for too long. Eventually, the heart stops, breathing stops, and death results.

▶ Tracking Your Progress

After reading this chapter, can you:	Page Reference	Objective Met?
• Describe possible causes of cardiogenic shock?	436	☐
• Differentiate between hemorrhagic shock and hypovolemic shock and describe possible causes of each?	436	☐
• Describe possible causes of obstructive shock?	436	☐
• Describe possible causes of distributive shock?	436	☐
• Discuss the stages of shock?	437	☐
• Describe common assessment findings and symptoms of shock?	438	☐
• Describe the emergency medical care of the patient with signs and symptoms of shock?	439	☐

Chapter Quiz

Multiple Choice

In the space provided, identify the letter of the choice that best completes each statement or answers each question.

_____ 1. Pump failure is one possible cause of shock. Another name for failure of the pump is
   a. neurogenic shock.
   b. cardiogenic shock.
   c. hypovolemic shock.
   d. hemorrhagic shock.

_____ 2. Which of the following regarding the response to shock in children and infants is correct?
   a. Children and infants will compensate much longer than adults.
   b. Children and infants will show the signs of shock much earlier than adults.
   c. Children and infants will show the signs of shock at the same rate as adults.
   d. Children and infants have healthy hearts and blood vessels and never go into shock.

_____ 3. Shock is a condition that develops as a response to injury or insult. Which of the following organs will suffer damage earliest as a result of shock?
   a. The skin
   b. The brain
   c. The kidneys and liver
   d. The large muscles of the arms and legs

_____ **4.** You and your partner have been called to the home of an 8-month-old female patient. Her mother informs you that the child has had diarrhea for the last 3 days and has refused her bottle for the last 36 hours. The child is pale with a capillary refill time of 3 to 4 seconds. This child is most likely

    a. not in shock.

    b. in shock due to fluid loss.

    c. in shock due to pump failure.

    d. in shock due to container failure.

_____ **5.** Which of the following is considered a late sign of shock?

    a. Altered mental status

    b. Rapid, shallow breathing

    c. Dropping blood pressure

    d. Persistent rapid, weak pulse

Sentence Completion

In the blanks provided, write the words that best complete each sentence.

    6. _____ shock is the most common type of shock.

    7. _____ shock occurs because of a massive infection.

Short Answer

Answer each question in the space provided.

    8. List the three stages of shock.

      1.

      2.

      3.

    9. List four major causes of distributive shock.

      1.

      2.

      3.

      4.

    10. List four signs or symptoms of early shock.

      1.

      2.

      3.

      4.

Answer Section

Multiple Choice

1. b

   Cardiogenic shock is shock brought on by the inability of the heart (the pump) to keep up with the body's demand. Neurogenic shock is "container failure" shock, which occurs when the impulse from the brain to the arteries is cut off (such as when the spinal cord is damaged). In the absence of a nervous impulse, the vessels of the body relax and dilate. When the vessels are fully dilated, the average body can hold approximately five times its normal volume of blood. Hypovolemic shock occurs from a loss of fluid, either blood or plasma. Hemorrhagic shock occurs from the loss of blood.

   Objective: Describe possible causes of cardiogenic shock.

2. a

   Typically, children and infants have a more efficient compensatory mechanism than adults. Children can compensate for massive blood loss, for example, much longer than an adult can. In a previously healthy adult, a sudden episode of blood loss will usually not produce vital-sign changes until the patient has lost 15% to 30% of his blood volume. Then the blood pressure will begin to creep down. Children may not show hemodynamic (blood pressure) compromise until 25% of the total blood volume is lost. By the time a child begins to show the more measurable signs of shock, the child may be very deep into the progression of shock. Do not let a good blood pressure and healthy appearance fool you into undertreating a child.

   Objective: Describe common assessment findings and symptoms of shock.

3. b

   The brain, the heart, and the lungs are among the organs most sensitive to oxygen deprivation. Within 4 to 6 minutes, these organs will begin to suffer as a result of hypoperfusion. Because the brain is so sensitive to oxygen deprivation, one of the first signs of shock is an altered mental status (anxiety, restlessness, confusion). The skin and muscles will suffer damage after about 4 to 8 hours, and the kidneys and liver will suffer damage after about 45 to 90 minutes.

   Objective: Describe common assessment findings and symptoms of shock.

4. b

   A patient does not have to bleed to be in shock from fluid loss. The body may also become depleted of fluid by excessive sweating, urinating, vomiting, or diarrhea or as a result of a burn injury.

   Objective: Describe common assessment findings and symptoms of shock.

5. c

   Decreasing blood pressure values are a late sign of shock. Altered mental status (anxiety, dizziness, restlessness) is an early sign, since the brain is one of the first organs to be affected by hypoperfusion. Shallow, rapid breathing and a rapid, weak pulse are also early signs as compared to a drop in blood pressure.

   Objective: Describe common assessment findings and symptoms of shock.

Sentence Completion

6. **Hypovolemic** shock is the most common type of shock.

   Objective: Differentiate between hemorrhagic shock and hypovolemic shock, and describe possible causes of each.

7. **Septic** shock occurs because of a massive infection.

   Objective: Describe possible causes of distributive shock.

Short Answer

8. Shock occurs in three stages: early (compensated), late (decompensated), and irreversible (terminal).

Objective: Discuss the stages of shock.

9. The four major causes of distributive shock are:

1. Injury to the spinal cord (neurogenic shock)
2. Severe infection (septic shock)
3. Severe allergic reaction (anaphylactic shock)
4. Psychological causes (psychogenic shock)

Objective: Describe possible causes of distributive shock.

10. Signs or symptoms of early shock include:

- Anxiety, restlessness
- Thirst
- Nausea and vomiting
- Increased respiratory rate
- Slight increase in heart rate
- Pale, cool, moist skin
- Delayed capillary refill in an infant or young child
- Blood pressure in normal range

Objective: Discuss the stages of shock.

Module 8

Trauma

▶ CHAPTER **26**

Trauma Overview 187

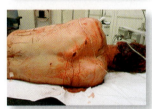

▶ CHAPTER **27**

Bleeding and Soft Tissue Trauma 193

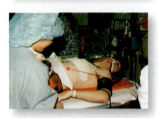

▶ CHAPTER **28**

Chest Trauma 204

▶ CHAPTER **29**

Abdominal and Genitourinary Trauma 209

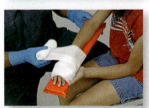

▶ CHAPTER **30**

Trauma to Muscles and Bones 214

▶ CHAPTER **31**

Head, Face, Neck, and Spine Trauma 222

▶ CHAPTER **32**

Special Considerations in Trauma 229

▶ CHAPTER **33**

Environmental Emergencies 237

▶ CHAPTER **34**

Multisystem Trauma 243

26 Trauma Overview

READING ASSIGNMENT ▶ Read Chapter 26, pages 441 to 448 in your textbook.

Sum It Up

- At a scene that involves trauma, perform a scene size-up and primary survey and then reconsider the mechanism of injury. Mechanism of injury (MOI) is the way in which an injury occurs, as well as the forces involved in producing the injury. By evaluating the MOI, you can often predict the types of injuries the patient is most likely to experience.

- If the MOI is significant, time is of the essence. If a patient has experienced a significant MOI, follow the primary survey with a rapid trauma assessment. Begin the rapid trauma assessment by reassessing the patient's mental status and then checking the patient's head. Then examine the neck, chest, abdomen, pelvis, lower extremities, upper extremities, and back. Compare one side of the body to the other. For example, if an injury involves one side of the body, use the uninjured side as the normal finding for comparison.

- If a trauma patient has no significant MOI, perform a focused physical examination. The focused physical exam concentrates on the specific injury site (and related structures) based on what the patient states is wrong and your suspicions based on the MOI and initial assessment findings.

▶ Tracking Your Progress

After reading this chapter, can you:	Page Reference	Objective Met?
• Discuss the reasons for reconsideration of the mechanism of injury?	444	☐
• State the reasons for performing a rapid trauma assessment?	445	☐
• Recite examples of and explain why patients should receive a rapid trauma assessment?	445	☐
• Describe the areas included in the rapid trauma assessment and discuss what should be evaluated?	446	☐
• Discuss the reason for performing a focused history and physical exam?	447	☐

Chapter Quiz

True/False

Decide whether each statement is true or false. In the space provided, write T for true or F for false.

_____ 1. You should perform a rapid trauma assessment if you determine the MOI is not significant.

_____ 2. On the basis of the mechanism of injury, you can often predict the types of injuries the patient is most likely to experience.

Multiple Choice

In the space provided, identify the letter of the choice that best completes each statement or answers each question.

_____ 3. If a life-threatening condition is discovered during the primary survey, you should immediately
   a. treat the condition.
   b. repeat the primary survey.
   c. assess the patient's baseline vital signs.
   d. perform a head-to-toe physical examination.

_____ 4. The rapid trauma assessment
   a. is necessary only for adult patients.
   b. is performed immediately following scene size-up.
   c. involves assessing the body to identify potential injuries.
   d. is performed only if life-threatening injuries are reported.

_____ 5. Your ambulance is called to the home of a 23-year-old woman who has cut her finger on a knife. On your arrival, the patient is up and walking in no apparent distress. She informs you that, while opening a package, she cut her finger. She has a half-inch partial-thickness laceration to her index finger, and bleeding is controlled. Which of the following reflects your *best* course of action in this situation?
   a. You should perform a head-to-toe physical examination.
   b. You should perform a focused physical examination on the area of injury.
   c. You should perform a focused physical examination on the area of injury, obtain baseline vital signs, and obtain a SAMPLE history.
   d. You should perform a head-to-toe physical examination, obtain baseline vital signs, and obtain a SAMPLE history.

Questions 6 to 10 pertain to the following scenario:

Your rescue crew is dispatched to the scene of a motor vehicle collision. You find a 34-year-old man supine on the pavement. Bystanders state that he was struck by a vehicle that has fled the scene. During your primary survey, you identify that the patient is in moderate distress, complaining of right-leg pain. His airway, breathing, and circulatory status seem within acceptable range. He is alert and answers questions appropriately.

_____ 6. For treatment purposes, reevaluating the mechanism of injury may indicate
   a. that there is a need for advanced life support personnel.
   b. that you should take down the names of all witnesses on the scene.
   c. that you should concern yourself with getting a vehicle description from the bystanders.
   d. that you should allow law enforcement personnel to speak with the patient before transporting him to the appropriate receiving facility.

_____ 7. While stabilizing this patient, your crew takes measures to stabilize his spine. Your partner begins manual in-line stabilization of the patient's head and neck. When may your partner release manual stabilization?
   a. After application of the cervical collar
   b. On arrival at the appropriate receiving facility
   c. After the patient is completely immobilized on a long backboard
   d. After you determine that the patient does not have head or neck pain

_____ 8. In this situation, the secondary survey should address

   a. the patient's entire body.
   b. only the patient's right leg.
   c. only the lower half of the body.
   d. only the areas that the patient says are painful.

_____ 9. Which of the following memory aids would assist you in performing a rapid trauma assessment on this patient?

   a. ABC
   b. ALS
   c. DOT
   d. DCAP-BTLS

_____ 10. While assessing the patient's right leg, you find that the thigh is twisted at an unusual angle, suggesting a probable femur injury. This finding

   a. is common and not overly alarming.
   b. does not require any emergency care.
   c. is frequently associated with significant blood loss.
   d. can be corrected in the field without the need for hospital intervention.

Questions 11 and 12 pertain to the following scenario:

Your rescue crew is called to the scene of a "motorcyclist down." On arrival, you find a 32-year-old male patient lying supine (on his back) in the middle of a parking lot. He informs you that his motorcycle slid on a patch of ice while he was turning at approximately 20 miles per hour. He is complaining of head, neck, and left-hip pain.

_____ 11. To facilitate the assessment of his head for the presence of blood, you should

   a. have the patient sit up.
   b. turn the patient's head from side to side to visualize the entire scalp.
   c. palpate the entire skull and periodically check your gloves for blood.
   d. wrap the patient's head with gauze and check for spots of blood leaking through.

_____ 12. How would you address the assessment of this patient's posterior body?

   a. Stand the patient up before taking full spinal precautions.
   b. An assessment cannot be accomplished due to the patient's position.
   c. Logroll the patient while manually maintaining in-line spinal stabilization.
   d. Apply a long backboard to the patient, and then roll the patient into the prone position on a second backboard and remove the first backboard to expose his back

Short Answer

Answer each question in the space provided.

13. A 40-year-old woman is complaining of abdominal pain after a motorcycle crash. Describe how you will examine this patient's abdomen.

14. List six factors to consider in a motor vehicle crash.

1.

2.

3.

4.

5.

6.

15. List five findings that you should look for when assessing the abdomen of a trauma patient.

1.

2.

3.

4.

5.

Answer Section

True/False

1. False

    If you determine the MOI is not significant, perform a primary survey and then begin the secondary survey with an assessment of the injured body part. This is called a focused physical exam. Examine other areas of the body as needed.

    Objective: Discuss the reason for performing a focused history and physical exam.

2. True

    By evaluating the mechanism of injury, you can often predict the types of injuries the patient is most likely to experience.

    Objective: Discuss the reasons for reconsideration of the mechanism of injury.

Multiple Choice

3. a

    The purpose of the primary survey is to identify life-threatening problems, begin treatment, and initiate rapid transport for critical patients. If a life-threatening condition is found, begin immediate emergency care and transportation. Some patients will be so seriously ill or injured that you may never fully address a head-to-toe physical examination, and obtaining a medical history or complete set of baseline vital signs may not be possible until the patient can be stabilized (or more resources become available).

    Objective: List and describe the components of patient assessment and the purpose of each component.

4. c

    A rapid trauma assessment should be conducted on all patients who have a significant mechanism of injury, regardless of whether the injuries appear initially to be life-threatening. The assessment should be performed on children and infants as well as adults. It is performed after the initial assessment (not immediately following the scene size-up).

    Objective: State the reasons for performing a rapid trauma assessment.

5. c

    Since no significant mechanism of injury exists, this patient should receive an appropriate focused history and physical examination that includes a full assessment of the injury site, baseline vital signs, and a SAMPLE history.

    Objective: Discuss the reason for performing a focused history and physical exam.

6. a

    A vehicle-pedestrian collision is a significant mechanism of injury. While legal ramifications certainly surround this collision, your attention should be on providing the appropriate level of stabilization for the patient. Given the mechanism of injury, advanced life support personnel should be called to the scene.

    Objective: Discuss the reasons for reconsideration of the mechanism of injury.

7. c

    Not until the patient is completely immobilized can you release manual stabilization regardless of the patient's denial of head or neck pain. The mechanism of injury suggests that this patient may have spinal compromise, regardless of current physical status. The cervical collar by itself does not provide sufficient support to maintain spinal alignment.

    Objective: State reasons for management of the cervical spine once the patient has been determined to be a trauma patient.

8. a

    Although the patient's complaint was initially limited to the right leg, the mechanism of injury (vehicle striking a pedestrian) suggests that other injuries may be present. Therefore, the entire body should be rapidly inspected (looked at), auscultated (listened to), and palpated (felt).

Objective: Recite examples of and explain why patients should receive a rapid trauma assessment.

9. d

DCAP-BTLS is a mnemonic designed to assist rescuers in remembering what signs to look for on a trauma patient. It stands for **d**eformities, **c**ontusions (bruises), **a**brasions (scrapes), **p**unctures or penetrating wounds, **b**urns, **t**enderness to palpation, **l**acerations (cuts), and **s**welling. ABC is a memory aid for the initial assessment: **a**irway, **b**reathing, and **c**irculation. ALS refers to advanced life support (advanced EMTs and paramedics). DOT stands for the Department of Transportation.

Objective: Describe the areas included in the rapid trauma assessment, and discuss what should be evaluated.

10. c

A significant amount of blood can be lost due to a femur fracture. Emergency care should include a full assessment of the extremity and application of the appropriate splint. This condition may be aided by on-scene stabilization; however, it is important that this patient be transported to an appropriate medical facility.

Objective: Discuss the reasons for reconsideration of the mechanism of injury.

11. c

The best way to check for bleeding without manipulating the patient's spine is to periodically inspect your gloves while palpating the patient's head. Standing the patient or turning the patient's head are unacceptable techniques because they jeopardize the integrity of full spinal immobilization. Wrapping the patient's head in gauze dressing is not a practical alternative.

Objective: Describe the steps EMS professionals should take for personal protection from airborne and bloodborne pathogens.

12. c

The best method for assessing the patient's posterior body is the logroll method. When performing this maneuver, one rescuer is positioned at the head for manual stabilization of the patient's head and neck. Additional rescuers

are positioned at the patient's side, and an assistant prepares the backboard for positioning. The rescuer at the patient's head is in charge of all patient movement and coordinates the logroll. Another rescuer is necessary to assess the patient's back once he is rolled onto his side. The backboard is then put in place, and the patient is rolled back onto the backboard and secured.

Objective: Describe the areas included in the rapid trauma assessment, and discuss what should be evaluated.

Short Answer

13. The abdomen is normally soft and is not painful or tender to touch. To examine the abdomen, place one hand on top of the other. Use the pads of the fingers of the lower hand, and gently feel the upper and lower areas of the abdomen for injuries or tenderness. If the patient is responsive, ask her to point to the area that hurts (point tenderness). Assess the area that hurts last. Determine if the abdomen feels soft or firm. During your examination, watch the patient's facial expression for signs of tenderness.

Objective: Describe the areas included in the rapid trauma assessment, and discuss what should be evaluated.

14. Factors to consider in a motor vehicle crash include the following:

- Rate of speed
- Seat belt use
- Impact site
- Amount of intrusion
- Airbag deployment
- Vehicle size
- Condition of steering wheel
- Condition of windshield

Objective: Discuss the reasons for reconsideration of the mechanism of injury.

15. Assess the abdomen for DCAP-BTLS, and look for the following:

- Surgical scars
- Bruising
- Open wounds
- Protruding abdominal organs
- An impaled object
- Distention
- Signs of obvious pregnancy

Objective: Describe the areas included in the rapid trauma assessment, and discuss what should be evaluated.

27 Bleeding and Soft Tissue Trauma

READING ASSIGNMENT ▶ Read Chapter 27, pages 449 to 481 in your textbook.

Sum It Up

- The skin is the body's first line of defense against bacteria and other organisms, ultraviolet rays from the sun, harmful chemicals, and cuts and tears.
- A wound is an injury to soft tissues. A closed wound occurs when the soft tissues under the skin are damaged but the surface of the skin is not broken (for example, a bruise). An open wound results when the skin surface is broken (for example, a cut or scrape).
- Hemorrhage (also called major bleeding) is an extreme loss of blood from a blood vessel. It is a life-threatening condition that requires *immediate* attention. If it is not controlled, hemorrhage can lead to shock and potentially to death.
- Hemophilia is a disorder in which the blood does not clot normally. A person with hemophilia may have major bleeding from minor injuries and may bleed for no apparent reason. Some medications or a serious injury may also prevent effective clotting.
- Arterial bleeding is the most serious type of bleeding. The blood from an artery is bright red, oxygen-rich blood. A bleeding artery can quickly lead to the loss of a large amount of blood.
- Venous bleeding is usually easier to control than arterial bleeding because it is under less pressure. Blood lost from a vein flows as a steady stream and is dark red or maroon because it is oxygen-poor blood.
- Capillary bleeding is common because the walls of the capillaries are fragile and many are close to the skin's surface. Bleeding from capillaries is usually dark red. When a capillary is torn, blood oozes slowly from the site of the injury because the pressure within the capillaries is low. Capillary bleeding often clots and stops by itself within a few minutes.
- External bleeding is bleeding that you can see. Clotting normally occurs within minutes. However, external bleeding must be controlled with your gloved hands and dressings until a clot is formed and the bleeding has stopped.
- You *must* wear PPE when you anticipate exposure to blood or other potentially infectious material. HIV and the hepatitis virus are examples of diseases to which you may be exposed that can be transmitted by exposure to blood.

- Three methods may be used to control external bleeding. You must know the methods of external bleeding control that are approved by medical direction and your local protocol.
  - Applying direct pressure slows blood flow and allows clotting to take place.
  - A splint is a device used to limit the movement of an injured arm or leg and reduce bleeding. After applying the splint, make sure to check the patient's fingers (or toes) often for color, warmth, and feeling. A pressure splint (also called an air or pneumatic splint) can help control bleeding from soft tissue injuries or broken bones. It can also help stabilize a broken bone.
  - A tourniquet is a tight bandage that surrounds an arm or leg. It is used to stop the flow of blood in an extremity. A tourniquet should be used to control life-threatening bleeding in an arm or leg when you cannot control the bleeding with direct pressure.
- Internal bleeding is bleeding that occurs inside body tissues and cavities. A bruise is a collection of blood under the skin caused by bleeding capillaries. A bruise is an example of internal bleeding that is not life-threatening.
- Closed soft tissue injuries occur because of blunt trauma. In blunt trauma, a forceful impact occurs to the body, but there is no break in the skin. In a closed soft tissue injury, there is no actual break in the skin, but the tissues and vessels may be crushed or ruptured. When assessing a closed soft tissue injury, it is important to evaluate surface damage and consider possible damage to the organs and major vessels beneath the area of impact.
- Closed soft tissue injuries include contusions, hematomas, and crush injuries. A contusion is a bruise. In a contusion, the epidermis remains intact. Cells are damaged and blood vessels torn in the dermis. Localized swelling and pain are typically present. A buildup of blood causes discoloration (ecchymosis). A hematoma is the collection of blood beneath the skin. A larger amount of tissue is damaged in a hematoma than in a a contusion. Larger blood vessels are damaged. Hematomas frequently occur with trauma sufficient to break bones. Crush injuries are caused by a crushing force applied to the body. These injuries can cause internal organ rupture. Internal bleeding may be severe and lead to shock.
- In open soft tissue injuries, a break occurs in the continuity of the skin. Because of the break in the skin, open injuries are susceptible to external hemorrhage and infection. In an abrasion, the outermost layer of skin (epidermis) is damaged by shearing forces (e.g., rubbing or scraping). A laceration is a break in the skin of varying depth. A laceration may be linear (regular) or stellate (irregular). Lacerations may occur in isolation or with other types of soft tissue injury. A puncture results when the skin is pierced with a pointed object such as a nail, pencil, ice pick, splinter, piece of glass, bullet, or knife. An object that remains embedded in the open wound is called an impaled object. In an avulsion, a flap of skin or tissue is torn loose or pulled completely off. In a degloving avulsion injury, the skin and fatty tissue are stripped away. In an amputation, extremities or other body parts are severed from the body. In an open crush injury, soft tissue and internal organs are damaged. These injuries may cause painful, swollen, deformed extremities. Internal bleeding may be severe.
- An evisceration occurs when an organ sticks out through an open wound. In providing care, do not touch the exposed organ or try to place it back into the body. Carefully remove clothing from around the wound. Lightly cover the exposed organ and wound with a thick, moist dressing. Secure the dressing in place with a large bandage to keep moisture in and prevent heat loss.
- An impaled object is an object that remains embedded in an open wound. Do not remove an impaled object unless it interferes with CPR or is impaled through the cheek and interferes with care of the patient's airway. Control bleeding and

stabilize the object with bulky dressings, bandaging them in place. Assess the patient for signs of shock, and treat if present.

- In the case of an amputated body part, control bleeding at the stump. In most cases, direct pressure will be enough to control the bleeding. Ask an assistant to find the amputated part, as it may be able to be reattached at the hospital. Put the amputated part in a dry plastic bag or waterproof container. Carefully seal the bag or container and place it in water that contains a few ice cubes.

- There are three categories of burns:
  - A superficial (first-degree) burn affects only the epidermis. It results in only minor tissue damage (such as sunburn). The skin is red, tender, and very painful. This type of burn does not usually require medical care and heals in 2 to 5 days with no scarring.
  - A partial-thickness (second-degree) burn involves the epidermis and dermis. The hair follicles and sweat glands are spared in this degree of burn. A partial-thickness burn produces intense pain and some swelling. Blistering may be present. The skin appears pink, red, or mottled and is sensitive to air current and pressure. This type of burn usually heals within 5 to 34 days. Scarring may or may not occur, depending on the depth of the burn.
  - A full-thickness (third-degree) burn destroys both the epidermis and the dermis and may include subcutaneous tissue, muscle, and bone. The color of the patient's skin may vary from yellow or pale to black. The skin has a dry, waxy, or leathery appearance. Because the skin is so severely damaged in this type of burn, it cannot perform its usual protective functions. Rapid fluid loss often occurs. Be ready to treat the patient for shock.

- The rule of nines is a guide used to estimate the total body surface area burned. The rule of nines divides the adult body into sections that are 9% or are mutiples of 9%. This guideline has also been modified for children and infants. To estimate the extent of a burn by using the rule of nines, add the percentages of the areas burned.

- A dressing is an absorbent material placed directly over a wound. A bandage is used to secure a dressing in place. A pressure bandage is a bandage applied with enough pressure over a wound site to control bleeding. Dressings and bandages serve the following functions:
  - Help to stop bleeding
  - Absorb blood and other drainage from the wound
  - Protect the wound from further injury
  - Reduce contamination and the risk of infection

▶ Tracking Your Progress

After reading this chapter, can you:	Page Reference	Objective Met?
• State the major functions of the skin?	451	☐
• List the layers of the skin?	451	☐
• Define wound and differentiate between an open wound and a closed wound?	451	☐
• Differentiate among arterial, venous, and capillary bleeding?	452	☐
• Establish the relationship between standard precautions and bleeding and soft tissue injuries?	453	☐
• Describe methods of controlling external bleeding?	453	☐
• Establish the relationship between mechanism of injury and internal bleeding?	457	☐

After reading this chapter, can you:

	Page Reference	Objective Met?
• List the signs of internal bleeding?	457	☐
• List the steps in the emergency medical care of the patient with signs and symptoms of internal bleeding?	457	☐
• Differentiate between open and closed soft tissue injuries?	458	☐
• List the types of closed soft tissue injuries?	459	☐
• Describe the emergency care of the patient with a closed soft tissue injury?	459	☐
• State the types of open soft tissue injuries?	460	☐
• Describe the emergency medical care of the patient with an open soft tissue injury?	463	☐
• Discuss the emergency medical care considerations for a patient with a penetrating chest injury?	463	☐
• Describe the emergency medical care of the patient with an evisceration?	464	☐
• Describe the emergency medical care of the patient with an impaled object?	465	☐
• Describe the emergency medical care of the patient with an amputation?	465	☐
• Describe the emergency medical care of the patient with an open neck injury?	465	☐
• Describe the emergency medical care of the patient with an eye injury?	466	☐
• Describe the emergency medical care of the patient with a mouth injury?	468	☐
• Describe the emergency medical care of the patient with an ear laceration?	468	☐
• Identify factors that determine the severity of a burn?	468	☐
• List the classifications of burns?	469	☐
• Define superficial burn?	469	☐
• List the characteristics of a superficial burn?	469	☐
• Define partial-thickness burn?	469	☐
• List the characteristics of a partial-thickness burn?	469	☐
• Define full-thickness burn?	470	☐
• List the characteristics of a full-thickness burn?	470	☐
• Discuss the use of the rule of nines to estimate the total body surface area burned?	470	☐
• Describe the emergency medical care of the patient with a superficial burn?	472	☐
• Describe the emergency medical care of the patient with a partial-thickness burn?	472	☐
• Describe the emergency medical care of the patient with a full-thickness burn?	472	☐
• Describe the emergency care for a chemical burn?	473	☐
• Describe the emergency care for an electrical burn?	474	☐
• List the functions of dressing and bandaging?	475	☐
• Describe the purpose of a bandage?	477	☐
• Describe the steps in applying a pressure dressing?	478	☐

Chapter Quiz

Multiple Choice

In the space provided, identify the letter of the choice that best completes each statement or answers each question.

_____ 1. An average adult man has a normal blood volume of about
   a. 3 to 4 liters.
   c. 5 to 6 liters.
   b. 4 to 5 liters.
   d. 6 to 7 liters.

_____ 2. Your rescue crew has been called to the scene of a high-speed vehicle collision. While triaging the patients, you note that one patient has an eyeball dangling out of its socket (an extruded eyeball). Appropriate management of this injury would be to
   a. replace the eyeball into the socket and cover both eyes.
   b. submerge the eyeball in water and cover the affected eye.
   c. replace the eyeball into the socket and cover the affected eye.
   d. cover the eyeball with a moist sterile dressing, protect it from further injury, and cover both eyes.

_____ 3. A 23-year-old man has been stabbed multiple times in his chest and abdomen. As you approach him and form your general impression, you see he is having difficulty breathing. There is a large pool of blood around him, and his shirt is soaked with blood. In this situation, you should first
   a. cover all wounds with a dressing.
   b. assess for signs of internal bleeding.
   c. apply direct pressure to the most severe wounds.
   d. assess and manage the patient's airway and breathing.

_____ 4. Which of the following is *not* an example of an occlusive dressing?
   a. Vaseline gauze
   c. Petroleum dressing
   b. Kerlix gauze
   d. Plastic wrap

_____ 5. You have been called to the home of a 3-year-old child who was burned while getting into a bathtub. His mother states that the child burned himself getting into the bath when the water was too hot. The child is conscious and crying. Both legs show scald-type burns up to the buttocks. The percent of body surface area burned would be
   a. 18%.
   c. 45%.
   b. 27%.
   d. 54%.

Questions 6–7 pertain to the following scenario:

Your rescue crew is called to a construction site for a 28-year-old woman who cut her hand with a saw. You arrive to find the patient holding a blood-soaked towel over her left hand. She states that blood was "spurting out with every heartbeat."

_____ 6. This type of bleeding is consistent with laceration of a(n)
   a. vein.
   c. artery.
   b. tendon.
   d. capillary bed.

_____ 7. The first step in controlling the bleeding associated with the injury is to
   a. apply a tourniquet.
   b. apply direct pressure at the injury site.
   c. apply pressure to the nearest pressure point.
   d. apply a blood pressure cuff to the upper arm and inflate it until the bleeding stops.

Questions 8–9 pertain to the following scenario:

Your ambulance has been called to the scene of a high-rise fire. You are assigned responsibility for a 66-year-old man with burns to his chest and arms. You note the jacket he is wearing is still smoldering. He is conscious and alert, complaining of difficulty breathing and severe arm pain.

_____ **8.** Which of the following should be done first?

    a. Remove the patient's burning clothing.

    b. Attempt to calculate the total burn area.

    c. Cover the burns with a dry, sterile dressing.

    d. Begin high-flow oxygen therapy with a nonrebreather mask if breathing status is adequate.

_____ **9.** The burns to the patient's upper arms are red and blistered, while the burns to the lower arms and hands are dry and leathery. The burns to the upper arms are most likely _____, while the burns to the lower arms are probably _____.

    a. third degree, first degree   **c.** first degree, second degree

    b. first degree, third degree   **d.** second degree, third degree

Questions 10–12 pertain to the following scenario:

Your rescue crew is called to an apartment complex for a fight. Local law enforcement has secured the scene. Your patient is a 16-year-old male complaining of chest pain and severe difficulty breathing. He states that he was stabbed several times in the back. On examination, you find five stab wounds to the upper back and a knife protruding from one of the wounds. There is also a 3-inch laceration to the patient's lower-left abdominal quadrant.

_____ **10.** The wounds on the patient's upper back should be covered with

    a. sterile gauze and wrap.

    b. an occlusive dressing and elastic wrap.

    c. an occlusive dressing taped on one side.

    d. an occlusive dressing taped on three sides.

_____ **11.** According to bystanders, the knife's blade is about 3 to 4 inches long. About 1 inch of the blade is exposed; the rest is in the patient. You should

    a. stabilize the knife with bulky dressings and secure in place.

    b. seat the knife (push it in the remaining 1 inch) and then secure in place.

    c. remove the knife if it compromises the ability to immobilize the patient's spine.

    d. attempt to remove the knife once but stop and secure in place if you meet any resistance.

_____ **12.** While examining the abdominal injury, you note that a loop of what appears to be intestine is hanging out about 2 inches. Appropriate management of this injury would be to

    a. push the loop back into the abdominal cavity.

    b. cover the loop with dry sterile gauze and secure with tape.

    c. cover with a large sterile dressing moistened with sterile saline, secure with a large bandage, and prevent heat loss.

    d. cover the loop with an occlusive dressing, apply ice packs or cool compresses, and secure with a gauze wrap.

Matching

Match the key terms in the right column with the definitions in the left column by placing the letter of each correct answer in the space provided.

_____ 13. A soft tissue injury in which a flap of skin or tissue is torn loose or pulled completely off

_____ 14. An injury that occurs when the soft tissues under the skin are damaged but the surface of the skin is not broken

_____ 15. Another phrase for hemorrhage

_____ 16. Circulation of blood through an organ or a part of the body

_____ 17. The entry of air into the circulation through a blood vessel that is torn and exposed to the air

_____ 18. Bleeding that you can see

_____ 19. An injury in which the skin surface is broken

_____ 20. Firm force applied to a bleeding site with gloved hands or bandages to control bleeding

_____ 21. Bleeding that occurs inside body tissues and cavities

_____ 22. Damage to the outermost layer of skin (epidermis) by shearing forces (such as rubbing or scraping)

_____ 23. Material, such as roller gauze, that is applied snugly to create pressure on a wound and hold a dressing in place over it

_____ 24. A device used to limit the movement of an injured arm or leg and reduce bleeding and discomfort

_____ 25. Piercing of the skin with a pointed object such as a nail or ice pick

_____ 26. A tight bandage that surrounds an arm or leg and is used to stop the flow of blood in the extremity

_____ 27. A collection of blood under the skin due to bleeding capillaries

_____ 28. A broken bone that penetrates the skin

_____ 29. An injury to the soft tissues of the body

_____ 30. An extreme loss of blood from a blood vessel

_____ 31. Absorbent material placed directly over a wound

_____ 32. A disorder in which the blood does not clot normally

_____ 33. A guide used to estimate the total body surface area burned

A. Air embolism

B. Dressing

C. Major bleeding

D. Internal bleeding

E. Tourniquet

F. Pressure bandage

G. Compound fracture

H. Hemophilia

I. Open wound

J. Puncture wound

K. Abrasion

L. External bleeding

M. Closed wound

N. Wound

O. Rule of nines

P. Bruise

Q. Splint

R. Hemorrhage

S. Perfusion

T. Avulsion

U. Direct pressure

Short Answer

Answer each question in the space provided.

34. What are the two most common causes of internal bleeding?

35. Complete the following table regarding the types of bleeding.

	Arterial	Venous	Capillary
Color			
Blood flow			
Bleeding control			

36. List four factors that determine the severity of a burn.
1.
2.
3.
4.

37. What is the most urgent type of injury to the eye?

38. List four types of open wounds.

39. List the characteristics of a partial-thickness burn.

40. List the characteristics of a full-thickness burn.

Answer Section

Multiple Choice

1. c

An average adult man has a normal blood volume of about 5 to 6 liters (5,000 to 6,000 mL).

Objective: Describe the components and functions of the circulatory system.

2. d

Replacing the eyeball may cause further damage and would increase the opportunity for infection. Do not attempt to replace misplaced body parts. Instead, you should attempt to keep the eyeball moist and protected.

Objective: Describe the emergency medical care of the patient with an eye injury.

3. d

Bleeding may be obvious when you approach a patient. However, remember that making sure the patient has an open airway and adequate breathing takes priority over other care. Stabilize the cervical spine if needed. During your assessment of the patient's circulation, control major (severe) bleeding.

Objective: List and describe the components of patient assessment and the purpose of each component.

4. b

Kerlix is porous and allows air to pass through it easily.

Objective: List the functions of dressing and bandaging.

5. b

The rule of nines differs for children and infants because their heads are proportionally larger than the heads of adults. The head is given twice the adult value, or 18%. The anterior chest, posterior chest, arms, and genitalia have the same values as the adult counterparts, while the legs are given a value of 13.5% each rather than 18%. This patient's percentage of BSA burned is 27%. Something about the characteristics of this burn should catch your attention: If the water was too hot, why would the patient put both legs completely under the surface of the water? The "story" from the parent does not make sense. When treating injured dependent patients (such as children, older adults, mentally challenged persons), be aware that abuse can exist. While it is not the role of an EMR to investigate abuse, it is your responsibility to notify the appropriate agency (law enforcement or medical direction) of circumstances that suggest abuse.

Objective: Discuss the use of the rule of nines to estimate the total body surface area burned.

6. c

Arteries (as compared to veins) flow blood under high pressure. Blood flowing through the arteries of the body is oxygenated and bright red. Therefore, arterial bleeds are characterized by the spurting of bright red blood. Veins carry deoxygenated blood from the cells of the body back to the heart. Deoxygenated blood is darker than oxygenated blood, and veins do not flow blood under pressure as high as do arteries. Venous bleeding is characterized by the constant flow of dark red or maroon blood. Capillaries are very small vessels. Red blood cells literally line up single file to flow through capillaries. Bleeding associated with capillary injury is an oozing of plasma with a scant amount of blood (like a "carpet burn").

Objective: Differentiate among arterial, venous, and capillary bleeding.

7. b

The steps to control bleeding are as follows: Begin by applying direct pressure at the bleeding point. If possible, elevate the injury above the level of the heart. If applicable, splint the extremity to decrease movement. If the wound continues to bleed uncontrollably, locate the nearest arterial pressure point. Apply pressure to the pressure point while still maintaining direct pressure on the wound. An arterial pressure point is a point where an artery comes close to the surface of the skin and runs over a bone. By compressing the arterial pressure point, the flow of blood to the injury will decrease. If direct pressure, elevation, splinting, and indirect pressure fail to control bleeding, a tourniquet may be considered. If you have the means to contact medical direction, do so before applying a tourniquet.

Objective: Describe methods of controlling external bleeding.

8. a

Your immediate concern should be to protect the patient from further harm. This means stopping the burning process and moving the patient to a safe place. Calculating the burn area, applying sterile dressings, and initiating oxygen therapy should be done only after ensuring the safety of the patient. *Note:* While oxygen is not flammable, it does support and accelerate combustion. Do not use oxygen around an open or smoldering flame.

Objective: Describe the emergency medical care of the patient with a partial-thickness burn.

9. d

Partial-thickness burns, also known as *second-degree burns*, are characterized by painful red or mottled skin that ultimately develops blisters. Both the epidermis and the dermis are damaged in a partial-thickness burn, whereas a superficial burn involves damage only to the epidermis. Full-thickness burns, also known as *third-degree burns,* may appear white, brown, or charred. Because the dermal layer is destroyed in full-thickness burns, no pain is associated with these burns (the nerves that sense pain in the skin are located in the dermal layer); however, a full-thickness burn is usually associated with superficial and partial-thickness burns, which are painful.

Objective: List the classifications of burns.

10. d

Air will always follow the path of least resistance. If there is a hole in the chest wall, air will enter the hole during inhalation. This air may become trapped in the chest cavity, leading to life-threatening compromise (pneumothorax or tension pneumothorax). An airtight barrier is critical. Sealing the occlusive dressing on three sides creates an airtight seal while allowing an avenue (the unsecured fourth side) for trapped air to escape.

Objective: Describe the emergency medical care of the patient with an open soft tissue injury.

11. a

The proper technique for securing an impaled object is to wrap the object with a bulky dressing and then secure the bulky dressing. Pushing the knife in any further may cause additional harm. Removing the knife to perform spinal immobilization is not appropriate. In this case, spinal immobilization would be indicated, since the possibility exists that the spinal cord may have been lacerated. However, you must improvise immobilization to facilitate transporting the patient with the knife in place (possibly immobilizing the patient on his side).

Objective: Describe the emergency medical care of the patient with an impaled object.

12. c

Never touch or attempt to replace exposed abdominal organs. Protect the organs from further harm by applying a large sterile dressing moistened with sterile water or saline over the area. Retain moisture and preserve body heat by securing the dressing with a large bandage. Replacing the organs into the abdomen increases the risk of infection. Allowing the organs to dry out or freeze may result in surgical removal of the affected section of bowel.

Objective: Describe the emergency medical care of the patient with an evisceration.

Matching

13.	T	24.	Q
14.	M	25.	J
15.	C	26.	E
16.	S	27.	P
17.	A	28.	G
18.	L	29.	N
19.	I	30.	R
20.	U	31.	B
21.	D	32.	H
22.	K	33.	O
23.	F		

Answer Section

True/False

1. **False**

   Children are less likely to sustain rib fractures than adults are because a child's chest wall is more flexible than that of an adult.

   Objective: Describe the causes, signs and symptoms, and emergency care for rib fractures.

2. **True**

   Paradoxical movement is probably most readily seen in an unresponsive patient. In patients with thick or muscular chest walls, it may be difficult to observe paradoxical movement. In some conscious patients, spasm and splinting of the chest muscles may cause paradoxical motion to go unnoticed.

   Objective: Describe the causes, signs and symptoms, and emergency care for flail chest.

Multiple Choice

3. **c**

   Not all open chest wounds are sucking chest wounds (although as a precaution all open wounds of the chest are treated as if they are sucking chest wounds). A sucking chest wound occurs when air is drawn into the chest cavity as the patient inhales. Some air may escape during exhalation. The main problem with a sucking chest wound is that air is not drawn into the lungs; rather, it is drawn into the pleural space. As air builds up in the pleural space, the amount of space available for lung expansion decreases. This is a simple pneumothorax. A tension pneumothorax occurs when one side of the lung has completely collapsed and pressure begins to be exerted on the opposite side.

   Objective: Describe the causes, signs and symptoms, and emergency care for open pneumothorax.

4. **d**

   Fractured ribs will cause an increase in discomfort during normal breathing. To compensate for this, patients will commonly breathe faster and more shallowly (almost like a panting dog). The pain associated with rib fractures is localized and sharp, unlike typical cardiac-type chest pain. Dull, squeezing pain, pain that radiates down the arms, or pain that started before the injury should all be considered cardiac (heart) in origin until proved otherwise at the hospital.

   Objective: Describe the causes, signs and symptoms, and emergency care for rib fractures.

5. **a**

   The liver is located just underneath the lower right rib cage. Fractures of ribs 5 through 9 on the right side may result in laceration of the liver. Fractures of ribs 9 through 11 on the left side may result in laceration of the spleen. The kidneys may be lacerated by posterior (backside) rib fractures. The bladder may be lacerated if the pelvis is fractured.

   Objective: Describe the causes, signs and symptoms, and emergency care for rib fractures.

6. **c**

   On the basis of the mechanism of injury, spinal stabilization is indicated. Providing high-concentration oxygen should maximize oxygen delivery. To keep the lungs properly inflated, the patient should be encouraged to breathe deeply or cough. Simple rib fractures do not generally necessitate rapid (lights and siren) transport.

   Objective: Describe the causes, signs and symptoms, and emergency care for rib fractures.

Short Answer

7. Signs and symptoms of a tension pneumothorax include:

   - Cool, clammy skin
   - Increased pulse rate
   - Cyanosis (late sign)
   - JVD
   - Decreased blood pressure
   - Severe respiratory distress
   - Agitation, restlessness, anxiety
   - Bulging of intercostal muscles on the affected side
   - Decreased or absent breath sounds on the affected side
   - Tracheal deviation toward the unaffected side (late sign)
   - Possible subcutaneous emphysema in the face, neck, or chest wall

   Objective: Describe the causes, signs and symptoms, and emergency care for tension pneumothorax.

8. Signs and symptoms of flail chest include:

   - Crepitus
   - Breathing difficulty
   - Bruising of the chest wall
   - Increased heart rate (tachycardia)
   - Pain and splinting of the affected side
   - Increased respiratory rate (tachypnea)
   - Pain in the chest associated with breathing
   - Paradoxical chest wall movement

   Objective: Describe the causes, signs and symptoms, and emergency care for flail chest.

29 Abdominal and Genitourinary Trauma

READING ASSIGNMENT ▶ Read Chapter 29, pages 491 to 497 in your textbook.

Sum It Up

- Injuries to the abdomen and pelvis can result from blunt or penetrating trauma. Deaths from abdominal trauma result mainly from hemorrhage or infection. Trauma to the genitourinary system seldom occurs separately from trauma to other body systems and is most often associated with abdominal trauma.

- It is best to assume that an injury to the chest or abdomen involves both body cavities. In this way, injuries are less likely to be overlooked.

- Knowing the organs found within each of the four abdominal quadrants will help you describe the location of a patient's injury and anticipate possible complications of the injury.

- The abdomen contains both hollow and solid organs. If hollow organs are cut or ruptured, their contents spill into the abdominal cavity, causing inflammation. Open wounds of hollow organs, such as the stomach or small intestine, may be accompanied by intense pain. Infection is a delayed complication that may be fatal. Severe bleeding may result if a solid organ is cut or ruptures. However, abdominal pain from solid-organ penetration or rupture typically is of slow onset and generally does not occur immediately.

- Types of abdominal injuries include open injuries, in which the skin is broken, and closed injuries, in which the skin is not broken.

- Trauma sustained from a motor vehicle crash, fall, or assault produces compression and deceleration injuries. A compression injury occurs when abdominal contents are squeezed between the vertebral column and the impacting object. In a deceleration injury, the individual's body stops its forward movement on impact but the abdominal organs continue to move forward until structural impact, tear, or rupture occurs.

- Penetrating trauma to the abdomen can result from low-, medium-, or high-energy weapons. A knife or ice pick is an example of a low-energy weapon. Medium-energy weapons include handguns and shotguns. High-energy weapons include military and hunting rifles.

- The genitourinary system consists of the kidneys, ureters, bladder, urethra, and external genitalia. An injury of the kidneys, ureters, bladder, or urethra can result in hematuria. Injuries to the external male genitalia include cuts, bruises, penetrating objects, amputations, and avulsions. The internal female genitalia are rarely injured except in the pregnant patient or in cases of sexual assault with penetration. Injuries to the external female genitalia usually result from straddle injuries or lacerations produced by sexual activity, such as foreign objects in the vagina, or sexual assault.

▶ Tracking Your Progress

After reading this chapter, can you:	Page Reference	Objective Met?
• State the possible causes, signs, and symptoms of an abdominal injury?	492	☐
• Differentiate between closed and open abdominal injuries?	494	☐
• State the possible causes, signs, and symptoms of a genitourinary injury?	495	☐
• Describe the assessment and emergency care for a patient with a possible abdominal injury?	494	☐
• Describe the assessment and emergency care for a patient with injuries to the external male genitalia?	495	☐
• Describe the assessment and emergency care for a patient with injuries to the external female genitalia?	495	☐

Chapter Quiz

True/False

Decide whether each statement is true or false. In the space provided, write T for true or F for false.

_____ 1. If exposed abdominal organs are present, make at least one attempt to reinsert them into the abdominal cavity.

_____ 2. Stab wounds to the abdomen most commonly involve the liver.

Multiple Choice

In the space provided, identify the letter of the choice that best completes each statement or answers each question.

_____ 3. The abdomen contains both solid and hollow organs. The liver, for example, is considered solid, while the stomach is considered hollow. Perforation of a solid abdominal organ is most commonly associated with

    a. paralysis.
    b. severe hemorrhage.
    c. tension pneumothorax.
    d. inflammation and infection.

_____ 4. Your rescue crew is called to a local park for a male assault victim. On the crew's arrival, your patient is found lying on the ground, moaning in pain. He does not speak English, and you are unable to understand what he is trying to explain to you. Which of the following physical findings would be consistent with an abdominal injury?

    a. The patient's abdomen is large and soft.
    b. The patient is coughing up bright red blood.
    c. The patient's blood pressure is high, and his pulse rate is low.
    d. The patient is in the fetal position and appears to be in shock.

_____ **5.** Injuries to the large intestine are usually caused by

    a. the lap portion of seat belts.

    b. direct blows to the abdomen.

    c. gunshot wounds and stabbings.

    d. frontal-impact motor vehicle crashes.

_____ **6.** Your rescue crew has been called to the scene of a sexual assault. Local law enforcement personnel have secured the scene. The police inform you that while trying to commit a rape, a 34-year-old man had his penis severed from his body. The amputated body part is on the ground. The patient is bleeding lightly from the groin. Appropriate management would be to

    a. control bleeding with a tourniquet, leave the amputated part at the crime scene, and transport the patient to the emergency department.

    b. control bleeding with a tourniquet, pack the amputated part in a bag filled with ice, and transport the patient and the bag to the emergency department.

    c. control bleeding with direct pressure, submerge the amputated part in a cup of water, and transport the patient and the cup to the emergency department.

    d. control bleeding with direct pressure; wrap the amputated part in sterile gauze, place it in a plastic bag, and keep it cool; and transport the patient and the bag to the emergency department.

_____ **7.** Blunt trauma to the kidney is usually caused by

    a. stabbings.

    b. gunshot wounds.

    c. an assault or straddle injury.

    d. motor vehicle crashes, falls, or contact sports.

_____ **8.** Your rescue crew is called to a local recreation area for a 23-year-old woman who injured herself while mountain biking. The patient states that she slipped off the seat while going over a bump and landed on the bar. There is a slow stream of blood building up in her groin. She tells you that there is a 1-inch laceration between her vagina and anus. Appropriate management of this injury would include

    a. applying ice directly to the wound.

    b. packing the vaginal opening with tampons or sterile gauze.

    c. controlling bleeding with external pressure and trauma pads.

    d. protecting the patient's modesty by not evaluating or treating the injury.

Answer Section

True/False

1. **False**

   If exposed abdominal organs are present, do not attempt to reinsert them into the abdominal cavity. Cover them with a moist, sterile dressing.

   Objective: Describe the assessment and emergency care for a patient with a possible abdominal injury.

2. **True**

   In order of frequency, stab wounds to the abdomen most commonly involve the liver, small intestine, diaphragm, and large intestine.

   Objective: State the possible causes, signs, and symptoms of an abdominal injury.

Multiple Choice

3. b

   The solid organs of the abdominal cavity (the spleen, liver, pancreas, and kidneys) are extremely vascular structures. Damage to these organs commonly results in significant blood loss. The abdominal organs may be injured by either penetrating or blunt trauma. For example, unrestrained patients in motor vehicle crashes are highly susceptible to spleen damage from striking the steering wheel during impact. Paralysis is most commonly associated with nerve damage, while a tension pneumothorax is a thoracic (chest) injury.

   Objective: State the possible causes, signs, and symptoms of an abdominal injury.

4. d

   Sometimes your best indicator of injury and level of distress will be the patient's initial presentation. Patients with abdominal injuries will commonly assume the fetal position (lying on the side with the legs drawn up). Not all

people with large abdomens have an abdominal injury (obviously), and a soft abdomen is a normal finding. Rigidity, however, may suggest injury. Coughing up blood is generally associated with an injury to the respiratory tract.

   Objective: State the possible causes, signs, and symptoms of an abdominal injury.

5. c

   Injuries to the large intestine are usually the result of gunshot wounds and stabbings.

   Objective: State the possible causes, signs, and symptoms of an abdominal injury.

6. d

   Amputated genital organs are treated like any other amputation injury, but with a more concerned emphasis placed on patient modesty and privacy. Bleeding should be controlled with direct pressure. Cold packs (not direct ice application) may relieve pain and swelling. The amputated body part should be wrapped in sterile gauze, placed in a bag, kept cool, and transported with the patient. As with all crime scenes, you must communicate closely with local law enforcement personnel.

   Objective: Describe the assessment and emergency care for a patient with injuries to the external male genitalia.

7. d

   Injury to the kidney is usually caused by blunt trauma from motor vehicle crashes, falls, or contact sports. Penetrating injury to the kidney can result from gunshot or stab wounds.

   Objective: State the possible causes, signs, and symptoms of a genitourinary injury.

8. c

   This injury is treated like any other soft tissue injury: Apply direct pressure with a sterile dressing. Protecting the patient's modesty is important; however, not treating the patient due to the location of the injury is inappropriate. If possible, have a female rescuer examine and treat this injury. Be professional. Ice should never be applied directly to any wound due to the possibility of tissue damage. Vaginal bleeding should not be treated with the internal application of gauze or any other product in the prehospital setting.

Objective: Describe the assessment and emergency care for a patient with injuries to the external female genitalia.

30 Trauma to Muscles and Bones

READING ASSIGNMENT ▶ Read Chapter 30, pages 498 to 523 in your textbook.

Sum It Up

- The skeletal system is divided into the axial and appendicular skeletons. The axial skeleton includes the skull, spinal column, sternum, and ribs. The appendicular skeleton is made up of the upper and lower extremities (arms and legs), the shoulder girdle, and the pelvic girdle.

- Skeletal muscles produce movement of the bones to which they are attached. Most skeletal muscles are attached to bones by means of tendons. Tendons create a pull between bones when muscles contract. The tendons of many muscles cross over joints, and this contributes to the stability of the joint. Tendons can be damaged from overextension or overuse. Ligaments connect bone to bone.

- A skeletal muscle has three main parts: The origin is the stationary attachment of the muscle to a bone, the insertion is the movable attachment to a bone, and the body is the main part of the muscle.

- The mechanism of injury to bones and joints can be caused by direct forces, indirect forces, and twisting forces:
  —A direct force causes injury at the point of impact.
  —An indirect force causes injury at a site other than the point of impact.
  —A twisting force causes one part of an extremity to remain in place while the rest twists. Twisting injuries commonly affect the joints such as ankles, knees, and wrists. Twisting forces cause ligaments to stretch and tear.

- Injuries to bones and joints may be open or closed. In an open injury, the skin surface is broken. An open injury increases the risk of contamination and infection. These injuries can also result in serious blood loss. In closed injuries of bones and joints, the skin surface is not broken. The injury is often painful, swollen, and deformed.

- A fracture is a break in a bone. If a bone is broken, chipped, cracked, or splintered, it is said to be fractured.

- A greenstick fracture occurs when the bone breaks on one side but not the other, like bending a green tree branch.

- Typical blood loss in an uncomplicated fracture of the tibia or fibula during the first 2 hours can be as much as 550 mL. A broken femur can result in the loss of up to 1 L of blood, and a fractured pelvis can result in the loss of 2 L.

- A dislocation occurs when the end of a bone is forced from its normal position in a joint. A partial dislocation (subluxation) means the bone is partially out of the joint. Luxation, a complete dislocation, means it is all the way out. Dislocations and subluxations usually result in temporary deformity of the affected joints, loss of limb function, immediate swelling, and point tenderness, and they may result in sudden and severe pain.
- A sprain is a stretching or tearing of a ligament, the connective tissue that joins the end of one bone with another. Sprains are classified as mild, moderate, and severe.
- A strain is a twisting, pulling, or tearing of a muscle or tendon. A muscle strain usually occurs when a muscle is stretched beyond its limit. A strain often occurs near the point where the muscle joins the tough connective tissue of the tendon.
- Most sprains and strains can be treated with rest, ice, and elevation.
- In assessing extremity injuries, check the **p**ulse, **m**ovement, and **s**ensation (PMS) in each extremity.
- A splint is a device used to immobilize (limit movement of) a body part to prevent pain and further injury.
  — In some situations, the patient will have already splinted the injury by holding the injured part close to her body in a comfortable position. The use of the body as a splint is called a self-splint or anatomic splint.
  — Before splinting an injured hand or foot, place it in the position of function. The natural position of the hand at rest looks as if the hand were gently grasping a small object, such as a baseball.
- Rigid splints are made of hard material, such as wood, strong cardboard, or plastic. This type of splint is useful for immobilizing injuries that occur to the middle portion (midshaft) of a bone. Some rigid splints are padded, but others must be padded before they are applied to the patient.
- Semirigid (flexible) splints are very useful for immobilizing joint injuries. These splints can be molded to the shape of the extremity. Examples include the SAM Splint and aluminum ladder splints. Semirigid splints can be used in combination with other splints, such as a sling and swathe.
- Soft splints are flexible and useful for immobilizing injuries of the lower leg or forearm. Examples of soft splints include sling and swathe combinations, blanket rolls, pillows, and towels. A sling and swathe are used to immobilize injuries to the shoulder, collarbone, or upper arm bone. A triangular bandage is often used to make a sling. A swathe is a piece of soft material used to secure the injured extremity to the body.
- A traction splint is a device used to immobilize a closed fracture of the thighbone. This type of splint maintains a constant steady pull on the bone. A traction splint keeps broken bone ends in a near-normal position. Controversy exists regarding whether or not a traction splint can or should be used to immobilize an open fracture of the femur. Be sure to ask your instructor, EMS agency coordinator, or medical director regarding the use of a traction splint for this type of injury in your area.
- A pneumatic splint requires air to be pumped in or suctioned out of it. The air splint, vacuum splint, and pneumatic antishock garment (PASG) are examples of pneumatic splints. A pneumatic splint is placed around the injured area and is inflated (air splint or PASG) or deflated (vacuum splint) until it becomes firm.

▶ Tracking Your Progress

After reading this chapter, can you:	Page Reference	Objective Met?
• Describe the anatomy and physiology of the musculoskeletal system?	499	☐
• List the major bones or bone groupings of the spinal column, the thorax, the upper extremities, and the lower extremities?	499	☐
• Discuss orthopedic trauma caused by direct and indirect forces?	504	☐
• Differentiate between open and closed orthopedic injuries?	504	☐
• Define and discuss fractures and dislocations?	504	☐
• Differentiate between sprains and strains?	507	☐
• Discuss the assessment findings and symptoms associated with musculoskeletal injuries?	507	☐
• List the six Ps of musculoskeletal injury assessment?	508	☐
• Describe the emergency medical care for a patient with orthopedic trauma?	508	☐
• Define splint and state the reasons for splinting?	509	☐
• List possible hazards of improper splinting?	509	☐
• List the general rules of splinting?	510	☐
• Discuss types of splints and give examples of situations in which each type might be used?	511	☐
• List warning signs of a splint that is too tight?	511	☐

Chapter Quiz

True/False

Decide whether each statement is true or false. In the space provided, write T for true or F for false.

_____ **1.** Most muscles are attached to bones by tendons.

_____ **2.** Ice should be applied to a sprain or strain for 40 minutes and removed for 20 minutes.

_____ **3.** Before being applied to a patient, a splint should be padded to prevent pressure and discomfort.

Multiple Choice

In the space provided, identify the letter of the choice that best completes each statement or answers each question.

_____ **4.** When immobilizing an extremity, it is important to check pulses
   a. after the splint is applied.
   b. before the splint is applied.
   c. before and after the splint is applied.
   d. during immobilization of the affected extremity.

_____ **5.** Which of the following indicates an open fracture?
   a. A wound over the injury
   b. No pulse distal to the injury
   c. Severe deformity
   d. The extremity is cool and pale

Questions 6–10 pertain to the following scenario:

Your crew is called to the scene of a motor vehicle collision. A 41-year-old woman crashed her motorcycle when she hit a patch of ice in the road. She was wearing a helmet and is complaining of severe right leg pain. She tells you the motorcycle came down on her leg when she crashed. You observe deformity and swelling at the middle of her thigh. She is also complaining that she felt her right knee "pop" when she went down.

_____ 6. Which of the following procedures takes priority?

 a. Perform a rapid trauma assessment.
 b. Begin stabilizing the patient's spine.
 c. Obtain a SAMPLE history from the patient.
 d. Assess distal movement, sensation, and circulation, and begin splinting the affected limb.

_____ 7. After exposing the entire limb, you notice that the patient is wearing a gold hoop anklet (bracelet on the ankle). It is slightly larger than the diameter of the ankle and does not appear to be affected by swelling. You should

 a. remove the jewelry.
 b. leave it in place unless it is affecting circulation.
 c. leave the anklet in place as a gauge to monitor distal swelling.
 d. place ice packs on the foot and ankle to ensure that swelling does not disturb circulation past the anklet.

_____ 8. Which of the following devices should be used to immobilize this patient's injury?

 a. A scoop stretcher
 b. A backboard and traction splint
 c. A backboard and sling and swathe
 d. A backboard and padded board splints

_____ 9. After properly treating this patient, you reassess her injuries. You are able to palpate a distal pulse on the top of the patient's right foot. You should

 a. mark this spot with an ink pen.
 b. attempt to palpate a blood pressure in the extremity.
 c. leave your hand in the same spot throughout patient care.
 d. mark this spot by scratching the skin at the pulse site until it turns red.

_____ 10. The bones of the foot are called

 a. tarsals.
 b. carpals.
 c. metatarsals.
 d. metacarpals.

_____ 11. The bones of the wrist are called

 a. tarsals.
 b. carpals.
 c. metatarsals.
 d. metacarpals.

_____ 12. Which of the following is an example of a ball-and-socket joint?

 a. The elbow
 b. The shoulder
 c. The fingers
 d. The knee

Sentence Completion

In the blanks provided, write the words that best complete each sentence.

13. The three major parts of a skeletal muscle are the _____, the _____, and the _____.

14. The two main divisions of the skeleton are the _____ and the _____ skeletons.

15. The appendicular skeleton consists of the upper and lower extremities, the _____ _____, and the _____ _____.

16. The lowermost portion of the sternum is called the _____ _____.

17. In children and adolescents, an area of growing tissue called the _____ _____ can be found near each end of a long bone.

18. The thoracic spine consists of _____ vertebrae.

19. The cervical spine consists of _____ vertebrae.

Short Answer

Answer each question in the space provided.

20. What is a dislocation?

21. What are the three most common signs and symptoms of a musculoskeletal injury?
    1.
    2.
    3.

22. List four reasons for splinting a musculoskeletal injury.
    1.
    2.
    3.
    4.

23. List three hazards of improper splinting.
    1.
    2.
    3.

24. What three things should you assess before and after applying a splint?
    1.
    2.
    3.

Answer Section

True/False

1. True

   Most skeletal muscles are attached to bones by means of tendons. Tendons create a pull between bones when muscles contract. The tendons of many muscles cross over joints, and this contributes to the stability of the joint.

   Objective: Describe the anatomy and physiology of the musculoskeletal system.

2. False

   Apply ice to a sprain or strain for 20 minutes, and then remove it for 40 minutes. Follow this rotation hourly. Ice reduces blood flow into the affected area, and this in turn reduces swelling.

   Objective: Describe the emergency medical care for a patient with orthopedic trauma.

3. True

   Pad a rigid or semirigid splint before applying it. Padding helps lessen patient discomfort due to pressure, especially around bony areas.

   Objective: List the general rules of splinting.

Multiple Choice

4. c

   Assess the presence of pulses, movement, and sensation in each of your patient's extremities *before* and *after* immobilization.

   Objective: List the general rules of splinting.

5. a

   If the continuity of the skin is broken at or near the injury site, the wound is classified as open. Any open wound over a fracture site indicates the possibility of an open fracture. Open wounds present an additional hazard to the patient because contaminants can now enter the body. When treating open injuries, you must cover them with a sterile dressing prior to splinting.

   Objective: Differentiate between open and closed orthopedic injuries.

6. b

   Spinal stabilization is a high priority and should begin during the primary survey as you address the airway. It is not necessary to secure the patient to a long backboard before beginning the SAMPLE history, nor should you move the patient until distal neurovascular status is assessed in all limbs. However, it is necessary based on the mechanism of injury to immediately begin manual stabilization of the spine.

   Objective: Describe the emergency medical care for a patient with orthopedic trauma.

7. a

   Don't wait for distal jewelry to become a problem before you address it. Remove the jewelry, ask the patient where she would like it kept (pocket, purse, with a friend, etc.), and then show her that you are putting it there. You must be extremely careful when handling valuables (jewelry, wallets, purses, and money)—if they are misplaced, some patients may blame you. Professionalism and good communication skills with the patient allow you to avoid unpleasant situations.

   Objective: List the general rules of splinting.

8. d

   This patient informed you that her knee "popped" when she crashed. You must assume that the joint has been damaged; therefore, a traction splint is contraindicated. EMRs do not typically use traction splints unless they receive specialized training and medical direction authorization to do so. A backboard should be used to immobilize the entire body. An injury to the knee can be immobilized using a pillow, padded board splint, SAM Splint, air splint, or vacuum splint, or the other leg can be used as a splint. A sling and swathe are used to care for a fracture of the upper arm (humerus), clavicle, or shoulder.

Objective: Describe the emergency medical care for a patient with orthopedic trauma.

9. a

Marking the pulse point with a pen allows you to quickly reassess distal circulatory status. It is not practical to keep your finger on the pulse throughout patient care, nor is it necessary to assess a distal blood pressure.

Objective: Describe the emergency medical care for a patient with orthopedic trauma.

10. c

The lower leg attaches to the foot by the ankle, which is made up of seven tarsal bones. The largest tarsal bone, the calcaneus, makes up the heel. The metatarsals make up the main part of the foot. The toes (phalanges) are the foot's equivalent to the fingers. Carpals make up the wrists, and metacarpals make up the hands.

Objective: List the major bones or bone groupings of the spinal column, the thorax, the upper extremities, and the lower extremities.

11. b

The forearm is connected to the wrist (carpals) and then to the hand (metacarpals) and fingers (phalanges).

Objective: Describe the anatomy and physiology of the musculoskeletal system.

12. b

Ball-and-socket joints allow movement in all directions. The only ball-and-socket joints in the body are the hip joint (pelvic bone and femur) and shoulder joint (scapula and humerus). A hinge joint allows only flexion and extension. Examples include the elbow (humerus and ulna), knee (femur and tibia), fingers, and toes.

Objective: Describe the anatomy and physiology of the musculoskeletal system.

Sentence Completion

13. The three major parts of a skeletal muscle are the **insertion,** the **body,** and the **origin.**

Objective: Describe the anatomy and physiology of the musculoskeletal system.

14. The two main divisions of the skeleton are the **axial** and the **appendicular** skeletons.

Objective: Describe the anatomy and physiology of the musculoskeletal system.

15. The appendicular skeleton consists of the upper and lower extremities, the **shoulder girdle,** and the **pelvic girdle.**

Objective: List the major bones or bone groupings of the spinal column, the thorax, the upper extremities, and the lower extremities.

16. The lowermost portion of the sternum is called the **xiphoid process.**

Objective: List the major bones or bone groupings of the spinal column, the thorax, the upper extremities, and the lower extremities.

17. In children and adolescents, an area of growing tissue called the **growth plate** (epiphyseal plate) can be found near each end of a long bone.

Objective: Describe the anatomy and physiology of the musculoskeletal system.

18. The thoracic spine consists of **12** vertebrae.

Objective: Describe the anatomy and physiology of the musculoskeletal system.

19. The cervical spine consists of **7** vertebrae.

Objective: Describe the anatomy and physiology of the musculoskeletal system.

Short Answer

20. A dislocation occurs when the ends of bones are forced from their normal positions in a joint. A partial dislocation (subluxation) means the bone is partially out of the joint. A complete dislocation means it is all the way out.

Objective: Define and discuss fractures and dislocations.

21. The three most common signs and symptoms of a musculoskeletal injury are pain, deformity, and swelling.

Objective: Discuss the assessment findings and symptoms associated with musculoskeletal injuries.

22. The reasons for splinting include the following:

• Limit motion of bone fragments, bone ends, or dislocated joints
• Lessen the damage to muscles, nerves, or blood vessels caused by broken bones

- Help prevent a closed injury from becoming an open injury
- Lessen the restriction of blood flow caused by bone ends or dislocations compressing blood vessels
- Reduce bleeding due to tissue damage caused by bone ends
- Reduce pain associated with the movement of the bone and the joint
- Reduce the risk of paralysis due to a damaged spine

Objective: Define splint, and state the reasons for splinting.

23. The hazards of improper splinting include the following:

- The compression of nerves, tissues, and blood vessels from the splint
- A delay in transport of a patient with a life-threatening injury
- Distal circulation that is reduced due to the splint's being applied too tightly to the extremity
- Aggravation of the musculoskeletal injury
- Cause or aggravation of tissue, nerve, vessel, or muscle damage from excessive bone or joint movement

Objective: List possible hazards of improper splinting.

24. Before and after applying a splint, you should assess distal pulses, movement, and sensation in the injured extremity.

Objective: List the general rules of splinting.

31 Head, Face, Neck, and Spine Trauma

READING ASSIGNMENT ▶ Read Chapter 31, pages 524 to 545 in your textbook.

Sum It Up

- A head injury is a traumatic insult to the head that may result in injury to soft tissue, bony structures, and/or the brain. A traumatic brain injury occurs when an external force to the head causes the brain to move within the skull or the force causes the skull to break and directly injures the brain.

- Blunt trauma to the head usually is caused by motor vehicle crashes, falls, sports, and assaults with blunt weapons. Gunshot and stab wounds are the usual mechanisms of penetrating trauma to the head. Appropriate airway management and breathing support are critical when treating a patient with a head injury.

- A scalp injury may or may not cause an injury to the brain. When injured, the scalp may bleed heavily. In children, the amount of blood loss from a scalp wound may be enough to produce shock. In adults, shock is usually not caused by a scalp wound or internal skull injuries. More often, in adults, shock results from an injury elsewhere.

- A head injury may be closed or open. In a closed head injury, the skull remains intact. However, the brain can still be injured by the forces or objects that struck the skull. The forces that impact the skull cause the brain to move within the skull. The brain strikes the inside of the skull, causing injuries to the brain tissue. The impact and shearing forces that affect the brain can cause direct damage to the brain tissue. If bleeding occurs within the skull, the pressure within the skull increases as the blood takes up more space within the closed container. If the bleeding continues and the pressure continues to rise, the patient can suffer severe brain damage and even death.

- In an open head injury, the skull is not intact and the risk of infection is increased. It is important to emphasize that the phrase "open head injury" refers to the condition of the skull and not the brain. Broken bones or foreign objects forced through the skull can cut, tear, or bruise the brain tissue itself. If the skull is cracked, the blood and CSF that normally surround the brain and spinal cord can leak through the crack in the skull and into the surrounding tissues. If the forces are strong enough to cause an open head injury, the brain will most likely sustain an injury as well.

- A depressed skull fracture exists when the broken portion of the skull moves in toward the brain. In a compound skull fracture, the scalp is cut and the skull is fractured. A fracture at the base of the skull is called a basilar skull fracture.

- Trauma to the face is usually the result of blunt trauma, most commonly from fists and clubs, falls, and windshields, dashboards, and steering wheels in motor vehicle crashes. Penetrating trauma may result from gunshot wounds, stabbings, dog bites, human bites, or biting of the tongue. An increasing number of patients (adults and children) with facial trauma are victims of intimate-partner violence.

- An injury to the nose can result in significant bleeding and a possible airway obstruction. Injuries to the ear include abrasions, contusions, lacerations, avulsions, and hematomas, which are treated like any other soft tissue injury. Never put anything into the ear to control bleeding.

- A buildup of blood in the anterior chamber of the eye is called a hyphema, a sight-threatening injury. Unless contraindicated, elevate the patient's head to maintain low pressure within the eye.

- A blowout fracture refers to cracks or breaks in the facial bones that make up the orbit of the eye. Typical assessment findings and symptoms of a severe blowout fracture include recession of the eyeball within the orbit, numbness over the cheek, epistaxis on the same side as the impact, and an inability to move one eye upward. Paralysis of upward gaze occurs because muscles in the eye become entrapped in the fracture.

- Injuries to the midface are most often caused by blunt trauma from an assault or motor vehicle crash. Fractures involving multiple bones of the midface are often associated with significant bleeding into the nose or mouth. These patients will require constant airway monitoring and frequent suctioning to maintain an open airway.

- Injuries to the mandible are common and most often caused by blunt trauma from an assault or motor vehicle crash. The patient who has a mandible fracture or a combined fracture of the nose, maxilla, and mandible is at risk of an airway obstruction.

- An impaled object in the cheek may be removed if bleeding obstructs the airway. After removing an object from the cheek, apply direct pressure to the bleeding site by reaching inside the patient's mouth with gloved fingers. A patient with an impaled object in the check may be more comfortable sitting up, if there is no risk of spinal injury.

- A blunt or penetrating neck injury can rapidly become a life-threatening emergency because the neck houses many critical structures. Call for additional EMS resources immediately. A neck injury can be caused by a hanging, impact with a steering wheel, a knife or gunshot wound, strangulation, a sports injury, or a "clothesline" injury, in which a person runs into a stretched wire or cord that strikes the throat. The patient with a neck injury may also have an underlying spinal injury.

- A concussion is a traumatic brain injury that results in a temporary loss of function in some or all of the brain. A concussion occurs when the head strikes an object or is struck by an object. The injury may or may not cause a loss of consciousness. A headache, loss of appetite, vomiting, and pale skin are common soon after the injury.

- A cerebral contusion is a brain injury in which brain tissue is bruised and damaged in a local area. Bruising may occur at both the area of direct impact (coup) and on the side opposite the impact (contrecoup).

- An altered or decreasing mental status is the best indicator of a brain injury.
- Most spinal injuries occur to the cervical spine. The next most commonly injured areas are the thoracic spine and lumbar spine. A spinal column injury (bony injury) can occur with or without a spinal cord injury. A spinal cord injury can also occur with or without an injury to the spinal column. The spinal cord does not have to be severed for a loss of function to occur.
- An injury to the spinal cord may be complete or incomplete. A complete spinal cord injury occurs when the spinal cord is severed. The patient has no voluntary movement or sensation below the level of the injury. Both sides of the body are equally affected. Paraplegia is the loss of movement and sensation of the lower half of the body from the waist down. Paraplegia results from a spinal cord injury at the level of the thoracic or lumbar vertebrae. Quadriplegia (also called tetraplegia) is a loss of movement and sensation in both arms, both legs, and the parts of the body below the area of injury to the spinal cord. Quadriplegia results from a spinal cord injury at the level of the cervical vertebrae. With an incomplete spinal cord injury, some parts of the spinal cord remain intact. The patient has some function below the level of the injury. With this type of injury, there is a potential for recovery because function may be only temporarily lost.
- Manual stabilization of the head and neck is also called in-line stabilization. Manual stabilization of the head and neck helps prevent further injury to the spine.

▶ Tracking Your Progress

After reading this chapter, can you:	Page Reference	Objective Met?
• Describe the components, anatomy, and physiology of the nervous system?	525	☐
• Define the structure of the skeletal system as it relates to the nervous system?	527	☐
• Distinguish between head injury and brain injury?	528	☐
• Relate mechanism of injury to potential injuries of the head and spine?	528	☐
• Differentiate between closed and open head injuries?	528	☐
• Discuss types of skull fractures?	529	☐
• Describe the possible causes, signs, and symptoms of a head injury?	529	☐
• Describe the emergency care of the patient with a head injury?	530	☐
• Describe the anatomy and physiology of the structures of the face?	531	☐
• Relate mechanism of injury to potential injuries of the face?	532	☐
• Describe the signs and symptoms of an injury to the face?	533	☐
• Describe the emergency care of the patient with an injury to the face?	534	☐
• Describe the anatomy and physiology of the structures of the neck?	535	☐
• Relate mechanism of injury to potential injuries of the neck?	536	☐
• Describe the signs and symptoms of an injury to the neck?	537	☐
• Describe the emergency care of the patient with an injury to the neck?	537	☐

After reading this chapter, can you:

	Page Reference	Objective Met?
• Describe the possible causes, signs, and symptoms of a concussion?	538	☐
• Describe the possible causes, signs, and symptoms of a cerebral contusion?	538	☐
• Describe the emergency care of the patient with a possible brain injury?	538	☐
• Differentiate between a spinal cord injury and a spinal column injury?	539	☐
• State the signs and symptoms of a potential spine injury?	539	☐
• Describe the method of determining whether a responsive patient may have a spine injury?	541	☐
• Relate the airway emergency medical care techniques to the patient with a suspected spine injury?	541	☐
• Describe the emergency care of the patient with a possible spine injury?	543	☐
• Describe how to manually stabilize the cervical spine?	543	☐

Chapter Quiz

True/False

Decide whether each statement is true or false. In the space provided, write T for true or F for false.

_____ 1. An absence of sensation on one side of the body is the best indicator of a brain injury.

_____ 2. A fractured mandible is unlikely to affect the patient's ability to maintain her airway.

_____ 3. The patient with a neck injury may also have an underlying spinal injury.

_____ 4. The mandible is the most common fracture of the face.

_____ 5. A blowout fracture refers to cracks or breaks in the maxilla or mandible.

_____ 6. An increasing number of patients with facial trauma are victims of intimate-partner violence.

Multiple Choice

In the space provided, identify the letter of the choice that best completes each statement or answers each question.

_____ 7. You are assessing a patient who hit his head on the steering wheel. You note some clear drainage coming from his left ear. What should you do next?
    a. Place a loose sterile dressing over the ear.
    b. Apply direct pressure to the ear to stop the flow.
    c. Place a cotton ball or other absorbent dressing in the ear.
    d. Have the patient turn his head to the left to prevent the drainage from coming out his left ear.

_____ 8. Which of the following statements regarding facial trauma is true?
    a. Patients with facial trauma should not be given oxygen.
    b. Never suction the mouth of a patient with facial trauma.
    c. Patients with suspected facial bone fractures should have an oral airway inserted to protect the airway.
    d. Injuries to the face may complicate airway management due to increased salivation and decreased movement.

Sentence Completion

In the blanks provided, write the words that best complete each sentence.

9. The _____ is the outermost part of the head that contains tissue, hair follicles, sweat glands, oil glands, and a rich supply of blood vessels.

10. The _____ nervous system is made up of the brain and spinal cord.

11. The _____ nervous system consists of all nervous tissue found outside the brain and spinal cord.

Short Answer

Answer each question in the space provided.

12. List the three areas of the spine that are most commonly injured.
    1.
    2.
    3.

13. Briefly explain the difference between paraplegia and quadriplegia.

14. What is a concussion?

Answer Section

True/False

1. False

   An altered or decreasing mental status is the best indicator of a brain injury.

   Objective: Describe the emergency care of the patient with a possible brain injury.

2. False

   Remember that the tongue is attached by muscles to the mandible. Therefore, a fractured mandible can affect the patient's ability to maintain her airway. This is particularly true when the patient is placed in a supine position and the tongue falls posteriorly, blocking the airway.

   Objective: Describe the signs and symptoms of an injury to the face.

3. True

   The patient with a neck injury may also have an underlying spinal injury.

   Objective: Relate mechanism of injury to potential injuries of the neck.

4. False

   After nasal fractures, the mandible is the next most common fracture of the face.

   Objective: Describe the signs and symptoms of an injury to the face.

5. False

   A blowout fracture refers to cracks or breaks in the facial bones that make up the orbit of the eye. Significant blunt trauma to the eye, such as getting hit by a bat, baseball, hockey stick, or puck or getting kicked in the face, may not injure the eye itself but may fracture an orbital bone. The sudden rise in pressure generated by the trauma is transmitted to the orbit, where the thinnest portion of the orbit ruptures.

   Objective: Relate mechanism of injury to potential injuries of the face.

6. True

   An increasing number of patients (adults and children) with facial trauma are victims of intimate-partner violence. Be particularly observant when assessing the scene involving a patient with facial trauma. Be alert for subtle signs of intimate-partner violence throughout your patient assessment and when obtaining the patient's medical history.

   Objective: Relate mechanism of injury to potential injuries of the face.

Multiple Choice

7. a

   If fluid is seen in the ear, do not attempt to stop the flow. Cover the ear with a loose, sterile dressing.

   Objective: Describe the emergency care of the patient with a head injury.

8. d

   Facial fractures may cause an increase in the production of saliva, and due to the fracture the ability to swallow the saliva becomes impaired. Constant attention to airway status must be maintained. Anticipate the need for frequent suctioning. An oral airway may be inserted if the patient is unconscious and does not have a gag reflex; however, the insertion of an oral airway does not replace the need to constantly reevaluate the patient's airway status.

   Objective: Describe the emergency care of the patient with an injury to the face.

Sentence Completion

9. The **scalp** is the outermost part of the head that contains tissue, hair follicles, sweat glands, oil glands, and a rich supply of blood vessels.

   Objective: Describe the components, anatomy, and physiology of the nervous system.

10. The **central** nervous system is made up of the brain and spinal cord.

    Objective: Describe the components, anatomy, and physiology of the nervous system.

11. The **peripheral** nervous system consists of all nervous tissue found outside the brain and spinal cord.

    Objective: Describe the components, anatomy, and physiology of the nervous system.

Short Answer

12. The three most commonly injured areas of the spine are the following:

    1. Cervical (neck) spine—most commonly injured

    2. Thoracic (chest) spine

    3. Lumbar (low-back) spine

    Objective: Relate mechanism of injury to potential injuries of the head and spine.

13. Paraplegia is loss of movement and sensation of the lower half of the body from the waist down. Quadriplegia (also called tetraplegia) is loss of movement and sensation in both arms, both legs, and the parts of the body below an area of injury to the spinal cord.

    Objective: State the signs and symptoms of a potential spine injury.

14. A concussion is a traumatic brain injury that results in a temporary loss of function in some or all of the brain.

    Objective: Describe the possible causes, signs, and symptoms of a concussion.

CHAPTER
32
Special Considerations in Trauma

READING ASSIGNMENT ▶ Read Chapter 32, pages 546 to 560 in your textbook.

Sum It Up

- Trauma is the leading cause of death in pregnant patients and the leading cause of death in women of childbearing age. Although pregnant patients can sustain all types of trauma, motor vehicle crashes are the most frequent cause of injury, followed by falls and intimate-partner violence. Direct or indirect trauma to a pregnant uterus can cause injury to the uterine muscle. This can cause the release of chemicals that cause uterine contractions, perhaps inducing premature labor. The effects of trauma on the fetus depend on the length of the pregnancy (the age of the fetus), the type and severity of the trauma, and the severity of blood flow and oxygen disruption to the uterus.
- The frequency of falls during pregnancy becomes more common after the 20th week of pregnancy. A woman's center of gravity shifts as the size of her abdomen increases during pregnancy and her pelvic ligaments loosen. As a result, a pregnant patient must readjust her body alignment and balance, and this increases her risk for falls and injury.
- Anatomic changes occur during pregnancy that affect nearly every organ system. In the respiratory system, the diaphragm becomes elevated and the mother's resting respiratory rate increases because of the enlarging uterus. The mother's blood volume circulates through the uterus every 8 to 11 minutes at term. As a result, the uterus can be a source of significant blood loss if injured. After the 12th week of pregnancy, the uterus begins to rise out of the pelvis and becomes susceptible to injury. As the uterus increases in size, the mother's abdominal organs are displaced superiorly. This displacement increases the likelihood of uterine and fetal injury.
- Early in the pregnancy, the mother's body begins to produce more blood to carry oxygen and nutrients to the fetus, resulting in an increased plasma volume and an increased volume of red blood cells. Her heart rate gradually increases by as much as 10 to 15 beats/min during pregnancy. During the first 6 months of pregnancy, the mother's systolic blood pressure may drop by 5 to 10 mm Hg. Her diastolic blood pressure may drop by 10 to 15 mm Hg. During the last 3 months of pregnancy, her blood pressure gradually returns to near normal. The changes in vital signs that typically occur during pregnancy can make it difficult to detect shock, particularly in late pregnancy.

- When shock occurs, the mother's blood pressure is preserved by the shunting of blood from nonvital organs, such as the uterus, to vital organs. Constriction of the uterine arteries decreases perfusion to the uterus, potentially compromising the fetus to save the mother. The fetus will often show signs of distress before any change in maternal vital signs. The healthy pregnant patient can lose 30% to 35% of her blood volume with no change in vital signs.
- A woman who is 20 weeks pregnant or more should be positioned on her left side. Positioning the patient on her left side shifts the weight of her uterus off the abdominal vessels. If the patient is immobilized on a backboard, tilt the board slightly to the left by placing a rolled towel, small pillow, blanket, or other padding under the right side of the board.
- Fetal death may occur because of death of the mother, separation of the placenta, maternal shock, uterine rupture, or a fetal head injury. Of these, maternal death is the number-one cause of fetal death. The second most common cause of fetal death is abruptio placentae. Abruptio placentae (also called placental abruption) occurs when a normally implanted placenta separates prematurely from the wall of the uterus (endometrium) during the last trimester of pregnancy. Partial separation may allow time for treatment of the mother and fetus. Separation of more than 50% of the placental surface often results in death of the fetus.
- A ruptured uterus is the actual tearing of the uterus. Uterine rupture can occur when the patient has been in strong labor for a long period; this is the most common cause. It can also occur when the patient has sustained abdominal trauma, such as a severe fall or a sudden stop in a motor vehicle collision.
- Correct seat belt use can significantly reduce both maternal and fetal injury following motor vehicle crashes. Injuries can occur if restraints are improperly worn. In a motor vehicle crash, uterine rupture can occur if a lap belt is worn too high over the pregnant uterus. Wearing a lap belt without a shoulder strap can result in compression of the uterus, with possible uterine rupture or abruptio placentae.
- Penetrating trauma in pregnancy is usually the result of gunshot or knife wounds, of which gunshot wounds are more common. Although the maternal outcome of penetrating trauma in pregnancy is usually favorable, the fetal death rate is high.
- Cardiac arrest in the pregnant trauma patient poses some unique challenges. Because the pregnant patient's diaphragm is elevated during pregnancy, it may be necessary to ventilate using less volume. Chest compressions should be performed higher on the sternum, slightly above the center of the sternum. If the patient is 20 weeks pregnant or more, it will be necessary to perform chest compressions with the patient on a backboard tilted 15 to 30 degrees to the left to offset the problems associated with supine hypotension.
- In situations involving major trauma, call for additional EMS personnel as soon as possible. Generally, the pregnant trauma patient who has a heart rate of more than 110 beats/min, chest or abdominal pain, or loss of consciousness or who is in her third trimester of pregnancy should be transported to a trauma center. Follow your local protocols.
- Injuries are the leading cause of death in infants and children. Blunt trauma is the most common mechanism of serious injury in the pediatric patient. The injury pattern seen in a child may be different from that seen in an adult. For example, if an adult is about to be struck by an oncoming vehicle, she will typically turn away from the vehicle. This results in injuries to the side or back of the body. In contrast, a child will usually face an oncoming vehicle, resulting in injuries to the front of the body.
- Falls are a common cause of injury in infants and children. Infants and young children have large heads in comparison to their body size, making them more

prone to falls. Note the distance of the fall, the surface on which the child landed, and the body area(s) struck. Any fall more than 10 feet or more than two to three times the child's height should be considered serious.

- Shaken baby syndrome is a group of signs and symptoms resulting from violent shaking or shaking and impacting of the head of an infant or small child. Shaken baby syndrome occurs when an infant or child is shaken by the arms, legs, or shoulders with enough force to cause the baby's brain to bounce against the skull.

- The younger the patient, the softer and more flexible the ribs are. Therefore, rib fractures are less common in children than in adults. However, the force of the injury can be transferred to the internal organs of the chest, resulting in major damage.

- Bruising of the lung (pulmonary contusion) is one of the most frequently observed chest injuries in children. This injury is potentially life-threatening.

- Abdominal trauma is the most common cause of unrecognized fatal injury in children. The abdominal organs of an infant or child are prone to injury because the organs are large and the abdominal wall is thin. As a result, the organs are closer to the surface of the abdomen and less protected.

- Extremity trauma is common in children. Fractures of both thighs can cause a major blood loss, resulting in shock. Extremity injuries in children are managed in the same way as are those in adults.

- In an injured child, delayed capillary refill time (if the child is 6 years of age or younger), cool distal extremities, and decreases in peripheral versus central pulse quality are generally more reliable signs of shock than blood pressure. This is because a healthy child can maintain a normal blood pressure until he has lost 25% to 30% of his total blood volume.

- Falls are the most common cause of injury in older adults, followed by motor vehicle crashes, pedestrian-vehicle incidents, and assaults. Most falls involving older adults occur at home and are low-level falls (falls from a standing height).

- Injuries sustained by older adults in MVCs are similar to those of younger patients except that adults over 65 years of age have an increased incidence of sternal fractures from seatbelts.

- Any older adult who has experienced a burn injury should be triaged to a burn center, if available in your area.

- As the brain shrinks with age, there is a higher risk of cerebral bleeding following head trauma. Loss of strength, sensory impairment, and medical illnesses increase the risk of falls. Skeletal changes cause curvature of the upper spine that may require padding when stabilizing the spine.

- In some situations, a "normal" blood pressure in an older adult who is usually hypertensive may actually represent hypotension.

- Because the older adult's ability to regulate body heat production and heat loss is altered, it is important to minimize the areas of the body exposed, keeping the patient covered as much as possible to maintain warmth.

- Bear in mind that an older adult's pulse may be irregular and that a slower-than-expected heart rate may be caused by prescribed cardiac medications.

- Generally, it is a good idea to do a head-to-toe examination of any older adult who has been injured, including repeated vital sign assessments. A thorough examination is important because even minor injuries in an older adult can be significant. Carefully assess the patient using the DCAP-BTLS memory aid to ensure injuries are not missed.

- The musculoskeletal system is the most commonly injured organ system in older adult trauma patients. Nontraditional immobilization techniques and extra padding may be necessary to adapt to musculoskeletal changes, such as curvature of the upper spine.

- Cognition refers to mental functions including memory, learning, awareness, reasoning, judgment, and the ability to think, plan, form and comprehend speech, process information, and understand and solve problems. A cognitive impairment is a change in a person's mental functioning caused by an injury or a disease process. Individuals who are cognitively impaired may have a condition such as Alzheimer's disease, vascular dementia, Down syndrome, an autistic disorder, or a traumatic brain injury or may have a history of stroke. Family members and caregivers often are important resources that should be tapped when you are called to provide care to a cognitively impaired patient.

▶ Tracking Your Progress

After reading this chapter, can you:	Page Reference	Objective Met?
• Discuss mechanisms of injury associated with trauma in pregnancy?	547	☐
• Discuss the unique anatomy, physiology, and pathophysiology considerations of the pregnant trauma patient?	548	☐
• Discuss the assessment findings associated with trauma in the pregnant patient?	550	☐
• Describe the emergency care of the pregnant trauma patient?	551	☐
• Discuss mechanisms of injury associated with pediatric trauma?	551	☐
• Discuss the unique anatomy, physiology, and pathophysiology considerations of the pediatric trauma patient?	552	☐
• Discuss the assessment findings associated with trauma in infants and children?	553	☐
• Describe the emergency care of the pediatric trauma patient?	554	☐
• Discuss mechanisms of injury associated with trauma in older adults?	555	☐
• Discuss the unique anatomy, physiology, and pathophysiology considerations of the older adult trauma patient?	555	☐
• Discuss the assessment findings associated with trauma in older adults?	556	☐
• Describe the emergency care of the older adult trauma patient?	556	☐
• Define cognitive impairment and discuss challenges in assessing the cognitively impaired patient?	557	☐

Chapter Quiz

True/False

Decide whether each statement is true or false. In the space provided, write T for true or F for false.

_____ **1.** Use of the AVPU scale to assess level of consciousness is unreliable in the pregnant trauma patient.

_____ **2.** A laceration of the face or scalp can lead to major blood loss in a child.

_____ **3.** Any older adult who has experienced a burn injury should be triaged to a burn center, if available in your area.

_____ **4.** Rib fractures are less common in children than in adults.

Multiple Choice

In the space provided, identify the letter of the choice that best completes each statement or answers each question.

_____ 5. Which of the following conditions is most likely to be associated with cognitive impairment?

    a. Hemophilia
    b. Depression
    c. Down syndrome
    d. Sickle cell disease

Questions 6–8 pertain to the following scenario:

Your rescue crew is dispatched to a motor vehicle collision on a local highway. Information at the time of dispatch is that there are three cars involved and the accident "appears serious."

_____ 6. Your first action when arriving on the scene should be to

    a. perform a scene size-up.
    b. begin immediate extrication of all trapped patients.
    c. perform a primary survey on all critical patients.
    d. perform a rapid physical examination on all unconscious patients.

_____ 7. You are assigned to assess and treat a 32-year-old woman who was the driver of one of the vehicles involved. She tells you she was not wearing her seat belt and was traveling about 40 miles per hour when another car pulled out in front of her. She is alert and answering all questions appropriately. She is 8½ months pregnant and is in severe distress. Which of the following findings would be consistent with an abruptio placenta?

    a. Elevated blood pressure, pedal edema, and severe headache
    b. Nausea, vomiting, elevated blood pressure, and subsequent seizures
    c. Painless, bright-red bloody discharge from the vagina and signs of shock
    d. Severe abdominal pain, dark red bloody discharge from the vagina, and signs of shock

_____ 8. Appropriate interventions for this patient would be

    a. positioning of the patient sitting upright, high-flow oxygen, and rapid transport
    b. full spinal stabilization with the backboard tilted to the left, high-flow oxygen, and rapid transport
    c. positioning of the patient on her left side, high-flow oxygen, and slow transport without lights or siren
    d. full spinal stabilization with the head of the backboard elevated, high-flow oxygen, and transport

Short Answer

Answer each question in the space provided.

9. Explain why a woman in late pregnancy should not lie flat on her back.

10. What is the leading cause of death in infants and children?

11. Why is the pregnant trauma patient at increased risk of vomiting and aspiration?

12. What is shaken baby syndrome?

13. A 25-year-old female stab wound victim who is 8 months pregnant has suffered a cardiac arrest. Describe the modifications in cardiopulmonary resuscitation procedures that should be used when providing emergency care for this patient.

14. Why are children prone to head injuries?

15. List four possible signs of elder abuse.
   1.
   2.
   3.
   4.

Answer Section

True/False

1. False

Use of the AVPU scale to assess level of consciousness may be unreliable in some older adults (such as those with Alzheimer's disease) and other cognitively impaired patients.

Objective: Discuss the assessment findings associated with trauma in the pregnant patient.

2. True

The blood vessels of the face and scalp bleed easily. In a child, even a small wound can lead to major blood loss.

Objective: Discuss the unique anatomy, physiology, and pathophysiology considerations of the pediatric trauma patient.

3. True

Although the frequency of burn injuries is lower in older adults than in younger patients, the death rate from burn injuries in older adults is high. Any older adult who has experienced a burn injury should be triaged to a burn center, if available in your area.

Objective: Discuss mechanisms of injury associated with trauma in older adults.

4. True

The younger the patient, the softer and more flexible the ribs are. Therefore, rib fractures are less common in children than in adults. However, the force of the injury can be transferred to the internal organs of the chest, resulting in major damage. The presence of a rib fracture in a child suggests that major force caused the injury.

Objective: Discuss the unique anatomy, physiology, and pathophysiology considerations of the pediatric trauma patient.

Multiple Choice

5. c

A cognitive impairment is a change in a person's mental functioning caused by an injury or a disease process. A cognitive impairment affects a person's ability to process, plan, reason, learn, understand, and remember information. Individuals who are cognitively impaired may have a condition such as Alzheimer's disease, vascular dementia, Down's syndrome, an autistic disorder, or a traumatic brain injury or may have a history of stroke.

Objective: Define cognitive impairment and discuss challenges in assessing the cognitively impaired patient.

6. a

Your initial responsibility is to assess the scene. Your scene size-up should address the number of patients, the mechanism of injury, the need for additional resources, safety (for you, your crew, the patients, and bystanders), and standard precautions. After the size-up, you can begin gaining access to and evaluating patients.

Objective: Determine if the scene is safe to enter.

7. d

Abruptio placenta may occur from trauma, high blood pressure, or multiple pregnancies. An abruptio placenta is the premature separation of the placenta from the uterine wall during the last trimester of pregnancy. Patients with this condition have severe abdominal pain. Bleeding may be present or absent depending on the location of the tear. Patients may also complain of decreased or absent fetal movement. Severe hypoxia slows the activity of the fetus.

Objective: Discuss the unique anatomy, physiology, and pathophysiology considerations of the pregnant trauma patient.

8. b

Since your patient has been involved in a motor vehicle collision, spinal stabilization is indicated. You must ensure that the fetus does not compress the blood vessels of the abdomen. To prevent this compression, tilt the backboard to the left. Provide high-flow oxygen and transport rapidly to the closest appropriate facility.

Objective: Describe the emergency care of the pregnant trauma patient.

Short Answer

9. A woman who is 20 weeks pregnant or more should be positioned on her left side. Positioning the patient on her left side shifts the weight of her uterus off the abdominal vessels. If the patient is immobilized on a backboard, tilt the board slightly to the left by placing a rolled towel, small pillow, blanket, or other padding under the right side of the board. Doing so will shift the weight of the patient's uterus and decrease the pressure on the abdominal blood vessels.

Objective: Discuss the unique anatomy, physiology, and pathophysiology considerations of the pregnant trauma patient.

10. Injuries are the leading cause of death in infants and children. Blunt trauma is the most common mechanism of serious injury in the pediatric patient.

Objective: Discuss mechanisms of injury associated with pediatric trauma.

11. During pregnancy, the speed with which food and liquids move through the gastrointestinal tract decreases, increasing the risk of vomiting and aspiration after trauma.

Objective: Discuss the unique anatomy, physiology, and pathophysiology considerations of the pregnant trauma patient.

12. Shaken baby syndrome is a severe form of head injury. It occurs when an infant or child is shaken by the arms, legs, or shoulders with enough force to cause the baby's brain to bounce against her skull. Just 2 to 3 seconds of shaking can cause bruising, swelling, and bleeding in and around the brain. It can lead to severe brain damage or death.

Objective: Discuss mechanisms of injury associated with pediatric trauma.

13. Cardiac arrest in the pregnant trauma patient poses some unique challenges. Because the pregnant patient's diaphragm is elevated during pregnancy, it may be necessary to ventilate using less volume. Chest compressions should be performed higher on the sternum, slightly above the center of the sternum. If the patient is 20 weeks pregnant or more, it will be necessary to perform chest compressions with the patient on a backboard tilted 15 to 30 degrees to the left to offset the problems associated with supine hypotension.

Objective: Describe the emergency care of the pregnant trauma patient.

14. Children are prone to head injuries because their heads are large and heavy compared with their body size. The younger the child, the softer and thinner the skull is. The force of injury is more likely to be transferred to the underlying brain instead of fracturing the skull. Striking the head jars the brain. The brain bounces back and forth, causing multiple bruised and injured areas.

Objective: Discuss the unique anatomy, physiology, and pathophysiology considerations of the pediatric trauma patient.

15. Possible signs of elder abuse include:

- Bruises, black eyes, welts, lacerations, rope marks
- Bone fractures, skull fractures
- Open wounds, cuts, punctures, untreated injuries in various stages of healing
- Older adult's report of being hit, slapped, kicked, or mistreated
- Physical signs of being subjected to punishment
- Signs of being restrained
- Older adult's sudden change in behavior Caregiver's refusal to allow visitors to see an older adult alone

Objective: Discuss mechanisms of injury associated with trauma in older adults.

CHAPTER

33 Environmental Emergencies

READING ASSIGNMENT Read Chapter 33, pages 561 to 588 in your textbook.

Sum It Up

- The skin plays a very important role in temperature regulation. Cold and warmth sensors (receptors) in the skin detect changes in temperature. These receptors relay the information to the hypothalamus. The hypothalamus (located in the brain) functions as the body's thermostat. It coordinates the body's response to temperature.
- The body loses heat to the environment in five ways:
  1. *Radiation:* Radiation is the transfer of heat from the surface of one object to the surface of another without contact between the two objects. When the temperature of the body is more than the temperature of the surroundings, the body will lose heat.
  2. *Convection:* Convection is the transfer of heat by the movement of air current. Wind speed affects heat loss by convection (wind-chill factor).
  3. *Conduction:* Conduction is the transfer of heat between objects that are in direct contact. Heat flows from warmer areas to cooler ones.
  4. *Evaporation:* Evaporation is a loss of heat by vaporization of moisture on the body surface. The body will lose heat by evaporation if the skin temperature is higher than the temperature of the surroundings.
  5. *Respiration:* The body loses heat through breathing. With normal breathing, the body continuously loses a relatively small amount of heat through the evaporation of moisture.
- Hypothermia is a core body temperature of less than 95°F (35°C). This condition results when the body loses more heat than it gains or produces.
  - A rectal temperature gives the most accurate measure of core temperature. However, obtaining a rectal temperature in the field often raises issues of patient sensitivity and welfare, such as exposure to cold by removal of clothing.
  - Your main concern in providing care should be to remove the patient from the environment. Use trained rescuers for this purpose when necessary. Perform a primary survey, keeping in mind that you need to move the patient to a warm location as quickly and as safely as possible. Remove any cold or wet clothing. Protect the patient from the environment. Assess the patient's

mental status, airway, breathing, and circulation. Keep in mind that mental status decreases as the patient's body temperature drops.

—You may need to rewarm the patient. The two main types of rewarming are passive and active.

- Passive rewarming is the warming of a patient with minimal or no use of heat sources other than the patient's own heat production. Passive rewarming methods include placing the patient in a warm environment, applying warm clothing and blankets, and preventing drafts.
- Active rewarming should be used only if sustained warmth can be ensured. Active rewarming involves adding heat directly to the surface of the patient's body. Warm blankets, heat packs, and/or hot-water bottles may be used, depending on how severe the hypothermia is.

- Local cold injury (also called frostbite) involves tissue damage to a specific area of the body. It occurs when a body part, such as the nose, ears, cheeks, chin, hands, or feet, is exposed to prolonged or intense cold. When the body is exposed to cold, blood is forced away from the extremities to the body's core. A local cold injury may be early (superficial frostbite) or late (deep frostbite).

- When the body gains or produces more heat than it loses, hyperthermia (a high core body temperature) results. The three main types of heat emergencies are heat cramps, heat exhaustion, and heat stroke.

  1. Heat cramps usually affect people who sweat a lot during strenuous activity in a warm environment. Water and electrolytes are lost from the body during sweating. This loss leads to dehydration and causes painful muscle spasms.
  2. Heat exhaustion is also a result of too much heat and dehydration. A patient with heat exhaustion usually sweats heavily. The body temperature is usually normal or slightly elevated. Severe heat exhaustion often requires IV fluids. Heat exhaustion may progress to heat stroke if it is not treated.
  3. Heat stroke is the most severe form of heat-related illness. It occurs when the body can no longer regulate its temperature. Most patients have hot, flushed skin and do not sweat. Individuals who wear heavy uniforms and perform strenuous activity for long periods in a hot environment are at risk for heat stroke.

- The first step in the emergency care of a patient suffering from a heat-related illness is to remove him from the hot environment. Move the patient to a cool (air-conditioned) location and follow treatment guidelines recommended for the patient's degree of heat-related illness.

- When providing emergency care for a drowning victim, ensure the safety of the rescue personnel. Suspect a possible spine injury if a diving accident is involved or unknown.

- Any breathless, pulseless patient who has been submerged in cold water should be resuscitated.

- Signs and symptoms of bites and stings typically include a history of a bite (spider, snake) or sting (insect, scorpion, marine animal), pain, redness, swelling, weakness, dizziness, chills, fever, nausea, and vomiting. Bite marks may be present.

- If a stinger is present, remove it by scraping the stinger out with the edge of card. Avoid using tweezers or forceps as these can squeeze venom from the venom sac into the wound.

- When caring for a victim of a bite or sting, watch closely for development of signs and symptoms of an allergic reaction; treat as needed.

▶ Tracking Your Progress

After reading this chapter, can you:	Page Reference	Objective Met?
• Describe the various ways that the body loses heat?	563	☐
• List the signs and symptoms of exposure to cold?	564	☐
• Explain the steps in providing emergency medical care to a patient exposed to cold?	567	☐
• List the signs and symptoms of exposure to heat?	570	☐
• Explain the steps in providing emergency care to a patient exposed to heat?	571	☐
• Recognize the signs and symptoms of water-related emergencies?	572	☐
• Describe the complications of drowning?	573	☐
• Discuss the emergency medical care of bites and stings?	577	☐

Chapter Quiz

Multiple Choice

In the space provided, identify the letter of the choice that best completes each statement or answers each question.

Questions 1–2 pertain to the following scenario:

Your crew has been called to a local park for a 65-year-old woman complaining of weakness and dizziness. It is a hot, humid summer day. You arrive to find the patient sitting in the sun on a park bench. Her skin condition is cool, pale, and moist. She greets you as you approach and is in a moderate level of distress.

_____ 1. Which of the following should you do first?
   a. Assess baseline vital signs.
   b. Perform a rapid trauma assessment.
   c. Assist the patient to the back of your air-conditioned ambulance.
   d. Begin cooling the patient with ice packs to the groin, armpits, and neck area.

_____ 2. This patient is responsive and does not complain of nausea. Which of the following regarding oral intake is correct?
   a. You may allow the patient to drink water.
   b. You may allow the patient to drink iced tea.
   c. You may allow the patient to eat but not drink.
   d. You may allow the patient to drink a cold beer.

_____ 3. Your crew is called to a construction site for a 29-year-old woman who has suffered a snakebite. She is complaining of weakness and nausea from a bite to the left hand that occurred about 1 hour ago. You should
   a. apply a tourniquet to the affected limb.
   b. apply cold packs to slow the absorption of the venom.
   c. provide oxygen by nonrebreather mask and position the affected extremity slightly below the level of the patient's heart.
   d. make an incision at the site of the bite and withdraw the venom using a syringe.

_____ 4. Which of the following are signs and symptoms associated with moderate hypothermia?
   a. Cardiopulmonary arrest
   b. Shivering gradually replaced by muscular rigidity, decreasing pulse and respirations, decreasing level of consciousness
   c. Low to absent blood pressure, muscular rigidity, slow or absent breathing, slowly responding pupils
   d. Shivering, increased pulse and respiratory rates, difficulty in speech and movement, confusion, poor judgment

_____ **5.** Which of the following is an example of a passive-warming method for cold-exposure patients?
   a. Placing the patient in a drafty atmosphere
   b. Placing the patient in a warm environment
   c. Having the patient do calisthenics (such as jumping jacks)
   d. Placing warming pads in the patient's groin, armpits, and neck areas

_____ **6.** Which of the following is appropriate management of a mildly hypothermic patient?
   a. Rub or massage cold extremities to increase distal perfusion.
   b. Whenever possible, transport the patient in the prone position.
   c. Cover the patient's head with a blanket, but leave the face exposed.
   d. Encourage the patient to drink coffee or hot tea if the patient is conscious and has an intact gag reflex.

Short Answer

Answer each question in the space provided.

7. List five factors that influence a drowning victim's chances for survival.
   1.
   2.
   3.
   4.
   5.

8. Describe how to monitor swelling in a stung or bitten extremity.

9. You are at the scene of a drowning incident. If observed, what circumstances would lead you to suspect a neck injury and the need for spinal stabilization?

10. List five signs or symptoms of a black widow spider bite.
   1.
   2.
   3.
   4.
   5.

Answer Section

Multiple Choice

1. c

Before obtaining your SAMPLE history and focused physical exam, you must prevent further injury to the patient. All other assessments and interventions should be conducted in an air-conditioned environment.

Objective: Explain the steps in providing emergency care to a patient exposed to heat.

2. a

If allowed by local protocol and medical direction, this patient may take sips of water. If, however, the patient complains of nausea or has an altered mental status, you should not allow any oral intake. Do not allow a heat (or cold) emergency patient to drink any caffeinated or alcoholic beverage.

Objective: Explain the steps in providing emergency care to a patient exposed to heat.

3. c

Supportive care such as oxygen therapy is best for managing this patient. Be prepared for nausea and vomiting. Do not apply a constricting band or tourniquet. A constricting band is not the same as a tourniquet. A tourniquet completely stops the flow of blood (arterial and venous) to and from the extremity. A constricting band slows the return of blood from an extremity (venous blood) but permits arterial blood flow. If a tourniquet or constricting band was applied to the affected arm or leg before your arrival and pulses are present in the extremity, leave it in place until the victim is evaluated at the hospital. If a tourniquet or constricting band was applied and pulses are absent in the extremity, consult medical direction for instructions. Cold packs should not be applied to the skin of snakebite victims. Do not incise and suck at the bite site.

Objective: Discuss the emergency medical care of bites and stings.

4. b

This response lists some of the more classic signs and symptoms of moderate hypothermia. There are four main body responses (other than temperature) that may give you a good idea of the patient's changing condition: mental status, airway and breathing status, circulatory status, and motor function status. Mental status may progress (decline) from difficulty speaking to confusion and memory lapse to combativeness to unresponsiveness. Airway and breathing status may progress from increased respirations to slow and shallow respirations to apnea (absence of breathing). Circulation may progress from rapid heart rate to irregular heart rate and low blood pressure to slow or absent heart rate with low or absent blood pressure. Motor function may progress from lack of coordination to shivering to rigidity.

Objective: List the signs and symptoms of exposure to cold.

5. b

Heating the passenger's area of the ambulance and covering the patient with a blanket are examples of passive warming. Placing warming pads on the patient is an example of active warming. Consult medical direction and local protocol before initiating active-warming measures. Placing a patient in a drafty area would result in decreased temperature due to convection (the movement of the air). Having the patient exercise is absolutely contraindicated.

Objective: Explain the steps in providing emergency medical care to a patient exposed to cold.

6. c

A considerable amount of body heat is lost through radiant energy escaping from the head. Therefore, protecting against this form of heat loss is essential. Leave the patient's face uncovered so that you may continuously assess the patient's airway and breathing. Never rub or massage a cold emergency patient. Transporting the patient prone (on the stomach) decreases your ability to assess the airway properly. Do not allow any cold (or heat) emergency patient to drink any fluid that contains caffeine or alcohol.

Objective: Explain the steps in providing emergency medical care to a patient exposed to cold.

Short Answer

7. Factors that influence a drowning victim's chances for survival include:

    - Length of immersion or submersion
    - Duration of hypoxia
    - Ability to swim
    - Age of victim
    - Cleanliness of the water
    - Temperature of the water
    - Duration and degree of hypothermia
    - Preexisting medical conditions
    - Presence of drugs and/or alcohol
    - Presence of associated injuries (especially to the cervical spine and head)
    - Response to initial resuscitation efforts

    Objective: Describe the complications of drowning.

8. If swelling is present in an extremity, mark the outer edge of the swelling and the time with a pen or marker. This allows other healthcare professionals to monitor the swelling progression.

    Objective: Discuss the emergency medical care of bites and stings.

9. When you are at the scene of a drowning incident, you should suspect a neck injury (and begin appropriate spinal stabilization procedures):

    - When the mechanism of injury is unknown
    - When signs of facial trauma are present
    - When signs of drug or alcohol use are present
    - In incidents involving use of a water slide and swimming, boating, waterskiing, or diving accidents

    Objective: Recognize the signs and symptoms of water-related emergencies.

10. Signs and symptoms of a black widow spider bite include the following:

    - Vague history of sharp pinprick followed by dull, numbing pain
    - Tiny red marks at the point of entry of the venom
    - Swelling
    - Difficulty breathing
    - Severe pain beginning 15 to 60 minutes after the bite and increasing for 12 to 48 hours
    - Lower-extremity bite: localized pain followed by abdominal pain and rigidity
    - Upper-extremity bite: pain and rigidity in chest, back, and shoulders

    Objective: Discuss the emergency medical care of bites and stings.

34 Multisystem Trauma

READING ASSIGNMENT ▶ Read Chapter 34, pages 589 to 593 in your textbook.

Sum It Up

- An individual who has been subjected to significant forces that affect more than one area of the body at the same time is a victim of multisystem trauma (also called polytrauma). Multisystem trauma should be suspected in any patient subjected to significant external forces.

- Patients who experience multisystem trauma are at a greater risk of developing shock and have a high frequency of serious injury and death. Short scene times and rapid transport to the closest appropriate facility, such as a trauma center, are essential to help ensure a positive patient outcome. You must know your local trauma system capabilities in advance to determine the appropriate destination for the multisystem trauma patient.

- When performing a scene size-up and recognizing that the mechanism of injury probably resulted in multisystem trauma, call for advanced life support personnel right away. In some situations, air medical transport may be necessary. Assess and treat the patient using the principles of prehospital trauma care.

- Blast injuries are one mechanism of injury that can produce multisystem trauma. Blast injuries result from pressure waves generated by an explosion. Blast waves cause disruption of major blood vessels, rupture of major organs, and lethal cardiac disturbances when the victim is close to the blast. Blast winds and ground shock can collapse buildings and cause trauma.

- Blast injuries are divided into five categories: primary, secondary, tertiary, quaternary, and quinary injuries. A primary blast injury occurs from the blast wave impacting the body surface. A secondary blast injury occurs from projectiles, such as bomb fragments, flying debris, and materials attached to the explosive device. A tertiary blast injury is caused by an individual's flying through the air because of displacement from the blast wind. A quaternary blast injury is any other injury from the blast not categorized as a primary, secondary, or tertiary blast injury. A quinary blast injury results from absorption of toxic materials associated with the blast, which can include bacteria and radiation. A blast victim should be reassessed often and transported as soon as possible to the closest appropriate facility.

▶ Tracking Your Progress

After reading this chapter, can you:	Page Reference	Objective Met?
● Define multisystem trauma?	590	☐
● Discuss the principles of prehospital trauma care?	591	☐
● Define blast injury and the categories of blast injuries?	591	☐
● Discuss the types of injuries that may result from each category of blast injury?	591	☐

Chapter Quiz

True/False

Decide whether each statement is true or false. In the space provided, write T for true or F for false.

_____ 1. Patients who experience multisystem trauma are at greater risk of developing shock than patients who have an injury of only one body system.

_____ 2. Definitive care for the multisystem trauma patient can generally be provided in the field.

_____ 3. The closer the person is to the site of the blast, the greater the injury.

Multiple Choice

In the space provided, identify the letter of the choice that best completes each statement or answers each question.

_____ 4. A 45-year-old man was injured as a result of a blast. Your assessment reveals the presence of dyspnea and hemoptysis. You suspect injury to the

    a. ear.
    b. lung.
    c. liver.
    d. intestines.

_____ 5. Which of the following is true of a secondary blast injury?

    a. A secondary blast injury occurs from projectiles.
    b. A secondary blast injury occurs from the blast wave impacting the body surface.
    c. A secondary blast injury results from absorption of toxic materials associated with the blast.
    d. A secondary blast injury is caused by an individual's flying through the air because of displacement from the blast wind.

Answer Section

True/False

1. True

   Patients who experience multisystem trauma are at greater risk of developing shock and have a high frequency of serious injury and death.

   Objective: Define multisystem trauma.

2. False

   Definitive care for multisystem trauma may include surgery, which cannot be done in the field. Short scene times and rapid transport to the closest appropriate facility, such as a trauma center, are essential to help ensure a positive patient outcome.

   Objective: Discuss the principles of prehospital trauma care.

3. True

   The closer the person is to the site of the blast, the greater the injury.

   Objective: Discuss the types of injuries that may result from each category of blast injury.

Multiple Choice

4. b

   Injury to the lung is the cause of greatest serious injury and death following a primary blast. Suspect a lung injury in anyone complaining of dyspnea, cough, hemoptysis, or chest pain following a blast.

   Objective: Discuss the types of injuries that may result from each category of blast injury.

5. a

   A secondary blast injury occurs from projectiles, such as bomb fragments, flying debris, and materials attached to the explosive device (such as screws, nails, bolts, ball bearings, or other small metal objects attached to grenades or bombs), resulting in blunt and/or penetrating trauma.

   Objective: Discuss the types of injuries that may result from each category of blast injury.

Module 9

Special Patient Populations

▶ CHAPTER **35**

Obstetrics   247

▶ CHAPTER **36**

Neonatal Care   253

▶ CHAPTER **37**

Pediatrics   259

▶ CHAPTER **38**

Older Adults   266

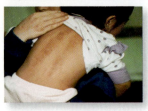

▶ CHAPTER **39**

Patients with Special Challenges   272

35 Obstetrics

READING ASSIGNMENT Read Chapter 35, pages 594 to 615 in your textbook.

Sum It Up

- The vagina is also called the birth canal. It is a muscular tube that serves as a passageway between the uterus and the outside of the body.
- The placenta is a specialized organ through which the fetus exchanges nourishment and waste products during pregnancy.
- The umbilical cord is the lifeline that connects the placenta to the fetus. It contains two arteries and one vein. The umbilical vein carries oxygen-rich blood to the fetus. The umbilical cord attaches to the umbilicus (navel) of the fetus.
- The amniotic sac is a membranous bag that surrounds the fetus inside the uterus. It contains fluid (amniotic fluid) that helps protect the fetus from injury.
- Pregnancy usually takes 40 weeks and is divided into three 90-day intervals called trimesters.
- The uterus and presenting part of the fetus descend into the pelvis in preparation for delivery about 10 days (average) before the onset of labor. This is called lightening. The presenting part is the part of the infant that comes out of the birth canal first. Premature labor (also called preterm labor) occurs when a woman has labor before her 37th week of pregnancy.
- Assessment of the pregnant patient is the same as that of other patients. However, because of the normal changes in vital signs that occur with pregnancy, the patient's vital signs may not be as diagnostically helpful as they are in a nonpregnant patient. Despite a significant amount of internal or external bleeding, young, healthy pregnant patients can maintain relatively normal vital signs for a significant time and then develop signs of shock very quickly.
- Labor is the process in which the uterus repeatedly contracts to push the fetus and placenta out of the mother's body. It begins with the first uterine muscle contraction and ends with delivery of the placenta. Delivery is the actual birth of the baby at the end of the second stage of labor. The first stage of labor begins with the first uterine contraction. This stage ends with a complete thinning and opening (dilation) of the cervix. The second stage of labor begins with the opening of the cervix and ends with delivery of the infant. During labor, the presenting part will eventually remain visible at the vaginal opening between contractions.

This is called crowning. The third stage of labor begins with delivery of the infant and ends with delivery of the placenta.

- Consider delivering at the scene in the following three circumstances:
  - —Delivery can be expected in a few minutes.
  - —No suitable transportation is available
  - —The hospital cannot be reached because of heavy traffic, bad weather, a natural disaster, or a similar situation.
- Because blood and amniotic fluid are expected during childbirth and may splash, you must use standard precautions, including gloves, mask, eye protection, and a gown.
- A premature infant is one born before the 37th week of gestation or one weighing less than 5.5 pounds (2.5 kilograms). Premature babies (also called preemies) can have many health challenges.
- A woman pregnant with twins (or more babies) usually goes into labor during or before her 37th week of pregnancy. The more babies a woman is expecting, the higher the risk of having a premature delivery.
- Request that ALS personnel be sent to the scene as soon as you recognize that you are dealing with a premature birth, a multiple gestation, or an abnormal presentation such as a breech presentation.
- A prolapsed cord is a serious emergency that endangers the life of the unborn fetus. A prolapsed cord occurs when a portion of the umbilical cord falls down below the presenting part of the fetus and presents through the birth canal before delivery of the head. When the umbilical cord is wrapped around the baby's neck, it is called a nuchal cord.

▶ Tracking Your Progress

After reading this chapter, can you:	Page Reference	Objective Met?
• Identify the following structures: uterus, vagina, fetus, placenta, umbilical cord, amniotic sac, and perineum?	597	☐
• Discuss the physiologic changes that normally occur during each trimester of pregnancy?	599	☐
• Discuss assessment of the pregnant patient?	600	☐
• Discuss obtaining a SAMPLE history from a pregnant patient?	600	☐
• Define the following terms: labor, delivery, presenting part, crowning, and Braxton-Hicks contractions?	601	☐
• Describe each of the stages of labor?	601	☐
• Differentiate between true and false labor contractions?	602	☐
• State indications of an imminent delivery?	604	☐
• Establish the relationship between standard precautions and childbirth?	604	☐
• Identify and explain the use of the contents of an obstetrics kit?	605	☐
• State the steps in the predelivery preparation of the mother?	605	☐
• State the steps in assisting in a delivery?	605	☐
• Describe care of the baby as the head appears?	606	☐

	Page Reference	Objective Met?
After reading this chapter, can you:		
• Describe how and when to cut the umbilical cord?	608	☐
• Discuss the steps in the delivery of the placenta?	608	☐
• List the steps in the emergency medical care of the mother after delivery?	609	☐
• Explain the purpose of uterine massage and describe how to perform this procedure?	609	☐
• Discuss the emergency medical care for a premature birth, multiple gestation, breech presentation, and prolapsed cord?	610	☐

Chapter Quiz

True/False

Decide whether each statement is true or false. In the space provided, write T for true or F for false.

_____ 1. While assisting with a delivery, you observe the umbilical cord wrapped around the baby's neck. Attempts to slide the cord over the baby's head or shoulder are unsuccessful. You should now place two umbilical clamps or ties on the cord approximately 12 inches apart and then cut the cord between the two clamps.

_____ 2. The ovaries are responsible for receiving and transporting the egg to the uterus.

Multiple Choice

In the space provided, identify the letter of the choice that best completes each statement or answers each question.

_____ 3. In a normal pregnancy, the egg will travel to the uterus through the
   a. cervix.
   b. vagina.
   c. urethra.
   d. fallopian tubes.

_____ 4. During delivery, especially very rapid deliveries, the tissue between the mother's anus and vagina may tear. This area is called the
   a. cervix.
   b. colon.
   c. perineum.
   d. labia majora.

_____ 5. The _____ of the female reproductive system produce(s) the hormones estrogen and progesterone and releases an egg once a month.
   a. ovaries
   b. fallopian tubes
   c. uterus
   d. cervix

_____ 6. You are called for a 26-year-old pregnant patient who states her water has broken. She is 9 months pregnant with her fourth child. On examination, you note that a loop of the umbilical cord is protruding from the vaginal opening. In addition to providing high-flow oxygen therapy and arranging for rapid transport, you should
   a. gently push the cord back into the birth canal and position the patient on her left side.
   b. position the patient in a knee-chest position, clamp and cut the cord, and prepare for delivery.
   c. position the patient in a knee-chest position, gently push the fetus way from the cord, and keep the cord moist.
   d. gently pull on the cord to ease delivery of the infant and transport with the patient on her back with the head slightly elevated.

_____ 7. In a normal pregnancy, the fertilized egg develops in the
  a. birth canal.
  b. uterus.
  c. fallopian tube.
  d. perineum.

_____ 8. Another term for the shedding of the uterine lining is
  a. menopause.
  b. menstruation.
  c. placental delivery.
  d. the first stage of labor.

_____ 9. Your crew is called to the home of a 32-year-old woman in labor. You arrive to find your patient lying in bed. She is alert and oriented to person, place, time, and event, and she is complaining of contractions. The patient informs you that she has been having contractions all morning, but they have increased in intensity over the last hour. Which of the following would suggest that delivery may be imminent?
  a. The patient has been urinating frequently.
  b. The patient feels like she needs to have a bowel movement.
  c. The patient feels weak and dizzy when lying flat on her back.
  d. The patient has been experiencing contractions that last about 30 seconds and are about 10 minutes apart.

Sentence Completion

In the blanks provided, write the words that best complete each sentence.

10. A breech birth occurs when the baby's _____ or _____ come out of the uterus first.

11. Preterm labor is labor that begins before the _____ week of gestation.

Short Answer

Answer each question in the space provided.

12. List three functions of the placenta.
  1.
  2.
  3.

13. An infant's head is crowning. You see that the bag of waters has not broken. What should you do now?

14. List the contents of an OB kit and explain the use of each item.

Answer Section

True/False

1. False

   If the cord is around the neck, gently loosen the cord and try to slip it over the baby's shoulder or head. If the umbilical cord is wrapped tightly around the baby's neck and cannot be loosened or is wrapped around the neck more than once, the cord must be removed. To do this, place two umbilical clamps or ties on the cord about 3 inches apart. Carefully cut the cord between the two clamps. Remove the cord from the baby's neck.

   Objective: Describe how and when to cut the umbilical cord.

2. False

   The ovaries are paired, almond-shaped organs located on either side of the uterus. The ovaries perform two main functions: producing eggs and secreting hormones, such as estrogen and progesterone.

   Objective: Identify the following structures: uterus, vagina, fetus, placenta, umbilical cord, amniotic sac, and perineum.

Multiple Choice

3. d

   The fallopian tubes receive and transport the egg to the uterus after ovulation. If fertilization occurs, the developing fetus (unborn infant) implants itself in the uterine wall and develops there.

   Objective: Identify the following structures: uterus, vagina, fetus, placenta, umbilical cord, amniotic sac, and perineum.

4. c

   The area between the anus and the vagina is the perineum. To help prevent tearing of the perineum, you may apply gentle pressure to the top of the infant's head as it emerges from the vagina. Be careful not to touch the fontanelles, the areas of the skull that have not yet formed. The pressure you apply should not halt delivery of the infant but should control it. Colon is another term for the large intestine. The cervix is the neck of the uterus. During pregnancy, it contains the mucus plug that protects the uterus from the invasion of bacteria. The passage of the plug may account for a light bloody show in the first stage of labor. The labia majora is the term given to the outermost folds of skin that enclose the vulva.

   Objective: Identify the following structures: uterus, vagina, fetus, placenta, umbilical cord, amniotic sac, and perineum.

5. a

   The almond-shaped ovaries are the organs that produce estrogen and progesterone and release eggs. Each month of her reproductive years, a woman typically releases one egg (except while pregnant).

   Objective: Identify the following structures: uterus, vagina, fetus, placenta, umbilical cord, amniotic sac, and perineum.

6. c

   This condition is called a prolapsed umbilical cord. Definitive care is achieved at the hospital. Your treatment should be aimed at ensuring adequate blood flow through the cord to the infant and providing oxygen therapy to the mother. To relieve the pressure of the infant on the cord, first place the mother in a knee-chest position. In this position, gravity will assist in moving the infant's head away from the birth canal. Using a gloved hand, gently apply pressure to the presenting part of the infant (usually the top of the head) until a pulse can be felt in the umbilical cord. Be mindful of the fontanelles (areas where the skull has not yet developed). The cord should be kept moist with warm (not hot), sterile water or normal saline.

Objective: Discuss the emergency medical care for a premature birth, multiple gestation, breech presentation, and prolapsed cord.

7. b

Pregnancy begins when an egg (ovum) joins with a sperm cell (fertilization). The fertilized egg (zygote) passes from the fallopian tube into the uterus. The zygote implants in the wall of the uterus (implantation).

Objective: Identify the following structures: uterus, vagina, fetus, placenta, umbilical cord, amniotic sac, and perineum.

8. b

At the end of each menstrual period, the uterus again begins to prepare to receive a fertilized egg. Generally, ovulation (release of an egg) occurs 14 days before the beginning of the next menstrual cycle. If the egg does not implant, the lining of the uterus will again shed.

Objective: Identify the following structures: uterus, vagina, fetus, placenta, umbilical cord, amniotic sac, and perineum.

9. b

Do not allow the patient to sit on the toilet to have a bowel movement. When the fetus enters the birth canal, it presses again the rectum. This sensation is often confused with the need to move one's bowels. Frequent urination is generally present throughout pregnancy due to the increasing size of the uterus pressing against the urinary bladder. Do not allow this patient to lie flat on her back. Dizziness and weakness are likely to occur because of the compression of the abdominal blood vessels by the fetus. If left on her back for a sustained period, perfusion to the fetus will be compromised. The contractions associated with imminent delivery generally last 45 to 60 seconds and occur every 2 to 3 minutes.

Objective: State indications of an imminent delivery.

Sentence Completion

10. A breech birth occurs when the baby's **buttocks** or **feet** come out of the uterus first.

Objective: Discuss complications of delivery including abnormal presentations and prolapsed cord.

11. Preterm labor is labor that begins before the **37th** week of gestation.

Objective: Discuss complications of labor including premature rupture of membranes and preterm labor.

Short Answer

12. The placenta is responsible for:

- Exchange of oxygen and carbon dioxide between the blood of the mother and fetus (the placenta serves the function of the lungs for the developing fetus)
- Removal of waste products
- Transport of nutrients from the mother to the fetus
- Production of a special hormone of pregnancy that maintains the pregnancy and stimulates changes in the mother's breasts, cervix, and vagina in preparation for delivery
- Maintaining a barrier against harmful substances

Objective: Identify the following structures: uterus, vagina, fetus, placenta, umbilical cord, amniotic sac, and perineum.

13. If the bag of waters does not break or has not broken, use your gloved fingers to tear it. Push the sac away from the infant's head and mouth as they appear.

Objective: State the steps in assisting in a delivery.

14. The contents of an OB kit and their uses are:

- Scissors or scalpel (used to cut the umbilical cord)
- Hemostats or cord clamps (used to clamp the umbilical cord)
- Umbilical tape or sterilized cord (used to tie the placenta side of the umbilical cord)
- Bulb syringe (used to suction the infant's mouth and nose)
- Towels (used to dry the infant)
- 2×10 gauze sponges (used to clear secretions from the infant's mouth)
- Sterile gloves (worn by the rescuer during delivery)
- One baby blanket (used to warm the infant)
- Sanitary napkins (used to absorb vaginal drainage after delivery)
- Plastic bag (used to transport the placenta to the hospital)
- Sterile sheet or drape paper (to create a sterile field around the vaginal opening)

Objective: Identify and explain the use of the contents of an obstetrics kit.

Neonatal Care

READING ASSIGNMENT ▶ Read Chapter 36, pages 616 to 621 in your textbook.

Sum It Up

- During labor and delivery, the newborn undergoes many changes as the change is made from fetal to neonatal circulation. The airways and alveoli of a fetus are filled with fluid. At birth, the newborn's respiratory system must suddenly begin and maintain oxygenation. If the newborn does not breathe sufficiently to force fluid from alveoli or if meconium blocks air from entering alveoli, hypoxia will result and permanent brain damage can occur.

- When the baby is born, look at the baby and ask yourself four questions at the time of birth:
  1. Term gestation?
  2. Clear of meconium?
  3. Breathing or crying?
  4. Good muscle tone?

- If the answer to all of those questions is yes, proceed with providing warmth, clearing the baby's airway, and drying. If the answer to any question is no, you will need to begin the initial steps of resuscitation.

- Meconium forms the first stools of a newborn. The presence of meconium in the amniotic fluid is an indication of possible fetal distress. If meconium is observed during delivery, be sure to suction the baby's mouth and nose as soon as the head is delivered. By suctioning the baby before the shoulders and chest are delivered and before the baby begins breathing, you reduce the baby's risk of sucking the meconium into her lungs.

- It is very important to keep a newborn warm. Newborns lose heat very quickly because they are wet and suddenly exposed to an environment that is cooler than that inside the uterus. Because most body heat is lost through the head as a result of evaporation, immediately dry the baby and cover its head as soon as possible. Wrap the baby's body and head in dry, warm blankets to prevent heat loss, keeping the face exposed.

- Assess the newborn immediately after birth, focusing on the baby's breathing rate and effort, the heart rate, and skin color. If the baby has not begun to breathe or is breathing very slowly, stimulate the baby.

- If the baby's breathing is not adequate and there is no improvement after 5 to 10 seconds, help the baby breathe by using mouth-to-mask breathing or an appropriately sized bag-mask device connected to 100% oxygen.

- Assess the baby's pulse by feeling the brachial pulse on the inside of the upper arm. If the baby's heart rate is less than 100 beats/min, immediately breathe for the baby by using mouth-to-mask breathing or a bag-mask device. Reassess the baby's breathing, heart rate, and color after 30 seconds. If there is no improvement and the baby's heart rate is less than 60 beats/min, begin chest compressions.
- Look at the color of the baby's face, chest, or inside of the mouth. A bluish tint in these areas is called central cyanosis. The skin of a newborn's extremities is often blue (acrocyanosis) immediately after delivery. This finding is common and requires no specific intervention. If the baby is breathing adequately and has a heart rate of more than 100 beats/min but central cyanosis is present, give blow-by oxygen.
- An Apgar score is used to assess an infant's condition at 1 and 5 minutes after birth. The Apgar score is used to assess 5 specific signs: *appearance* (color), *pulse* (heart rate), *grimace* (irritability), *activity* (muscle tone), and *respirations.*

▶ Tracking Your Progress

After reading this chapter, can you:	Page Reference	Objective Met?
• Discuss special considerations of meconium?	617	☐
• Explain the importance of keeping a newborn warm?	618	☐
• Identify the primary signs used for evaluating a newborn?	618	☐
• Give examples of appropriate techniques used to stimulate a newborn?	618	☐
• Determine when ventilatory assistance is appropriate for a newborn?	619	☐
• Determine when chest compressions are appropriate for a newborn?	619	☐
• Assess patient improvement due to chest compressions and ventilations?	619	☐
• Discuss central cyanosis and acrocyanosis and their importance when assessing a newborn?	619	☐
• Determine when blow-by oxygen delivery is appropriate for a newborn?	619	☐
• Discuss use of the Apgar score when caring for a newborn?	619	☐

Chapter Quiz

True/False

Decide whether each statement is true or false. In the space provided, write T for true or F for false.

_____ 1. When clearing a newborn's airway, suction the baby's nose first and then the mouth.

_____ 2. When you are providing emergency care for a newborn, chest compressions are not indicated unless the infant's pulse is absent.

Multiple Choice

In the space provided, identify the letter of the choice that best completes each statement or answers each question.

Questions 3–6 pertain to the following scenario:

Your rescue crew is called to the home of a 34-year-old woman whose bag of waters has broken. You arrive to find the patient supine on the floor of her apartment. The baby's head can be seen at the birth canal. You decide to remain on the scene and deliver the baby.

_____ 3. After the head has emerged from the birth canal, you should
  a. instruct the mother to give one last big push.
  b. suction the mouth and nose with a bulb syringe.
  c. apply gentle traction to the head to ease delivery of the shoulder.
  d. apply a pediatric oxygen mask to the baby and flow the oxygen at 5 L/min.

_____ 4. As soon as the entire baby has been delivered, you should immediately
  a. clamp the umbilical cord.
  b. clamp and cut the umbilical cord.
  c. Begin warming, drying, and stimulating the baby.
  d. Place the infant about 2 to 3 feet below the level of the birth canal.

_____ 5. Evaluation of this infant's condition after birth is conducted using which of the following memory aids?
  a. AVPU
  b. Apgar
  c. SAMPLE
  d. A-NU-BABY

_____ 6. Your assessment of the infant reveals that her body is pink, she has a strong cry, her pulse is about 140 beats/min, and her respiratory rate when quieted is about 40 breaths/min. She is actively moving all extremities. Based on this information, her Apgar score is
  a. 7.
  b. 8.
  c. 9.
  d. 10.

Sentence Completion

In the blanks provided, write the words that best complete each sentence.

7. A full-term baby's respiratory rate is normally between _____ and _____ breaths/min.

8. A full-term baby's heart rate is normally between _____ and _____ beats/min.

Short Answer

Answer each question in the space provided.

9. Why is it very important to keep a newborn warm?

10. Fill in the missing information regarding the Apgar scoring system.

Sign	0	1	2
Appearance (color)			
Pulse (heart rate)			
Grimace (irritability)			
Activity (muscle tone)			
Respirations (respiratory effort)			

Answer Section

True/False

1. False

   Suction the baby's mouth first to be sure there is nothing for the baby to suck into his lungs if he should gasp when you suction his nose.

   Objective: Describe care of the baby as the head appears.

2. False

   If the baby's heart rate is less than 100 beats/min, immediately breathe for the baby by using mouth-to-mask breathing or a bag-mask device. Reassess the baby's breathing, heart rate, and color after 30 seconds. If there is no improvement and the baby's heart rate is less than 60 beats/min, begin chest compressions.

   Objective: Determine when chest compressions are appropriate for a newborn.

Multiple Choice

3. b

   After the head emerges, instruct the mother to "breathe through" the next contraction until you can clear the infant's airway. Clear the airway with a bulb syringe. Make sure you depress (squeeze) the syringe before you put it into the infant's mouth and nose. Once the nose and mouth have been suctioned adequately, you may lower the infant's head slightly to ease delivery of the top shoulder. Then lift it up slightly to deliver the bottom shoulder. The shoulders are the widest part of the infant's body. Once the shoulders deliver, the rest of the baby will deliver rapidly. Be gentle but supportive as the infant emerges.

   Objective: Describe care of the baby as the head appears.

4. c

   Leave the infant at the level of the birth canal and immediately begin warming, drying, and stimulating the infant. Regardless of the infant's presentation (whether pink and crying or blue and slow to respond), warming, drying, and stimulating are the first steps in the resuscitation of a newborn.

   Objective: State the steps in assisting in a delivery.

5. b

   Newborns are evaluated using the Apgar scale: **A**ppearance (color), **P**ulse (heart rate), **G**rimace (irritability), **A**ctivity (muscle tone), and **R**espirations (breathing rate). Each category is rated from 0 to 2 (with 2 being normal and healthy) for a total of 10 possible points. The scale is evaluated at 1 minute and 5 minutes postbirth. If the 5-minute evaluation is less than 7, continue evaluating every 5 minutes. AVPU is a memory aid for assessing the level of consciousness for adults or children. SAMPLE is the history-taking acronym. A-NU-BABY is not an accepted acronym.

   Objective: Discuss use of the Apgar score when caring for a newborn.

6. c

   This infant would be scored as follows: pink body (1 point), pulse above 100/min (2 points), strong cry (2 points), respiratory rate 40 (2 points), active motion (2 points).

Sentence Completion

7. A full-term baby's respiratory rate is normally between __30__ and __60__ breaths/min.

   Objective: Identify the primary signs used for evaluating a newborn.

8. A full-term baby's heart rate is normally between __100__ and __180__ beats/min.

   Objective: Identify the primary signs used for evaluating a newborn.

Short Answer

9. Newborns lose heat very quickly because they are wet and suddenly exposed to an environment that is cooler than that inside the uterus. Quickly dry the baby's body and head to remove blood and amniotic fluid. Immediately remove the wet towel or blanket from the infant, and then quickly wrap the baby in a clean, warm blanket. Because most body heat is lost through the head, remember to cover the baby's head as soon as possible.

Objective: Explain the importance of keeping a newborn warm.

10. See table below.

Sign	0	1	2
Appearance (color)	Blue or pale	Body pink Extremities blue	Completely pink
Pulse (heart rate)	Absent	Below 100/min	Above 100/min
Grimace (irritability)	No response	Grimace	Cough, sneeze, cry
Activity (muscle tone)	Limp	Some flexion of extremities	Active motion
Respirations (respiratory effort)	Absent	Slow, irregular	Good, crying

Objective: Discuss use of the Apgar score when caring for a newborn.

READING ASSIGNMENT ▶ Read Chapter 37, pages 622 to 642 in your textbook.

Sum It Up

- Children are not small adults. Children have unique physical, mental, emotional, and developmental characteristics that you must consider when assessing and caring for them.

- Before responding to any call involving an infant or child, it is essential to know where pediatric equipment is located in your emergency bags. It is not appropriate to search for age-appropriate equipment for the first time at an emergency scene.

- While en route to a call involving an infant or child, think about age-appropriate vital signs and anticipated developmental stage based on the dispatch information given. If you have this information stored on a note card or in a pocket guide, locate it en route to the call and have it readily accessible (such as attached to your clipboard).

- Communicating with scared, concerned parents and family is an important aspect of your responsibilities at the scene of an ill infant or child. Be professional and compassionate and remember to include them while providing care to their loved one.

- Your assessment of an infant or child should begin "across the room." When forming a general impression of an infant or child, look at his appearance, breathing, and circulation. Quickly determine if the child appears sick or not sick.

- Once your general impression is complete, perform a hands-on ABCDE assessment to determine if life-threatening conditions are present. In a responsive infant or child, use a toes-to-head or trunk-to-head approach. This approach should help reduce the infant's or child's anxiety.

- If a child is unable to speak, cry, cough, or make any other sound, her airway is completely obstructed. If the child has noisy breathing, such as snoring or gurgling, she has a partial airway obstruction. You will need to intervene if the child has a complete airway obstruction.

- In children, pulse regularity normally changes with respirations (increases with inspiration, decreases with expiration).

- Use the carotid artery to assess the pulse in an unresponsive child older than 1 year of age. Feel for a brachial pulse in an unresponsive infant. Feel for a pulse for about 10 seconds. If there is no pulse, or if a pulse is present but the rate is less than 60 beats/min with signs of shock, you must begin chest compressions.

- In infants and children, it is important to compare the pulse of the central blood vessels (such as the femoral artery) with those found in peripheral areas of the body (such as the feet). They should feel the same. If they do not, a circulatory problem is present.

- Assess capillary refill in children 6 years of age or younger. Delayed capillary refill may occur because of shock or hypothermia, among other causes.

- Assess blood pressure in children older than 3 years of age. In children 1 to 10 years of age, the following formula may be used to determine the lower limit of a normal systolic blood pressure: 70 + (2 × child's age in years) = systolic blood pressure. The lower limit of normal systolic blood pressure for a child 10 or more years of age is 90 mm Hg. The diastolic blood pressure should be about two-thirds the systolic pressure.

- The most common medical emergencies in children are respiratory emergencies. Upper-airway problems usually occur suddenly. Lower-airway problems usually take longer to develop. Respiratory distress is an increased work of breathing (respiratory effort). Respiratory failure is a condition in which there is not enough oxygen in the blood and/or ventilation to meet the demands of body tissues. Respiratory failure becomes evident when the patient becomes tired and can no longer maintain good oxygenation and ventilation. Respiratory arrest occurs when a patient stops breathing.

- Cardiopulmonary arrest results when the heart and lungs stop working. When respiratory failure occurs together with shock, cardiopulmonary failure results. Cardiopulmonary failure will progress to cardiopulmonary arrest unless it is recognized and treated promptly.

- The most common causes of an altered mental status in a pediatric patient are a low level of oxygen in the blood, head trauma, seizures, infection, low blood sugar, and drug or alcohol ingestion. Any patient with an altered mental status is in danger of an airway obstruction. Be prepared to clear the patient's airway with suctioning.

- Shock rarely results from a primary cardiac problem in infants and children. Common causes of shock in infants and children include diarrhea and dehydration, trauma, vomiting, blood loss, infection, and abdominal injuries.

- Seizures from fever are most common in children younger than the age of 5. It is the rapid rise of the child's temperature in a short period—not how high the temperature is—that causes the seizure.

- Meningitis is an inflammation of the meninges, the membranes covering the brain and spinal cord. It may be caused by a virus (most common cause), fungus, or bacteria. One form of meningitis is potentially life-threatening when the organism that causes it enters the bloodstream. A fever and reddish-purple rash are present in more than half of the patients who develop this form of meningitis.

- A seizure is a temporary change in behavior or consciousness caused by abnormal electrical activity in one or more groups of brain cells. Status epilepticus is recurring seizures without an intervening period of consciousness. Status epilepticus is a medical emergency that can cause brain damage or death if it is not treated.

- Many calls involving a pediatric poisoning become very emotional. You will need to calm the situation, find out what the exposure was, and contact your local poison control center.

- Absence of adult supervision is a factor in most submersion incidents involving infants and children. Signs and symptoms of drowning will vary depending on the type and length of submersion. All drowning victims should be transported to the hospital.

- Sudden infant death syndrome (SIDS) is the sudden and unexpected death of an infant that remains unexplained after a thorough case investigation, including performance of a complete autopsy, examination of the death scene, and review of the clinical history. The cause of SIDS is not clearly understood.

After reading this chapter, can you:	Page Reference	Objective Met?
• Describe differences in anatomy and physiology of the infant, child, and adult patient?	624	☐
• Describe assessment of an infant and child?	628	☐
• Describe possible causes, signs and symptoms, and emergency care for an airway obstruction?	632	☐
• Describe possible causes, signs and symptoms, and emergency care for respiratory emergencies in an infant and child?	633	☐
• Differentiate between respiratory distress and respiratory failure?	634	☐
• Describe possible causes, signs and symptoms, and emergency care for cardiopulmonary failure?	635	☐
• Describe possible causes, signs and symptoms, and emergency care for altered mental status in an infant and child?	636	☐
• Describe possible causes, signs and symptoms, and emergency care for shock in an infant and child?	637	☐
• Describe possible causes, signs and symptoms, and emergency care for fever in an infant and child?	637	☐
• Describe possible causes, signs and symptoms, and emergency care for seizures in an infant and child?	638	☐
• Describe possible causes, signs and symptoms, and emergency care for poisoning in an infant and child?	639	☐
• Describe possible causes, signs and symptoms, and emergency care for drowning in an infant and child?	640	☐
• Describe possible causes, signs and symptoms, and emergency care for sudden infant death syndrome?	641	☐

Chapter Quiz

Multiple Choice

In the space provided, identify the letter of the choice that best completes each statement or answers each question.

_____ 1. Your rescue crew is called to the scene of an 8-month-old male patient who was found unresponsive in his crib. He is warm to the touch and was last observed playing in the crib only 10 minutes before your arrival. When assessing this patient's airway, you should perform a

    a. a head tilt–chin lift maneuver.

    b. a jaw-thrust maneuver.

    c. a head tilt–chin lift maneuver without hyperextending the neck.

    d. a head tilt–chin lift maneuver while hyperextending the neck.

Questions 2–4 pertain to the following scenario:

You are dispatched for a "sick child." When you arrive, you find a 7-year-old who is having difficulty breathing.

_____ 2. Which of the following accurately reflects your primary survey priorities when assessing this child?
   a. Determine pulse, get medical history, count breathing rate.
   b. Assess mental status, determine breathing effectiveness, count pulse rate.
   c. Count pulse rate, perform head-to-toes exam, determine breathing rate.
   d. Get medical history, count breathing rate, assess mental status.

_____ 3. Which breathing assessment would be abnormal for this child?
   a. Breathing is at a regular rate of 16 breaths/min.
   b. Breathing is noisy and you hear a whistling sound.
   c. Neck muscles are relaxed and the child is lying flat.
   d. Skin is pink, warm, and dry.

_____ 4. Which is an appropriate initial method to assess circulation in this child?
   a. Assess skin color of the nail beds, mouth, and eyelids.
   b. Count the pulse for 5 seconds and multiply by 12.
   c. Press on the nail bed or forehead to check capillary refill.
   d. Take the blood pressure in both arms.

_____ 5. A 3-year-old child had what her mother described as a seizure while watching TV on the couch. She is now very sleepy and is breathing at a rate of 24 breaths/min. What should you do?
   a. Elevate her legs.
   b. Assist ventilations.
   c. Immobilize the child on a spine board.
   d. Place the patient in the recovery position.

Questions 6–8 pertain to the following scenario:

Your crew is called to the home of a 4-month-old female infant with difficulty breathing and a history of an upper respiratory infection. You arrive on scene to find this patient pale and sleepy in her father's arms. There is a considerable amount of thick, yellow discharge coming from the patient's nose.

_____ 6. To open the airway of this patient, you should
   a. hyperextend the head and neck.
   b. place the head in a neutral position.
   c. place the patient's chin on her chest.
   d. perform a jaw-thrust maneuver.

_____ 7. Which of the following is true regarding this patient's airway and breathing?
   a. The tongue is proportionally smaller in children than in adults.
   b. An early sign of infant respiratory distress is a slow respiratory rate (bradypnea).
   c. It is a common but insignificant finding for children this age to grunt during exhalation.
   d. Children this age are obligate nose breathers, and she may not open her mouth to breathe if the nose is obstructed.

_____ 8. After assessing the airway, you determine a need for suctioning. Which of the following is a correct guideline for suctioning this patient's nasal passages?
   a. Use a rigid catheter, and suction for no more than 3 to 5 seconds.
   b. Use a bulb syringe, and suction on insertion for no more than 5 seconds.
   c. Use a rigid catheter, and suction on insertion for no more than 15 seconds.
   d. Use a bulb syringe, and suction on withdrawal for no more than 10 seconds.

Sentence Completion

In the blanks provided, write the words that best complete each sentence.

9. A school-age child is from _____ to _____ years of age.

10. A toddler is from _____ to _____ years of age.

Short Answer

Answer each question in the space provided.

11. List five possible causes of altered mental status.

    1.
    2.
    3.
    4.
    5.

12. What is the formula used to approximate the lower limit of systolic blood pressure in children 1 to 10 years of age?

Answer Section

Multiple Choice

1. c

The airways of infants are extremely delicate. Hyperextending the airway may cause the trachea to become damaged and swell (leading to further airway complications). When you are opening the airway of an infant, the patient's head should be placed somewhere between the neutral position (no extension and looking straight up while lying supine) and the "sniffing" position (nose slightly elevated up from the neutral position).

Objective: Describe the purpose, indications, contraindications, complications, and procedure for performing the head tilt–chin lift.

2. b

Your primary survey priorities include assessing the patient's level of responsiveness and noting the need for spinal precautions. Then assess the patient's ABCs (airway, breathing, and circulation), reassess mental status, and expose the patient as necessary for a more thorough physical exam.

Objective: Describe assessment of an infant and child.

3. b

Normal breathing is quiet and painless and occurs at a regular rate. Noisy breathing is abnormal breathing. Remember to approach the patient immediately and begin your focused assessment if the patient:

- Looks like he is struggling (laboring) to breathe
- Has noisy breathing
- Is breathing faster or slower than normal
- Looks as if his chest is not moving normally

Objective: Describe assessment of an infant and child.

4. a

While assessing the patient's pulse, quickly check the patient's skin. Assessing the patient's skin condition can provide important information about the flow of blood through the body's tissues (perfusion). Assess perfusion by evaluating skin color, temperature, condition (moist, dry).

Objective: Describe normal and abnormal findings when assessing skin color.

5. d

A patient who has had a seizure is likely to be confused and/or sleepy after the seizure. If no spinal injury is suspected, place the patient in the recovery position to allow gravity to help any secretions in the mouth drain out. Suction the child's mouth if necessary, and administer oxygen.

Objective: Describe possible causes, signs and symptoms, and emergency care for seizures in an infant and child.

6. b

A "sleepy" presentation in a distressed child is not a good sign. Infants and children do not generally become sleepy until their compensatory mechanisms are about to fail. The correct manner in which to position an infant's airway is to place the head in a neutral position or in a position with the head slightly elevated ("sniffing" position). Hyperextending the neck may result in kinking of the patient's delicate trachea. Placing the chin on the chest may cause the tongue to obstruct the airway. Since there is no indication or history of trauma, the jaw-thrust maneuver would not be necessary.

Objective: Relate mechanism of injury to opening the airway.

7. d

Until about 6 months of age, infants are obligate nose breathers. They depend on an open nasal passage for breathing. If the nasal passage is obstructed, infants may not "think" to breathe through their mouths. The tongue is proportionately larger in children and infants than in adults. A slow respiratory rate is a late and worrying sign of distress. Infants and children compensate for distress much longer than adults do, but when they crash, they crash fast. Do not wait for measurable signs of injury or illness before starting treatment. Grunting with each exhalation is a significant sign of possible respiratory collapse. If grunting is present and breathing is adequate, provide high-flow oxygen by nonrebreather mask and continuous reassessment. If breathing is inadequate, assist ventilations with a bag-valve-mask device and supplemental oxygen.

Objective: Describe differences in anatomy and physiology of the infant, child, and adult patient.

8. d

Bulb syringes are excellent for suctioning nasal and oral secretions in infants. You should provide oxygen before and immediately after suctioning. To correctly use the bulb syringe, you must first depress the bulb, then insert the tip gently into the patient's mouth or nose, and finally release the bulb. Remove the syringe from the airway, depress the bulb, and repeat as necessary. Do not suction for more than 10 seconds per attempt, and provide supplemental oxygen between suctioning attempts if possible. (Do not suction a newborn for more than 3 to 5 seconds per attempt.)

Objective: Describe the purpose, indications, contraindications, complications, and procedure for suctioning the upper airway.

Sentence Completion

9. A school-age child is from **6** to **12** years of age.

   Objective: Discuss the physiologic, cognitive, and psychosocial characteristics of a school-age child.

10. A toddler is from **1** to **3** years of age.

    Objective: Discuss the physiologic, cognitive, and psychosocial characteristics of a toddler.

Short Answer

11. Possible causes of altered mental status include:

    AEIOU-TIPPS

    Alcohol, abuse
    Epilepsy (seizures)
    Insulin (diabetic emergency)
    Overdose, (lack of) oxygen (hypoxia)
    Uremia (kidney failure)
    Trauma (head injury), temperature (fever, heat- or cold-related emergency)
    Infection
    Psychiatric conditions
    Poisoning (including drugs and alcohol)
    Shock, stroke

    Objective: Describe possible causes, signs and symptoms, and emergency care for altered mental status in an infant and child.

12. The formula used to approximate the lower limit of systolic blood pressure in children 1 to 10 years of age is $70 + (2 \times \text{age in years})$.

    Objective: Describe the methods of assessing blood pressure.

38 Older Adults

READING ASSIGNMENT ▶ Read Chapter 38, pages 643 to 654 in your text book.

Sum It Up

- The term elderly refers to persons 65 years of age and older. Elderly people are rapidly becoming the largest group of patients who are encountered in the prehospital setting.

- Assessment of an older adult should be approached in the same systematic manner as that of all other patients. Keep in mind that an older adult may not show severe symptoms, even if he is very ill.

- While communicating with the patient, face the patient and speak slowly, clearly, and respectfully at the patient's eye level. Make sure that lighting is adequate to enable the patient to see your face and lips when speaking to her. Locate the patient's hearing aid or eyeglasses if needed. Speak to the patient first rather than to family or others.

- Coronary artery disease is the leading cause of death and disability in persons aged 65 years and older. The frequency of sudden cardiac death as the initial sign of coronary artery disease increases with age. An older adult who is experiencing an acute coronary syndrome may not show the same signs and symptoms as a younger person. His signs and symptoms are often vague and can be masked by other diseases.

- Heart failure is a common condition in older adults. When the left ventricle fails as a pump, blood backs up into the lungs (pulmonary edema). When the right ventricle fails, blood returning to the heart backs up and causes congestion in the organs and tissues of the body.

- Asthma and chronic obstructive pulmonary disease (COPD) are common in older adults. In fact, the death rate from asthma has increased most significantly in those aged 65 or older. More than 50% of all pneumonia cases occur in individuals 65 years of age and older. A pulmonary embolism is the sudden blockage of a branch of the pulmonary artery by a venous clot. Experts say that the incidence of a pulmonary embolism triples between the ages of 65 and 90.

- The incidence of strokes and transient ischemic attacks increases with advancing age. It has been estimated that 75% of stroke patients are older than 65 years of age and that 40% of stroke survivors have significant dysfunction.

- Delirium (also known as acute brain syndrome) is a sudden change (onset of minutes, hours, days) in mental status that is generally caused by a reversible condition such as hypoglycemia, drug overdose, or trauma.

- Dementia involves a more gradual change in baseline mental status that causes a progressive and sometimes irreversible loss of intellectual functions, psychomotor skills, and social skills. Causes of potentially reversible dementia include alcoholism, organic poisons, trauma, depression, infections, eye and ear problems, and drug overdose. Alzheimer's disease is an example of an irreversible dementia. It has been estimated that more than 60% of all dementias are of the Alzheimer's type. The progression of symptoms of Alzheimer's disease and the time that it first appears vary by individual.

- Before labeling any patient who has a sudden deterioration in mental status as confused or disoriented, make sure that you have searched for and ruled out possible treatable causes such as hypoxia, hypoglycemia, infection, and dehydration (among many other possibilities).

- Dysphagia (difficulty swallowing) is a frequent complaint of older adults. The patient may describe this problem as "food getting stuck" shortly after swallowing.

- Constipation is a common complaint among older adults. Laxative use in older adults is common, even among those who are not constipated. Fecal impaction is the condition in which hardened feces become trapped in the rectum and cannot be expelled.

- The involuntary leakage of stool is called fecal incontinence. Urinary incontinence is the involuntary leakage of urine.

- Enlargement of the prostate gland is common in men older than 50 years of age. The gland slowly increases in size and gradually leads to problems with urination.

- Older adults are susceptible to urinary tract infections because of incomplete emptying of the bladder and the use of indwelling urinary catheters.

- Osteoarthritis is the major cause of knee, hip, and back pain in older adults. Osteoporosis can result in a loss of height because of compression fractures of the vertebrae and kyphosis (an abnormal curvature of the spine resulting in stooped posture).

- Older adults are at risk of toxicity because of factors that alter drug metabolism and excretion including decreased kidney function, altered gastrointestinal absorption, and decreased blood flow in the liver.

- Polypharmacy is the use of multiple medications, often prescribed by different doctors, which can cause adverse reactions in the patient. Be respectful but firm when questioning the patient about her medical history, including any prescribed medicines and their proper dosages.

- Cataracts, which cloud the lens of the eye, are the most common disorder of the eye in older adults.

- Glaucoma is a disease associated with a buildup of internal eye pressure that can damage the optic nerve, which sends visual information to the brain. If untreated, glaucoma will eventually cause blindness. Glaucoma is the second leading cause of blindness in the United States.

- Macular degeneration is the leading cause of vision loss and legal blindness in Americans aged 65 and older. The macula is the central part of the retina and is responsible for sharp vision, such as that needed to read or drive.

- Hearing loss because of aging is called presbycusis, which means "older hearing."

- If your older adult patient is complaining of pain or discomfort, ask carefully worded questions about the discomfort he is having. Acute pain is pain of sudden onset. Chronic pain is pain that is of long duration. Asking an older adult to rate his discomfort on a scale from 0 to 10 may not give a true picture of the pain he is experiencing.

After reading this chapter, can you:	Page Reference	Objective Met?
• Describe assessment of the older adult?	644	☐
• Discuss techniques that should be used to enhance communication with an older adult?	645	☐
• Describe cardiovascular system changes that occur in older adults?	646	☐
• Describe respiratory system changes that occur in older adults?	647	☐
• Describe nervous system changes that occur in older adults?	647	☐
• Differentiate between delirium and dementia?	648	☐
• Describe gastrointestinal system changes that occur in older adults?	649	☐
• Describe genitourinary system changes that occur in older adults?	650	☐
• Describe metabolic and endocrine disorders that occur in older adults?	650	☐
• Describe musculoskeletal system changes that occur in older adults?	651	☐
• Describe toxicological emergencies in older adults?	651	☐
• Describe the sensory changes that occur in older adults?	652	☐

Chapter Quiz

True/False

Decide whether each statement is true or false. In the space provided, write T for true or F for false.

_____ 1. Heart failure is a common condition in older adults. When the left ventricle fails as a pump, blood returning to the heart backs up and causes congestion in the organs and tissues of the body.

_____ 2. Delirium is irreversible.

_____ 3. All forms of dementia are irreversible.

_____ 4. Some forms of Alzheimer's disease may begin as early as age 30.

Multiple Choice

In the space provided, identify the letter of the choice that best completes each statement or answers each question.

_____ 5. To determine an older adult's normal level of responsiveness, it is best to
   a. contact the patient's physician for this information.
   b. assume that the patient's mental status is impaired.
   c. ask a family member or neighbor to give you this information.
   d. contact your billing department for this information from previous prehospital care reports.

_____ 6. Pain is not easily assessed in an older adult because older adults
   a. do not trust EMS personnel.
   b. may fear hospitalization.
   c. may make up symptoms.
   d. often abuse prescription pain medicine.

_____ 7. Which of the following strategies will help you effectively care for a person who is visually impaired?

  a. Call the person by name each time you speak to him.
  b. Have the family relay information to the patient.
  c. To guide the patient in walking, push him.
  d. Speak loudly to the patient.

_____ 8. A patient with signs and symptoms of heart failure (without hypotension) should be placed in a _____ position.

  a. prone
  b. supine
  c. sitting
  d. knee-chest

_____ 9. An 82-year-old man presents with shortness of breath that has worsened over the past week. His skin is hot, flushed, and dry. He has a cough that is occasionally productive of yellowish-green sputum. He states he has not had any appetite for the past 24 to 36 hours. On the basis of this information, you suspect that the patient is experiencing

  a. asthma.
  b. pneumonia.
  c. emphysema.
  d. pulmonary embolism.

_____ 10. In the early stage of Alzheimer's disease, the patient

  a. occasionally forgets where he put his car keys or glasses.
  b. makes up stories to compensate for memory loss and is disoriented to date and place.
  c. becomes disoriented to date, forgets messages, gets lost while driving, and has difficulty maintaining good hygiene.
  d. must be dressed, fed, bathed, and turned and his verbal responses are nearly unintelligible, consisting mainly of grunts and agitation to communicate.

Answer Section

True/False

1. **False**

   Although heart failure is a common condition in older adults, when the left ventricle fails as a pump, blood backs up into the lungs (pulmonary edema). The patient may be anxious and restless and experience mental status changes secondary to hypoxia. The patient is often short of breath with exertion and may experience orthopnea and paroxysmal nocturnal dyspnea. She may have a cough that produces frothy sputum that is sometimes blood-tinged. Accessory muscles are often used to improve breathing. The patient often complains of fatigue and recent weight gain. Her pulse is usually rapid and may be irregular. When the right ventricle fails, blood returning to the heart backs up and causes congestion in the organs and tissues of the body. Swelling of the feet and ankles and distention of the jugular veins is usually present. The patient typically complains of weakness, recent weight gain, and nausea and may complain of abdominal discomfort.

   Objective: Describe cardiovascular system changes that occur in older adults.

2. **False**

   Delirium (also known as acute brain syndrome) is a sudden change (onset of minutes, hours, days) in mental status that is generally caused by a reversible condition such as hypoglycemia, drug overdose, or trauma.

   Objective: Describe nervous system changes that occur in older adults.

3. **False**

   Dementia involves a more gradual change in baseline mental status that causes a progressive and *sometimes* irreversible loss of intellectual functions, psychomotor skills, and social skills. Causes of potentially reversible dementia include alcoholism, organic poisons, trauma, depression, infections, eye and ear problems, and drug overdose. Alzheimer's disease is an example of an irreversible dementia.

   Objective: Describe nervous system changes that occur in older adults.

4. **True**

   Dementia generally begins after the age of 60 years, but some forms of Alzheimer's disease may begin as early as age 30.

   Objective: Describe nervous system changes that occur in older adults.

Multiple Choice

5. **c**

   It may be difficult for you to find out whether the patient's symptoms are due to a medical emergency or an ongoing (chronic) medical problem or are a part of normal aging. To help find out what the patient's normal mental status is, ask someone who knows the patient to give you this information. For example, ask a family member or neighbor how the patient appears to him today. Ask the family, "What is different today? Is she confused? Behaving inappropriately? Having hallucinations? Does her speech sound normal to you?" Then ask the person providing information to compare how your patient appears today with how she was yesterday or 2 or 3 days ago.

   Objective: Describe assessment of the older adult.

6. **b**

   An older adult may not tell you about important symptoms because he is afraid of being hospitalized. He may be afraid that once he is at the hospital, he will never come home or he may not be able to make decisions about his care.

   Objective: Describe assessment of the older adult.

7. a

When you speak to a blind patient, address her by name. In guiding a patient who is blind, you should offer the patient your arm and lead her—do not push, pull, or grab a blind patient.

8. c

Place the patient in a sitting position and administer 100% oxygen. If the patient cannot tolerate a nonrebreather mask but his breathing is adequate, try using a nasal cannula. Patients with heart failure will often tell you that they feel like they are smothering when a nonrebreather mask is put on their face. If the patient's breathing is inadequate, you will need to assist his breathing with a bag-mask device. Provide calm reassurance to help reduce the patient's anxiety.

Objective: Describe cardiovascular system changes that occur in older adults.

9. b

Typical signs and symptoms of pneumonia include gradual onset, cough productive of sputum, shortness of breath with or without fever, fatigue, loss of appetite, and tightness in the chest. However, 25% to 30% of older adults who have pneumonia will not have an elevated temperature, and 25% will not have cough and sputum production.

Objective: Describe respiratory system changes that occur in older adults.

10. c

In the early stage of the disease, he becomes disoriented to date, has difficulty managing his finances (such as forgetting to pay bills), forgets messages, and misplaces items. He gets lost while driving, makes poor decisions, has difficulty maintaining good hygiene, complains of neglect by others, and is restless and impatient.

Objective: Describe nervous system changes that occur in older adults.

39 Patients with Special Challenges

READING ASSIGNMENT ▶ Read Chapter 39, pages 655 to 664 in your textbook.

Sum It Up

- Child maltreatment is an act or failure to act by a parent, caregiver, or other person as defined by state law that results in physical abuse, neglect, medical neglect, sexual abuse, and/or emotional abuse. It is also defined as an act or failure to act that presents an impending risk of serious harm to a child.

- There are four common types of abuse: physical abuse, sexual abuse, emotional abuse, and neglect. Physical abuse is physical acts that cause or could cause physical injury to a child. Sexual abuse is inappropriate adolescent or adult sexual behavior with a child. Emotional abuse is behaviors that harm a child's self-worth or emotional well-being. Neglect is the failure to provide for a child's basic physical, emotional, or educational needs or to protect a child from harm or potential harm. Medical neglect is a type of maltreatment caused by failure of the caregiver to provide for the appropriate healthcare of the child although financially able to do so.

- When providing care for an infant or child who is ill or injured due to neglect or abuse, show a professional and caring attitude for the patient. Report known or suspected child abuse as required by law in your state. Carefully document your physical exam findings as well as your observations of the child's environment. Document the caregiver's comments exactly as stated and enclose them in quotation marks. Your documentation must reflect the facts and not your opinion of what may or may not have occurred. Report your findings to appropriate personnel when transferring patient care.

- Elder abuse is any physical, sexual, or emotional abuse or neglect committed against an older adult. Domestic elder abuse refers to maltreatment of an older adult that occurs in the elder's home (or in the home of a caregiver) by an individual who has a special relationship with the elder (such as a spouse, sibling, child, friend, or caregiver). Institutional elder abuse occurs in residential facilities for older persons such as nursing homes, foster homes, group homes, or board and care facilities. Self-neglect or self-abuse is the conscious and voluntary behavior of a mentally competent older adult that threatens her own health or safety as a matter of personal choice. Types of elder abuse are similar to those encountered with children and include physical, sexual, and emotional abuse and neglect.

- EMS is often the primary route that the homeless use to access healthcare. Homeless people typically do not have health insurance or money to pay for healthcare services, and most do not have transportation. Talk with your patient and listen without making a moral judgment. Document your assessment findings and the care provided objectively.

- Bariatrics is the branch of medicine that deals with the causes, prevention, and treatment of obesity and weight-related health problems. Before moving a bariatric patient, know in advance the manufacturer's weight limitations on EMS equipment such as backboards, stair chairs, and stretchers.

- Patients with special needs may also be referred to as technology-assisted patients. These are patients experiencing a chronic or terminal illness who are being cared for at home and are dependent on high-technology equipment.

- Home care is professional assistance that a patient receives in his home. It does not require a doctor's prescription and does not include skilled nursing services. Home healthcare is medical care provided in the home that is deemed medically necessary by a physician (requires a physician's prescription). Home healthcare is provided by home healthcare agencies, which are regulated by state and federal laws.

- A central line is an intravenous line placed near the heart for long-term use. Central lines may be used to give medications and nutritional solutions directly into the venous circulation. A peripherally inserted central catheter is also called a PICC line. A PICC line is smaller than those routinely used for central lines.

- A gastrostomy tube is a special catheter placed directly into the stomach for feeding. It is most often used when passage of a tube through a patient's mouth, pharynx, or esophagus is contraindicated or impossible or when the tube must be maintained for a long period.

- Hydrocephalus is a condition in which there is an excess of cerebrospinal fluid (CSF) within the brain. A ventricular shunt is a drainage system used to remove the excess CSF.

- Palliative care (also called comfort care) is care provided to relieve symptoms of disease, such as pain, nausea and vomiting, rather than to cure the disease. Palliative care is usually provided for patients with a terminal illness and their families.

- Hospice care is a program of palliative and supportive care services providing physical, psychological, social, and spiritual care for dying persons, their families, and other loved ones. Most hospice care is provided in the patient's home.

▶ Tracking Your Progress

After reading this chapter, can you:	Page Reference	Objective Met?
• Define child maltreatment and differentiate among the four primary types of child abuse?	656	☐
• Describe possible signs and symptoms and emergency care for child abuse?	657	☐
• Define elder abuse and differentiate among the primary categories of elder abuse?	658	☐
• Describe the signs, symptoms, and emergency care for elder abuse?	659	☐
• Discuss common illnesses among the homeless?	659	☐
• Discuss possible challenges associated with the assessment and provision of emergency care to the homeless patient?	660	☐
• Discuss possible challenges associated with the assessment and provision of emergency care to the bariatric patient?	660	☐
• Differentiate between home care and home healthcare?	660	☐
• Discuss medical devices commonly used by patients with special healthcare needs?	661	☐
• Discuss the specific assessment and emergency care considerations for patients with special healthcare needs?	661	☐
• Differentiate between palliative care and hospice care?	662	☐

Chapter Quiz

Matching

Match the key terms in the right column with the definitions in the left column by placing the letter of each correct answer in the space provided.

_____ 1. Failure to provide for a patient's basic needs

_____ 2. Medical care provided in the home that is deemed medically necessary by a physician

_____ 3. A surgically created opening

_____ 4. A special catheter placed directly into the stomach for feeding

_____ 5. A healing remedy practiced by some cultures in which a coin is heated in hot oil and then rubbed along the patient's spine to heal an illness

_____ 6. A condition in which there is an excess of cerebrospinal fluid (CSF) within the brain

_____ 7. A contagious bacterial skin infection that can look like a burn

_____ 8. A drainage system used to remove excess cerebrospinal fluid in a patient who has hydrocephalus

_____ 9. The creation of a surgical opening into the trachea through the neck, with insertion of a tube to aid passage of air or removal of secretions

_____ 10. The conscious and voluntary behavior of a mentally competent older adult that threatens his own health or safety as a matter of personal choice

_____ 11. An intravenous line often used for neonates, young children, or patients requiring only short-term IV therapy for the delivery of medications and nutritional solutions directly into the venous circulation

_____ 12. Acts that cause or could cause physical injury to an individual

_____ 13. Maltreatment of an older adult that occurs in a nursing home, foster home, or similar location

_____ 14. The branch of medicine that deals with the causes, prevention, and treatment of obesity and weight-related health problems

_____ 15. An intravenous line placed near the heart for long-term use

_____ 16. Bluish areas usually seen in non-Caucasian infants and young children that may be mistaken for bruises

A. Central line

B. Tracheostomy

C. Peripherally inserted central catheter

D. Hydrocephalus

E. Coining

F. Neglect

G. Institutional elder abuse

H. Gastrostomy tube

I. Bariatrics

J. Stoma

K. Self-neglect or self-abuse

L. Mongolian spots

M. Ventricular shunt

N. Physical abuse

O. Home healthcare

P. Impetigo

Answer Section

Matching

1. F
2. O
3. J
4. H
5. E
6. D
7. P
8. M
9. B
10. K
11. C
12. N
13. G
14. I
15. A
16. L

Module 10

EMS Operations

▶ CHAPTER **40**

**Principles of Emergency
Response and Transportation**   279

▶ CHAPTER **41**

Incident Management   286

▶ CHAPTER **42**

Multiple-Casualty Incidents   289

▶ CHAPTER **43**

Air Medical Transport   293

► CHAPTER **44**

Vehicle Extrication 296

► CHAPTER **45**

Hazardous Materials Awareness 301

► CHAPTER **46**

Terrorism and Disaster Response 308

READING ASSIGNMENT ▶ Read Chapter 40, pages 665 to 681 in your textbook.

Sum It Up

- Preparations for an emergency call include having the appropriate personnel and equipment and an emergency response vehicle that is ready for use.
- Emergency transport vehicles are required to carry specific types and quantities of medical equipment to be certified as ambulances. In addition to basic medical supplies, nonmedical supplies that must be carried include personal safety equipment as required by local, state, and federal standards, as well as preplanned routes or comprehensive street maps.
- Daily inspections of the emergency response vehicle and its equipment are necessary to ensure it is in proper working order.
- In the dispatch phase of an EMS response, the patient or a witness reports the emergency by calling 9-1-1 or another emergency number. EMD receives the call and gathers information from the caller. The dispatcher then activates (dispatches) an appropriate EMS response based on the information received.
- En route to the reported emergency, begin to anticipate the knowledge, equipment, and skills you may need to provide appropriate patient care. Notify the dispatcher that you are responding to the call. Determine the responsibilities of the crew members before arriving on the scene.
- Laws pertaining to the proper methods of responding to an emergency vary from state to state. In general, most states require that emergency vehicle operators obey all traffic regulations unless a specific exemption has been made and documented in statute. Most states allow for such exemptions, as long as they do not endanger life or property. In addition, these exemptions are typically granted only when a true emergency exists. A true emergency is a situation in which there is a high possibility of death or serious injury and the rapid response of an emergency vehicle may lessen the risk of death or injury.
- When driving in emergency mode, the operator of an emergency vehicle must drive with due regard for the safety of others on the roadway. Due regard means that, in similar circumstances, a reasonable and responsible person would act in a way that is safe and considerate of others. Emergency vehicles should never operate at a speed greater than is warranted by the nature of the call or the condition of the

patient being transported. This speed must also not be greater than traffic, road, and weather conditions allow. All emergency vehicle warning systems should be used as intended by the manufacturer and must be in operation during an emergency response. All emergency vehicle warning systems must be functioning in the prescribed manner before entering any intersection.

- Escorts and multiple-vehicle responses are extremely dangerous. They should be used only if emergency responders are unfamiliar with the location of the patient or receiving facility. Provide a safe following distance (generally a minimum of 500 feet). Stop and then proceed through any intersection as directed by the standard right-of-way guidelines.

- While approaching the scene, be cautious, and look for dangers. Position the emergency vehicle with careful consideration of potential dangers such as fire, hazardous materials, downed power lines, crowds, heavy traffic flow, and potential violence. When you arrive on the scene, notify the EMD of your arrival. Before initiating patient care, put on appropriate PPE. Determine the mechanism of injury or nature of the patient's illness. Ask for additional resources before making patient contact and institute the Incident Command System if needed. When it is safe to do so, gain access to the patient. Perform an initial assessment and provide essential emergency care.

- If patient transport is needed, prepare the patient. Ask for assistance with lifting and moving the patient to the ambulance. Secure the patient to the stretcher, and lock the stretcher in place. Ensure that outside compartment doors are closed and secure.

- Notify the dispatcher when you are en route to your station and again when you arrive. Clean and disinfect the vehicle and equipment as needed in preparation for the next call. Replace supplies used during the run. Notify the dispatcher when your tasks are complete and you are ready for another call.

▶ Tracking Your Progress

After reading this chapter, can you:	Page Reference	Objective Met?
• Discuss the medical and nonmedical equipment needed to respond to a call?	669	☐
• Differentiate among the various methods of moving a patient to the unit on the basis of injury or illness?	669	☐
• Discuss the measures necessary to ensure safe operation of an emergency vehicle?	670	☐
• State what information is essential in order to respond to a call?	672	☐
• Describe the general provisions of state laws relating to the operation of the ambulance and privileges in any or all of the following categories: speed, warning lights, sirens, right-of-way, parking, and turning?	673	☐
• Discuss "due regard for the safety of others" while operating an emergency vehicle?	673	☐
• List factors contributing to unsafe driving conditions?	674	☐
• Give examples of possible driver distractions?	675	☐
• Describe the considerations that should be given to a request for escorts, following of an escort vehicle, and intersections?	676	☐
• Determine if the scene is safe to enter?	677	☐
• Describe the important factors to consider when placing an emergency vehicle at the emergency scene?	678	☐

	Page Reference	Objective Met?
After reading this chapter, can you:		
• Summarize the importance of preparing the unit for the next response?	679	☐
• Distinguish among the terms cleaning, low-level disinfection, intermediate-level disinfection, high-level disinfection, and sterilization?	680	☐
• Describe how to clean or disinfect items following patient care?	680	☐

Chapter Quiz

Multiple Choice

In the space provided, identify the letter of the choice that best completes each statement or answers each question.

_____ 1. Which of the following statements regarding vehicle operation is correct?
   a. The use of lights and siren automatically grants you the right of way.
   b. The light bar on the top of the vehicle is the most visible warning device on the vehicle.
   c. The standard rules of the road apply even if you are in the emergency response mode.
   d. Most drivers will not yield the right of way when they notice your approach with lights and siren.

_____ 2. Which of the following is correct regarding the operation of lights and siren for emergency response?
   a. Lights and siren should be used simultaneously when operating in the emergency response mode.
   b. Flashing lights must be used continuously, and the siren should be activated at intersections to control traffic.
   c. In the emergency response mode, activating the lights and siren is necessary only when operating in extremely heavy traffic conditions.
   d. In the emergency response mode, lights and siren should be turned on when local laws are being broken and turned off when local laws are obeyed.

Questions 3–7 pertain to the following scenario:

Your rescue crew has been called to the scene of a serious multivehicle collision on a local interstate highway. Several rescue units have been dispatched. As you get closer to the scene, you find yourself driving behind another responding rescue crew.

_____ 3. Both units are responding with lights and sirens activated. You should
   a. maintain a minimum following distance of at least 200 feet.
   b. select a different route to the scene even if it delays your response time.
   c. follow as closely as possible to the lead vehicle to maximize your visibility when entering intersections.
   d. use a different siren or audible tone to help motorists distinguish a multiple-vehicle response.

_____ 4. While responding to the emergency scene
   a. you must wear your seat belt at all times.
   b. you must wear your seat belt only if you are driving the vehicle.
   c. you need not wear your seat belt since you are using the red lights and siren to avoid a collision.
   d. you must wear your seat belt only if you are riding in a rear-facing seat (jump seat).

_____ 5. As you approach an intersection, the light is red for your direction of travel. You should
   a. slow to 20 to 25 miles per hour and proceed through the intersection.
   b. come to a complete stop, wait until the light changes to green, and then proceed through the intersection.
   c. come to a complete stop, ensure traffic has stopped in all directions, and then proceed through the intersection.
   d. proceed through the intersection maintaining no more than 10 miles per hour above the posted speed limit.

_____ 6. As you approach the scene, you observe that one of the involved vehicles has caught fire. What is the minimum distance you should park your rescue vehicle from the fire (assuming you do not have the training or responsibility for firefighting functions)?
  a. 100 feet
  b. 200 feet
  c. 2,000 feet
  d. 1 mile

_____ 7. Assuming you are the first unit to arrive at the scene, which of the following responsibilities should be addressed first?
  a. Gain access to all patients.
  b. Notify dispatch of your arrival at the scene.
  c. Perform a primary survey of all patients to determine care priorities.
  d. Provide essential emergency care to stabilize patients and prepare them for transport.

_____ 8. Your patient is a 31-year-old woman with an open head injury. Your crew provides prompt, efficient treatment, and the patient is transported to an appropriate facility. You have restocked your supplies and are prepared to return to service. On returning to the vehicle, you observe a small amount of blood on the handle of your door. Your best course of action would be to
  a. drive the vehicle through a commercial car wash.
  b. immediately scrub away the blood with undiluted household bleach.
  c. have the vehicle put out of service until an OSHA-approved vendor decontaminates it.
  d. put on appropriate personal protective equipment and personally decontaminate the handle with a bleach and water solution.

Matching

Match the key terms in the right column with the definitions in the left column by placing the letter of each correct answer in the space provided.

_____ 9. A method of decontamination that destroys all microorganisms including highly resistant bacterial spores

_____ 10. A situation in which there is a high possibility of death or serious injury and the rapid response of an emergency vehicle may lessen the risk of death or injury

_____ 11. Operation of an emergency vehicle while responding to a medical emergency

_____ 12. A method of decontamination that destroys most bacteria, some viruses and fungi, but not tuberculosis bacteria or bacterial spores

_____ 13. The use of physical or chemical means to remove, inactivate, or destroy bloodborne pathogens on a surface or item to the point where it is no longer capable of transmitting infectious particles and the surface or item is considered safe for handling, use, or disposal

_____ 14. A method of decontamination that destroys all microorganisms except large numbers of bacterial spores.

_____ 15. A method of decontamination that destroys tuberculosis bacteria, vegetative bacteria, and most viruses and fungi but not bacterial spores

A. Intermediate-level disinfection

B. True emergency

C. Decontamination

D. Low-level disinfection

E. High-level disinfection

F. Sterilization

G. Emergency response

Short Answer

Answer each question in the space provided.

16. List six contributing factors to unsafe driving conditions.

1.

2.

3.

4.

5.

6.

17. Where do most accidents involving emergency response vehicles occur?

18. List four important areas to consider when placing an emergency vehicle at the scene of an emergency.

1.

2.

3.

4.

19. Describe the correct procedure for transferring the patient to the ambulance.

20. State what information is essential in order to respond to a call.

Answer Section

Multiple Choice

1. c

Headlights are the most visible warning devices on an emergency vehicle because they are mounted at the eye level of other drivers. Use caution during any response that uses lights and siren due to the "excitement factor."

Objective: Discuss the measures necessary to ensure safe operation of an emergency vehicle.

2. a

All visual and audible warning devices should be activated when driving in the emergency response mode. Avoid turning the siren on and off repeatedly as you may surprise drivers by your sudden, unsuspected approach. There may be circumstances when operating the siren is not desired, such as when driving through a residential neighborhood in the middle of the night. Common sense and local protocol should prevail. However, if you are going to turn off the siren, you should consider turning off the flashing lights as well, thus returning to a normal response mode.

Objective: Discuss "due regard for the safety of others" while operating an emergency vehicle.

3. d

Provide a safe following distance (generally a minimum of 500 feet). Stop and then proceed through any intersection using standard right-of-way guidelines. Check your agency's policy regarding the use of siren and/or lights in these situations. Some agencies do not want them used because they may confuse other drivers. Other agencies specify that a different siren time and/or tone must be used to help other motorists distinguish multiple emergency vehicles.

Objective: Describe the considerations that should be given to a request for escorts, following of an escort vehicle, and intersections.

4. a

During transport, remember that your safety must be your priority. Wearing a seat belt is one way to ensure your safety. While some people may consider it cumbersome to wear a seat belt during transport, your risk of injury increases if you are not restrained. All passengers and patients should also be properly secured. Infants and children should always be appropriately secured.

Objective: Define the role of the EMR relative to the responsibility for personal safety and the safety of the crew, the patient, and the bystanders.

5. c

While it is not necessary to wait for the light to change to green, waiting until all vehicles in all lanes of traffic yield the right-of-way is absolutely necessary. Failure to operate with due regard for the safety of others may have detrimental effects on your health, the health of others, and your long-term financial and professional stability. Reckless, aggressive driving does not make a significant difference in response times and should never be tolerated.

Objective: Discuss "due regard for the safety of others" while operating an emergency vehicle.

6. a

You should park a minimum of 100 feet upwind from any burning vehicle. If the vehicle is very large or involves some other hazard, you would obviously want to increase your safety zone. A minimum safety zone of 2,000 feet should be observed at hazardous materials incidents.

Objective: Describe the important factors to consider when placing an emergency vehicle at the emergency scene.

7. b

When you arrive at the scene, you should notify dispatch of your arrival and provide a brief on-scene report to other emergency vehicles responding to the scene. Your report could be as simple as "Rescue 10 is on scene. Three-car collision with trapped patients. Appears serious." This brief report allows responding units to plan their actions and prepare for special assignments en route (such as extrication duties, firefighting, special approach considerations, or ALS-level care). This on-scene notification should be followed by the scene size-up, which includes body substance isolation precautions, scene safety control, and determination of the mechanism of injury. Next, you must gain access to the patients, perform primary surveys, provide emergency care, and prepare the patients for transport. If the number or severity of the patients outweighs your initial on-scene resources, triage should begin as part of the scene size-up.

Objective: List the correct radio procedures during each phase of a typical EMS call.

8. d

A strong solution of household bleach should remove and/or kill any biological contaminant especially on something nonporous like a metal handle. Be sure to readdress body substance isolation during any decontamination procedure. In this situation you should, at a minimum, wear disposable gloves.

Objective: Describe how to clean or disinfect items following patient care.

Matching

9.	F	13.	C
10.	B	14.	E
11.	G	15.	A
12.	D		

Short Answer

16. Contributing factors to unsafe driving conditions include:

- Escorts
- Road surface
- Excessive speed
- Reckless driving
- Weather conditions
- Multiple-vehicle response
- Inadequate dispatch information and unfamiliarity with the location
- Failure to heed traffic warning signals
- Disregarding of traffic rules and regulations

- Failure to anticipate the actions of other motorists
- Failure to obey traffic signals or posted speed limits

Objective: List factors contributing to unsafe driving conditions.

17. Most accidents involving emergency response vehicles occur in intersections.

Objective: Describe the considerations that should be given to a request for escorts, following an escort vehicle, and intersections.

18. There are four things to consider when placing an emergency vehicle at the emergency scene. They are scene safety, traffic volume and flow, egress from the scene, and distance from the patient(s) or scene.

Objective: Describe the important factors to consider when placing an emergency vehicle at the emergency scene.

19. The correct procedure for transferring the patient to the ambulance is as follows:

- Ensure that dressings and splints, if used, are secure.
- Transfer the patient to the transport vehicle. The lifting and moving method and the device used will depend on the patient's illness or injury and the safety of the scene (i.e., emergency move at an unsafe scene versus a move of a stable medical patient).
- Secure the patient to the stretcher, and lock the stretcher in place.
- Before leaving the scene, the driver should ensure that outside compartment doors are closed and secure.

Objective: Differentiate among the various methods of moving a patient to the unit on the basis of injury or illness.

20. Information that is essential in order to respond to a call includes:

- Location of the call
- Nature of the call
- Name, location, and callback number of the caller
- Location of the patient
- Number of patients and severity of the problem
- Other special problems (such as hazardous materials)

Objective: State what information is essential in order to respond to a call.

Incident Management

READING ASSIGNMENT ▶ Read Chapter 41, pages 682 to 686 in your textbook.

Sum It Up

- All field EMS professionals must know how to establish and work within the National Incident Management System (NIMS). Requirements for entry-level personnel include certification in Incident Command System (ICS)-100: Introduction to ICS, or equivalent, and the Federal Emergency Management Agency (FEMA) IS-700 course called NIMS: An Introduction.
- The National Incident Management System was created to provide a consistent nationwide template that allows all governmental, private sector, and nongovernmental agencies to work together during domestic incidents.
- The Incident Command System is an important part of NIMS. The ICS is a standardized system developed to assist with the control, direction, and coordination of emergency response resources. The ICS can be used at an incident of any type and size.
- An incident commander (IC) is the person who is responsible for managing all operations at the incident site. Depending on the size of the incident, the incident commander may assign to others the authority to perform certain activities. Scene operations may be broken down into groups, such as treatment and extrication.
- If you arrive on the scene of an MCI where the ICS has been established, report to the command post. Find out who the IC is. Identify yourself and your level of training. Follow the directions given by the IC about your assignment.

Chapter Quiz

True/False

Decide whether each statement is true or false. In the space provided, write T for true or F for false.

_____ 1. The incident commander is generally located in the staging area to enable rapid assignments as personnel arrive on the scene.

_____ 2. The Incident Command System has become the standard for incident management across the United States.

Short Answer

3. You are called to the scene of a multiple-casualty incident. The Incident Command System has been established. What should you do first when you arrive at the scene?

4. How should you communicate with others at the scene of a major incident?

Answer Section

True/False

1. False

   The incident commander is located at the command post.

   Objective: Describe basic concepts of incident management.

2. True

   The Incident Command System has become the standard for incident management across the United States.

   Objective: Describe basic concepts of incident management.

Short Answer

3. If you arrive on the scene of a multiple-casualty incident where the ICS has been established, report to the command post. Find out who the incident commander is, and identify yourself and your level of training. Follow the directions given by the incident commander about your assignment.

   Objective: Describe basic concepts of incident management.

4. When communicating with others on the scene, use plain English. Do not use "10-codes," radio codes, technical language, or other jargon. Using plain English helps ensure efficient, clear communications on the scene.

   Objective: Describe basic concepts of incident management.

 Multiple-Casualty Incidents

Sum It Up

- A multiple-casualty incident may also be called a mass-casualty incident or multiple-casualty situation. An MCI is any event that places a great demand on resources—equipment, personnel, or both.
- The START triage system is used by many systems in dealing with MCIs. START stands for *simple* *triage* and *rapid* *treatment*. On the basis of your assessment findings, you categorize each patient into one of four categories. Color-coded triage tags that correspond with these categories are placed on the patients and used to identify the level of injury sustained.
- The JumpSTART triage system was developed for use with children. It specifies how the four color-coded tags are applied to pediatric patients.

▶ Tracking Your Progress

After reading this chapter, can you:	Page Reference	Objective Met?
• Describe the criteria for a multiple-casualty situation?	688	☐
• Evaluate the role of the EMR in the multiple-casualty situation?	688	☐
• Summarize the components of basic triage?	699	☐

Chapter Quiz

Multiple Choice

In the space provided, identify the letter of the choice that best completes each statement or answers each question.

Questions 1–3 pertain to the following scenario:

Your ambulance crew is called to the scene of a "five-car pileup" on a local highway. Information at time of dispatch indicates that several people have been injured seriously. En route you request that a paramedic ambulance and the local fire department respond as well. When you arrive at the scene, you observe that 14 people have been injured in the collision. Their injuries range from minor to life-threatening. The other responding units are still about 8 minutes from the scene.

_____ 1. The initial on-scene needs far outweigh your initial resources. Which of the following is true about triaging this scene?
- **a.** CPR on a deceased patient takes priority over triage.
- **b.** Triage should wait until paramedics arrive at the scene.
- **c.** You should immediately begin full physical assessments on all patients.
- **d.** You should immediately begin triaging all patients rather than treating any one seriously injured patient.

_____ 2. During triage, which of the following patients should be considered the lowest priority at this scene?
- **a.** A 34-year-old man with swelling and deformity at the right arm and left lower leg.
- **b.** A 51-year-old woman who is pulseless and apneic with blood coming from both ears.
- **c.** A 24-year old woman complaining of chest pain after striking the steering wheel with her upper torso.
- **d.** A 60-year old man who is up and walking around the scene. He is awake but does not know his name, nor does he recall the accident.

_____ 3. Which of the following patients should be treated and transported first?
- **a.** A 24-year-old woman with blistering scald burns to one arm and both upper legs.
- **b.** A 74-year-old woman who was ejected from her vehicle. She is pulseless and apneic.
- **c.** A 13-year-old male complaining of abdominal pain who is showing the signs of shock.
- **d.** A 27-year-old man complaining of neck pain. He is unable to feel or move his arms or legs.

Short Answer

Answer each question in the space provided.

4. List the four categories used in the START triage system.

    1.

    2.

    3.

    4.

5. List the four areas evaluated during a primary survey using the START triage system.

    1.

    2.

    3.

    4.

Answer Section

Multiple Choice

1. d

   The most knowledgeable EMS professional arriving on the scene first should assume the responsibility of scene triage. Fully assessing each patient requires too much time and resources and is not a component of triage. Treating patients (such as performing CPR) is not a component of triage. Triage is a system of rapidly assessing each patient so that every patient may be "tagged" according to his priority. Typically, triage procedures evaluate three patient factors: breathing status, heart rate, and level of consciousness. Patients are categorized according to this brief assessment. Once resources have arrived to begin treating patients, assigned tasks should be based on the triage patient categorization.

   Objective: Evaluate the role of the EMR in a multiple-casualty situation.

2. b

   The woman who is pulseless and apneic with blood coming from both ears should be categorized as the lowest priority. The woman complaining of chest pain and the man who has an altered mental status should be considered the highest priority. The man with arm and leg trauma should be considered an intermediate priority.

   Objective: Summarize the components of basic triage.

3. c

   Patients showing the signs of shock are considered a high priority, especially when such a patient is young. Young patients do not typically show signs of shock until their compensatory mechanisms begin to crash rapidly. Burn patients without airway compromise and spinal injury patients are a second priority. Again, patients who are not breathing and pulseless are a last priority.

   Objective: Summarize the components of basic triage.

Short Answer

4. The four categories in the START triage system are:

   - Red: Immediate
   - Yellow: Delayed
   - Green: Ambulatory
   - Black: Dead or nonsalvageable

   Objective: Summarize the components of basic triage.

5. Four areas are evaluated during the primary survey using the START system: ability to walk (ambulatory), respirations, perfusion, and mental status.

   Objective: Summarize the components of basic triage.

43 Air Medical Transport

READING ASSIGNMENT ▶ Read Chapter 43, pages 693 to 696 in your textbook.

Sum It Up

- Air medical transport may be necessary when the condition of one or more patients is critical.
- Local standards and protocols for the use of air transport vary widely, even within a given region. It is essential that you become familiar with local guidelines regarding the use of air transport.
- Safety is critical around a helicopter. Remember to wear appropriate personal protective equipment (such as a helmet, turnout coat, eye shield, etc.). Also, remember to *never* approach a helicopter from the rear.
- If your unit is designated to land the helicopter, you will need to locate a secure landing zone. You must locate an area that is easily controlled for traffic and pedestrians. You should allow at least 100 feet by 100 feet to land any helicopter. The area should be free of overhead obstacles such as wires, trees, and light poles. It should also be free of debris and should be relatively level. The ground should be clear of rocks and grooves and must be firm enough to support the aircraft.

▶ Tracking Your Progress

After reading this chapter, can you:	Page Reference	Objective Met?
• Give examples of situations in which air medical transport may be indicated?	693	☐
• Discuss the general requirements for a helicopter landing zone?	694	☐
• Discuss general safety guidelines for use around helicopters?	695	☐

Chapter Quiz

True/False

Decide whether each statement is true or false. In the space provided, write T for true or F for false.

_____ **1.** Never move toward a helicopter until signaled by the flight crew.

_____ **2.** If an air medical crew transports a patient for whom you initially provided emergency care, it is not necessary for you to complete a prehospital care report.

_____ **3.** Secure any objects that may be blown away before approaching a helicopter.

Multiple Choice

In the space provided, identify the letter of the choice that best completes each statement or answers each question.

_____ **4.** When establishing a landing zone for a medical helicopter, the minimum size of the area secured should be
   a. 20 feet by 40 feet
   b. 100 feet by 100 feet
   c. 200 feet by 200 feet
   d. 500 feet by 500 feet

_____ **5.** Vehicles or nonaircraft personnel should not be allowed within _____ of a medical helicopter.
   a. 10 feet
   b. 30 feet
   c. 60 feet
   d. 90 feet

Answer Section

True/False

1. True

   Never move toward a helicopter until signaled by the flight crew.

   Objective: Discuss general safety guidelines for use around helicopters.

2. False

   In addition to your routine documentation of your patient assessment findings and emergency care provided, make sure to document the time patient care was transferred to the flight crew, the patient's condition at the time care was transferred, and the patient's destination.

   Objective: Describe what information is required in each section of the prehospital care report and how it should be entered.

3. True

   Secure any objects that may be blown away (hats, papers, blankets, etc.) before approaching the aircraft.

   Objective: Discuss general safety guidelines for use around helicopters.

Multiple Choice

4. b

   If your unit is designated to land a helicopter, you will need to locate a secure landing zone. You must locate an area that is easily controlled for traffic and pedestrians. You should allow at least 100 feet by 100 feet to land any helicopter. The area should be free of overhead obstacles such as wires, trees, and light poles. It should also be free of debris and should be relatively level. The ground should be clear of rocks and grooves and must be firm enough to support the aircraft.

   Objective: Discuss the general requirements for a helicopter landing zone.

5. c

   Do not allow vehicles or nonaircraft personnel within 60 feet of the aircraft.

   Objective: Discuss general safety guidelines for use around helicopters.

Vehicle Extrication

READING ASSIGNMENT ▶ Read Chapter 44, pages 697 to 705 in your textbook.

Sum It Up

- You may be called to assist with extrication. Your main duties will involve ensuring patient safety and delivering patient care by providing cervical spine stabilization, treating any injuries sustained by the patient(s), and assisting paramedics on the scene with any special needs.

- Extrication is the process of removing structural components from around a patient to facilitate patient care and transport. The EMR on the extrication scene has an important role both as a care provider for the patient and as a support member for the extrication team. Base the extrication on the patient's condition to ensure that the techniques used will provide the fastest access to and best egress for the patient from the vehicle.

- Protective clothing that is appropriate for the situation must be worn during extrication. This includes protective boots, pants, a coat, eye protection, a helmet, and gloves. Respiratory protection may also be needed.

- Scene size-up is an important step in the extrication process. A proper scene size-up will reveal any hazards present and also give a good indication of the number of persons injured, the types of injury, and which patient or patients require medical attention first.

- Once on the scene, fire apparatus should be parked in the fend-off position, which involves parking your unit in advance of the scene and in a way that allows traveling vehicles to strike your unit and not crew members.

- Alternative fuels and renewable fuels, such as hydrogen and ethanol, pose special challenges for emergency response personnel. If you know or suspect that a scene involves alternative or renewable fuels, contact your dispatch center so that this important information can be relayed to responding fire department crews. Do not approach unless you are trained and equipped with appropriate PPE for the situation or the scene has been deemed safe by the proper authorities.

- Stabilization is the process of rendering a vehicle motionless in the position in which it is found. The purpose of stabilization is to eliminate potential movement of a vehicle (or structure) that may cause further harm to entrapped patients or rescuers.

- Simple extrication is the use of hand tools to gain access and extricate the patient from the vehicle. Complex extrication involves the use of powered hydraulic rescue tools, such as cutters, spreaders, and rams. The patient's level of entrapment will determine whether the extrication will fall into the simple or complex category.
- Four levels of entrapment are possible during a motor vehicle crash. The first level is no entrapment. Light entrapment requires that a door or some other object will need to be opened or moved to get the patient out. Moderate entrapment is more involved, requiring removal of doors or the roof. Heavy entrapment is the highest level of entrapment and involves any situation that is above and beyond moderate entrapment.
- Disentanglement is the moving or removing of material that is trapping a victim.
- Continue your education beyond the information contained in this chapter in order to provide the best care for your patients and maintain and improve your skills as you gain more experience in EMS.

▶ Tracking Your Progress

After reading this chapter, can you:	Page Reference	Objective Met?
• Describe the purpose of extrication?	698	☐
• Discuss the role of the EMR in extrication?	698	☐
• Identify what equipment for personal safety is required for the EMR?	698	☐
• Define the fundamental components of extrication?	698	☐
• State the steps that should be taken to protect the patient during extrication?	700	☐
• Evaluate various methods of gaining access to the patient?	701	☐
• Distinguish between simple access and complex access?	702	☐

Chapter Quiz

True/False

Decide whether each statement is true or false. In the space provided, write T for true or F for false.

_____ 1. Cutters, spreaders, and rams are examples of tools used during a simple extrication.

_____ 2. All persons involved in an extrication operation should wear protective clothing.

_____ 3. Equipment for stabilization involves the use of hammers, hacksaws, cutters, and spreaders.

_____ 4. When attempting to gain access to a patient, it is best to use the path of least resistance first.

Multiple Choice

In the space provided, identify the letter of the choice that best completes the statement or answers each question.

_____ 5. Before removing a patient from a vehicle during extrication, what step should be taken?
  a. Take a full set of vital signs.
  b. Bandage all wounds.
  c. Maintain spinal stabilization.
  d. Obtain a complete history and perform a physical exam.

Questions 6 to 10 pertain to the following scenario:

Your rescue crew is called to the scene of a motor vehicle collision on a local four-lane highway. Information at the time of dispatch indicates that there are at least five vehicles involved. The posted speed limit is 55 mph. The crash occurred 45 miles from the nearest hospital.

_____ 6. Which of the following duties should be performed first?
  a. Gain access to the most critically injured patients.
  b. Triage patients according to the severity of their injuries.
  c. Determine the number of patients, the types of injuries, and additional resource needs.
  d. Assess the mental, airway, breathing, and circulation status of all patients, and begin treating life-threatening conditions.

_____ 7. One of the vehicles has come to rest on its side. There is one occupant in the vehicle. Before gaining access and assessing the occupants, you should consider
  a. removing the vehicle's battery.
  b. siphoning the fuel from the tank.
  c. cribbing the vehicle with wedges and boards.
  d. checking to see if the patient can get out of the vehicle without assistance.

_____ 8. After access has been made to this patient, you determine that he is critically injured and showing late signs of shock. Which of the following should you consider?
  a. Requesting a medical helicopter
  b. Applying an AED
  c. Stabilizing his spine with a vest-type extrication device
  d. Rocking the vehicle back onto its wheels to facilitate rapid extrication

_____ 9. To gain full access to this patient, you must go through one of the windows. Which of the following techniques would be indicated?
  a. Break either the front or rear window.
  b. Cover the patient with a blanket, and break the front windshield.
  c. Cover the patient with a blanket, and break a window far from the patient's location.
  d. Cover the patient with a blanket, and break the closest windshield to the patient's location.

_____ 10. Once you have gained access to this patient, which of the following should be done first?
  a. Check for a pulse.
  b. Perform a primary survey.
  c. Perform a rapid trauma assessment.
  d. Apply a nonrebreather mask connected to supplemental oxygen.

_____ 11. As an EMR, which of the following is your primary responsibility during extrication?
  a. Communicating with the dispatcher
  b. Coordinating the rescue operation
  c. Operating the rescue tools
  d. Protecting the patient

Answer Section

True/False

1. **False**

   Simple extrication is the use of hand tools to gain access and extricate the patient from the vehicle. Simple hand tools include tools such as hammers, hacksaws, battery-operated saws, and pry bars.

   Objective: Distinguish between simple and complex access.

2. **True**

   Remember that your personal safety is your priority on every call. Protective clothing that is appropriate for the situation must be worn during extrication. This includes protective boots, pants, a coat, eye protection, a helmet, and gloves. Respiratory protection may also be needed if there is the possibility of particulates from the extrication process entering the nose or mouth. Hearing protection may also be necessary depending on the amount of noise on the scene. If there is any possibility of a fire, structural firefighting gear should be worn. Additional protection may be required for bloodborne and airborne pathogens. Always wear the PPE that will give you the most protection from the hazards present at the extrication scene.

   Objective: Identify what equipment for personal safety is required for the EMR.

3. **False**

   Complex extrication involves the use of powered hydraulic rescue tools such as cutters, spreaders, and rams. Equipment for stabilization may include cribbing and wedges, airbags, step chocks, come-alongs (hand winches), hydraulic rams, jacks, and/or chains. Simple extrication involves the use of tools such as hammers, hacksaws, battery-operated saws, and pry bars.

   Objective: Distinguish between simple access and complex access.

4. **True**

   Gaining access to the patient inside an entangled vehicle should be accomplished as soon as safely possible after arriving on the scene. Use the path of least resistance. Try opening each door, roll down windows, or have the patient unlock doors.

   Objective: Distinguish between simple access and complex access.

Multiple Choice

5. **c**

   Before removing the patient from the vehicle during extrication, maintain spinal stabilization.

   Objective: Discuss the role of the EMR in extrication.

6. **c**

   The scene size-up is your first responsibility at the scene. Some of the components of the scene size-up include determining the number of patients and the types of injuries, assessing the need for additional resources, and noting the number of vehicles and the extent of damage to the vehicles. An important aspect of the size-up is the concern for the safety of yourself, your crew, the patient(s), and bystanders. Do not forget that taking standard precautions is part of the scene size-up. Gaining access to, triaging, and assessing patients all occur after the scene size-up.

   Objective: Evaluate the role of the EMR in the multiple-casualty situation.

7. **c**

   This vehicle is not secure in its present position (on its side). Before accessing the patient, rescue personnel should immediately begin stabilizing the vehicle with wedges, chocks, jacks, and so on. Removing the battery may actually slow your extrication efforts if an electrical seat in the vehicle needs to be moved to access the patient more fully.

Siphoning fuel from the tank may actually increase the possibility of explosion or exposure. Patients involved in MVCs should not be asked to crawl free of the wreckage unless imminent danger exists (such as the vehicle is on fire).

Objective: Define the fundamental components of extrication.

8. a

With the closest hospital 45 miles from the accident scene, it is safe to say that ground transport will exceed 15 minutes. This patient is in critical condition, and rapid transportation to an appropriate facility is just as vital as is rapid stabilization. The patient's condition warrants rapid extrication. The use of a vest-type extrication device would be appropriate if the patient's condition is stable. The AED may be applied if the patient is apneic and pulseless; currently, this is not the case. Rocking the vehicle back onto its wheels would compromise the patient's spinal stabilization and could aggravate any injury that exists.

Objective: Describe the indications for the use of rapid extrication.

9. c

Ideally, you should break a window remote from the patient. Modern passenger car side and rear windows are made of tempered glass. When broken, tempered glass fractures into hundreds of small rounded pieces rather than large shards of glass. The front windshield, however, is made of laminated safety glass. This glass is much more difficult to remove because the plates of glass are bonded to a clear laminate. Perhaps the best way to remove the front windshield is to remove the frame and rubber seal and then pop the window out. In any case, patients should be covered during extrication. Putting a rescuer in with the patient is ideal. Extrication can be very noisy and frightening for patients of any age. Close communication with the patient is essential.

Objective: State the steps that should be taken to protect the patient during extrication.

10. b

Once access is made, a primary survey should be performed. If the patient is unconscious or conscious but has an altered mental status, a rapid trauma assessment should follow the primary survey. If the patient is conscious and alert, a focused history and physical examination should follow the primary survey.

Objective: Discuss the reason for performing a focused history and physical exam.

11. d

EMRs are responsible for giving necessary care to the patient before extrication and making sure that the patient is removed in a way that minimizes further injury. Some EMRs are also responsible for extrication procedures.

Objective: Discuss the role of the EMR in extrication.

CHAPTER

45 Hazardous Materials Awareness

READING ASSIGNMENT ▶ Read Chapter 45, pages 706 to 713 in your textbook.

Sum It Up

- As defined by the NFPA, a hazardous material is any substance that causes or may cause adverse effects on the health or safety of employees, the general public, or the environment.
- A hazardous substance can be identified by using a number of resources:
  —U.S. DOT Emergency Response Guidebook
  —UN classification numbers
  —NFPA 704 placard system
  —UN/DOT placards
  —Shipping papers
  —MSDSs
- The first phase of dealing with a hazardous materials incident is recognizing that one exists. As always, your personal safety is your priority in any emergency scene. If there is no risk to you (and you are properly trained and equipped to do so), remove patients to a safe zone. The safe zone (also called the cold zone) is an area safe from exposure or the threat of exposure. The warm zone is a controlled area for entry into the hot zone. It also serves as the decontamination area after exiting the hot zone. All personnel in the warm zone must wear appropriate protective equipment. The hot zone is the danger zone.

After reading this chapter, can you:	Page Reference	Objective Met?
• Define hazardous materials and explain the EMR's role during a call involving them?	707	☐
• Describe what the EMR should do if there is reason to believe that there is a hazard at the scene?	707	☐
• Briefly describe the various types of chemical protective clothing?	707	☐
• State the role the EMR should perform until appropriately trained personnel arrive at the scene of a hazardous materials situation?	710	☐
• Discuss methods used to identify hazardous materials?	710	☐
• Discuss the establishment of safety zones at a scene involving hazardous materials?	711	☐

Chapter Quiz

Multiple Choice

In the space provided, identify the letter of the choice that best completes each statement or answers each question.

Questions 1–6 pertain to the following scenario:

Your rescue crew is called to the scene of a 22-year-old man who has been "burned" (according to the information at time of dispatch). You arrive at an industrial complex to find your patient standing in an assembly area. Bystanders state that a container of dry chlorine powder burst open and covered the patient. The material is used for pool maintenance and is all over the patient and his immediate area. The shipping container information states that the product may cause irritation to the skin and mucous membranes. You call for a hazardous materials team. Their estimated time to the scene is 20 minutes. Your crew has taken standard precautions with gloves, eye and respiratory protection, and gowns.

_____ 1. Your best course of action will be to
    a. form a general impression and primary survey.
    b. wait until the hazardous materials team arrives.
    c. remove the patient, your crew, and the bystanders from the area.
    d. begin irrigating the patient with water to remove the gross contaminants.

_____ 2. As performed by trained personnel, the first step in decontaminating this patient should be
    a. immediate flushing of the chemical from the skin with hot water and then wrapping exposed skin areas with dry, sterile dressings.
    b. immediate removal of dry powder and then irrigation with water.
    c. neutralization of the acid with a corresponding base (such as lye).
    d. immediate submersion of the patient in a chemical bath of bicarbonate of soda and water.

_____ 3. Which of the following is correct regarding the decontamination of this patient?
    a. All clothing and jewelry must be removed before or during irrigation
    b. The patient must strip down to his underwear before or during irrigation
    c. The patient should change into clean clothes if available before or during irrigation
    d. The patient should be decontaminated with his clothes on so the clothing becomes decontaminated as well

_____ 4. After continuous irrigation, the patient begins to complain of left eye discomfort. He states it feels like his eye is burning and itching. Appropriate treatment for this complaint would be to
    a. cover the left eye with a moistened, sterile gauze pad.
    b. lay the patient on his left side and continuously irrigate the left eye until arrival at the hospital.
    c. lay the patient on his right side and continuously irrigate the left eye until arrival at the hospital.
    d. have the patient submerse his head in a container of water and bicarbonate of soda until the discomfort is relieved.

_____ 5. Which of the following would suggest that this patient may have inhaled some chlorine powder?

    a. Abdominal cramping

    b. Nausea and vomiting

    c. Blisters on the chest and neck area

    d. Difficulty breathing, with crackles (rales)

_____ 6. Appropriate management of this patient en route to the hospital would be

    a. continuous irrigation and no oxygen due to an explosion hazard.

    b. continuous irrigation and low-flow oxygen (nasal cannula at 4 to 6 L/min).

    c. continuous irrigation and high-flow oxygen (nonrebreather mask at 15 L/min).

    d. continuous irrigation, high-flow oxygen (nonrebreather mask at 15 L/min), and application of occlusive dressings to all burned areas.

Questions 7–10 pertain to the following scenario:

Your rescue crew is called to assist another rescue crew at the scene of a chemical spill. The first arriving rescue crew attempted to rescue an unconscious male from an "empty" processing vat. When you arrive, you find the patient and three rescuers unconscious in a large metal vat. The vat is about 8 feet tall by 6 feet square and open on the top. There is no unusual odor in the immediate area.

_____ 7. The unconscious rescuers are wearing firefighter turnout clothing without a self-contained breathing apparatus (SCBA). This is also known as what level of protection?

    a. Level 1   **c.** Level D

    b. Level A   **d.** Level 0

_____ 8. An on-site foreman informs you that the worker was cleaning the vat with "XYZ SpeedeeKleen Cleanser." What document should the company have on hand that provides specific, detailed information about the chemical name, physical properties, fire and explosion hazard, and emergency first aid treatment?

    a. The UN/DOT placard

    b. The receipt of purchase

    c. The material safety data sheet (MSDS)

    d. The _Emergency Response Guidebook_ (ERG)

_____ 9. Additional information about the specific chemical may be rapidly obtained by contacting

    a. the United Nations.

    b. the company that shipped the chemical.

    c. the emergency department of a local hospital.

    d. the Chemical Transportation Emergency Center (CHEMTREC).

_____ 10. While investigating the chemicals involved in this incident, you decide to establish safety zones. The zone immediately surrounding the danger area is referred to as the

    a. hot zone.   **c.** level-1 zone.

    b. red zone.   **d.** level-A zone.

Questions 11–13 pertain to the following scenario:

The National Fire Protection Association developed a standard system of hazardous chemical identification. This system employs a diamond-shaped diagram divided into four quadrants each with a different color.

_____ 11. The red portion of the diagram refers to

    a. health hazards.

    b. flammability hazards.

    c. reactivity or stability hazards.

    d. the level of protective clothing required for entry into the scene.

_____ 12. A placard with a "1" rating in the blue field indicates that the

    a. substance will not burn.

    b. substance is extremely flammable.

    c. substance is slightly hazardous to health.

    d. substance may detonate—vacate area if material is exposed to fire.

_____ **13.** You are called to the scene of a hazardous materials spill. You should park the emergency vehicle
   a. at least 500 feet from the spill.
   b. at least 1,000 feet from the spill.
   c. at least 2,000 feet from the spill.
   d. as close to the spill as possible without endangering yourself.

Matching

Match the key terms in the right column with the definitions in the left column by placing the letter of each correct answer in the space provided.

_____ **14.** Triage

_____ **15.** National Incident Management System

_____ **16.** Warm zone

_____ **17.** Multiple-casualty incident

_____ **18.** Hazardous material

_____ **19.** Cold zone

_____ **20.** Decontamination (decon)

_____ **21.** Hot zone

_____ **22.** Incident commander

_____ **23.** Chemical protective clothing

_____ **24.** Exclusion zone

_____ **25.** Material safety data sheets

A. An identified safety zone at a hazardous materials incident that is an area safe from exposure or the threat of exposure and that serves as the staging area for personnel and equipment

B. Documents that the Occupational Safety and Health Association requires be kept on-site anywhere that chemicals are used

C. A standardized system that provides a consistent nationwide template allowing governmental, private sector, and nongovernmental agencies to work together during domestic incidents

D. An identified safety zone at a hazardous materials incident that contains the hazardous material (contaminant)

E. Sorting multiple victims into priorities for emergency medical care or transportation to definitive care

F. A substance (solid, liquid, or gas) that, when released, is capable of creating harm to people, the environment, and property

G. Physical and/or chemical processes used at a hazardous materials incident to reduce and prevent the spread of contamination from persons and equipment

H. Any event that places a great demand on resources—equipment, personnel, or both

I. The person who is responsible for managing all operations during domestic incidents

J. Another name for the hot zone at a hazardous materials incident

K. An identified safety zone at a hazardous materials incident that serves as a controlled area for entry into the hot zone and that is the area where most operations take place

L. Materials designed to protect the skin from exposure by either physical or chemical means

Answer Section

Multiple Choice

1. c

    Do not assume that because you have some prehospital education about treating exposed patients you are able or expected to be able to manage a hazardous materials incident. Once you recognize that your "medical" incident has a hazardous materials element, immediately return to the scene size-up mode. Ensure the safety of yourself, your crew, the patient, and all potential patients (bystanders). Call for available resources (fire department, hazmat team, on-site specialists, local public safety department, local public health department, etc.). Find out what your particular resources are *before* you encounter a hazardous materials incident.

    Your scene assessment reveals that you, your crew, the patient, and the bystanders may be harmed by staying in the immediate area. In all cases where your location may put you in harm's way, you need to move as quickly as the situation warrants. Since the patient is conscious and standing, it would be appropriate for you to instruct him to follow you out of the area. Have all bystanders leave the area, and direct them to a site other than the one to which you are directing the patient. Remember, as long as the patient is contaminated, everywhere he goes is contaminated until proved otherwise.

    Objective: State the role the EMR should perform until appropriately trained personnel arrive at the scene of a hazardous materials situation.

2. b

    Since the patient is covered in a dry product, you should attempt (or instruct the patient) to sweep off the material. Immediate and continuous irrigation with water should follow. Never attempt to "correct" a product's pH to reduce an injury or burn. Do not add an acid to an alkali or vice versa. The result could be fatal. The only substance you should use to irrigate is water.

    Objective: Define hazardous materials and explain the EMR's role during a call involving them.

3. a

    Protecting a patient's modesty and privacy is important; however, when decontaminating a patient, all clothing must be removed, including jewelry, wigs, toupees, and other body adornments. Do not be concerned with decontaminating these things, as your efforts should be directed toward saving the patient. Do not transport the clothing or other effects with the patient—it is contaminated. If you are concerned about the safety of valuables, ensure that law enforcement personnel secure the entire area from nonessential personnel. Allowing the patient to wear "clean" clothing during the decontamination may only result in ineffective decontamination. If bystanders and nonessential personnel are removed from the area, you have met the privacy concerns of the patient to the best of your ability.

    Objective: Define hazardous materials and explain the EMR's role during a call involving them.

4. b

    The correct method for treating an eye exposure is to have the patient lie down and continuously irrigate the affected eye with water or normal saline solution. The affected eye is lowered so that contaminants are not washed into the unaffected eye. If both eyes are affected, you may position the patient on either side. Laying the patient flat may cause the contaminated irrigation fluid to run down the face toward the nose and mouth.

5. d

    The signs and symptoms of inhaled poisoning include difficulty breathing, rales or crackles (typically from damage to the lungs leading to leaking fluid in the lung space), chest pain, cough or hoarseness (typically from damage to the larynx), dizziness (typically from shock and inadequate oxygenation), and headache, confusion, seizures, or altered mental status (typically from inadequate oxygen delivery to the brain). Abdominal cramping, vomiting, and nausea generally accompany ingested poisoning incidents. Blisters on the chest and neck area suggest an absorbed poisoning incident.

Objective: List common poisonings by inhalation and the signs and symptoms related to common poisonings by this route.

6. c

Continuously irrigate to ensure that most of the contaminants are washed away. *Caution:* Your patient may become extremely cold during continuous irrigation. The ideal way to warm the patient without stopping irrigation is to use the heater in the transport vehicle. Monitor your patient closely for signs of hypothermia, especially if severe burns are present. Oxygen should be delivered by nonrebreather mask at 10 to 15 L/min.

Objective: Discuss the emergency medical care for poisoning by inhalation.

7. c

Level D personal protective equipment provides limited body protection and no respiratory protection. These rescuers should have done a better job in sizing up the scene and recognizing potential hazards. Obviously, they ignored or downplayed the assessment of the mechanism of injury. Instead of helping to resolve the situation, they became part of the problem, and this may have cost them their lives. This scenario is based on countless similar, real-life incidents. Remember that personal safety is your priority!

Objective: Briefly describe the various types of chemical protective clothing.

8. c

Material safety data sheets are the first-responding emergency crew's best friend. They contain valuable information about specific chemicals. UN/DOT placards and the *Emergency Response Guidebook* (ERG) provide only generic information about similar types of chemicals. OSHA law mandates that businesses have immediate access to MSDSs for all chemicals used or stored on-site.

Objective: Discuss methods used to identify hazardous materials.

9. d

CHEMTREC provides a 24-hour hotline for product information and emergency response protocols. CHEMTREC is particularly useful as a resource for identifying the chemical components of a substance on the basis of the product's trade name. In this example, CHEMTREC may be able to provide information with regard to the ingredients and hazards of XYZ SpeedeeKleen Cleanser.

Objective: Discuss methods used to identify hazardous materials.

10. a

The hot zone should encompass the contamination area and potential contamination area. Therefore, the hot zone size may be influenced by ambient temperature, wind direction, and terrain, as well as by the characteristics of the contaminant. Only personnel with the appropriate level of personal protective equipment should enter the hot zone. Personnel entering the hot zone should have a specific purpose—no freelancing in the hot zone! The warm zone is a control area for entry into the hot zone. Also, personnel leaving the hot zone are decontaminated in the warm zone. The appropriate-level personal protective equipment must be observed in the warm zone. The cold zone is a safe area intended for support personnel and unused resources. The general public should be kept out of the cold zone.

Objective: Discuss the establishment of safety zones at a scene involving hazardous materials.

11. b

The red quadrant of the NFPA 704 diamond refers to flammability hazards. The blue quadrant refers to health hazards, while the yellow quadrant refers to reactivity hazards. The white quadrant contains information regarding special hazard concerns such as water reactivity or radioactivity. The three colored quadrants rate hazards on a scale of 1 to 4, with 4 being the highest level of hazard. The white quadrant contains symbols or words that indicate special hazard considerations, if applicable.

Objective: Discuss methods used to identify hazardous materials.

12. c

The blue field refers to health hazard, and a rating of 1 indicates that only a slight health hazard exists. A zero rating would indicate that there is no hazard present. A 4 rating would indicate that an extreme health hazard exists and that only trained personnel with proper attire should enter the hazard area.

Objective: Discuss methods used to identify hazardous materials.

13. c

Park at least 2,000 feet from a hazardous substance.

Objective: Describe what the EMR should do if there is reason to believe that there is a hazard at the scene.

Matching

14. F	20. G
15. L	21. D
16. B	22. I
17. H	23. K
18. A	24. C
19. E	25. J

46 Terrorism and Disaster Response

READING ASSIGNMENT ▶ Read Chapter 46, pages 714 to 723 in your textbook.

Sum It Up

- Weapons of mass destruction (WMD) are materials used by terrorists that have the potential to cause great harm over a large area.
- There are five main categories of WMDs. B-NICE is a simple way to remember these categories:
  - —Biological
  - —Nuclear or radiological
  - —Incendiary
  - —Chemical
  - —Explosive
- Biological weapons involve the use of bacteria, viruses, rickettsia, or toxins to cause disease or death. Diseases can be spread by inhalation of substances dispersed by spray devices (aerosols), ingestion of contaminated food or water supplies, or absorption through direct skin contact with the substance.
- The Centers for Disease Control and Prevention (CDC) categorizes biological weapons according to their risk to national security.
- Nuclear radiation gives off three main types of radiation: alpha, beta, and gamma. It is the charge that makes radiation an immediate problem and disruptive to cell function and structure. Alpha particles are large, heavy, and charged and cannot penetrate very far into matter. Because clothing or a sheet of paper is of sufficient thickness to stop them, external exposure to alpha particles usually has no effect on people. Beta particles are much smaller, travel more quickly, have less charge, and can penetrate more deeply than alpha particles. Beta particles can be stopped by layers of clothing or thin metal or plastic, such as several sheets of aluminum foil or Plexiglas.
- Gamma rays are waves of very high energy, similar to light. These waves of energy penetrate very deeply and can easily go right through a person. To reduce exposure from gamma rays, thick material such as lead must be used.
- According to the CDC, a dirty bomb is a mix of explosives, such as dynamite, with radioactive powder or pellets. A dirty bomb is also known as a radiological weapon. When the dynamite or other explosives are set off, the blast carries radioactive material into the surrounding area.
- Incendiary materials are substances that burn with a hot flame for a specific period.

- Chemical agents are poisonous substances that injure or kill people when inhaled, ingested, or absorbed through the skin or eyes. There are five broad categories of chemical weapons: nerve agents, blister agents, blood agents, choking agents, and irritants.

- Most terrorist attacks involve the use of explosives. Explosives are associated with a very rapid release of gas and heat.

- At a possible WMD incident, your primary responsibilities will be to isolate the scene, preserve evidence and deny entry, ask for additional help, and coordinate efforts with other responding fire, EMS, and law enforcement personnel; recognize signs of a potential WMD incident and alert the proper authorities; recognize the potential of a secondary explosion or attack on emergency responders; and make sure you, as well as additional responders, are safe.

- If hazardous substances or conditions are suspected, the scene must be secured by qualified personnel wearing appropriate equipment. If you are not qualified and do not have the appropriate equipment, you may need to wait for additional help to arrive before you can attempt entry into the scene.

- Access to any patient must not occur without the proper personal protective equipment. Standard personal protective equipment may not be sufficient or appropriate for this type of response.

▶ Tracking Your Progress

After reading this chapter, can you:	Page Reference	Objective Met?
• Define weapons of mass destruction?	715	☐
• Discuss the five main types of weapons of mass destruction?	715	☐
• Define biological weapons, give examples, and explain how they are spread?	716	☐
• Discuss the types of radiation that may be given off by nuclear weapons?	717	☐
• Define chemical agents, give examples of their use as weapons, and explain their effects on the human body?	718	☐
• Discuss your primary responsibilities at a suspected terrorist incident?	720	☐
• Discuss incident factors that may suggest possible terrorist activity or weapons of mass destruction?	720	☐

Chapter Quiz

Multiple Choice

In the space provided, identify the letter of the choice that best completes the statement or answers each question.

_____ 1. A blister agent is an example of a(n)

    a. biological weapon.

    b. chemical weapon.

    c. nuclear weapon.

    d. explosive.

_____ **2.** Cyanide is an example of a
   a. nerve agent.
   b. blister agent.
   c. blood agent.
   d. choking agent.

Short Answer

Answer each question in the space provided.

3. List four common types of biological agents.
   1.
   2.
   3.
   4.

4. List five categories of weapons of mass destruction a terrorist might use.
   1.
   2.
   3.
   4.
   5.

5. Fill in the missing information.

Disease/Agent	Group/Type
	Biological/virus/category A
Botulism/enterotoxin B/ricin	
	Rickettsia/category B
	Category C
Sarin, soman, tabun, VX	
	Blister agents
Cyanide, arsine, hydrogen chloride	
Chlorine, phosgene	
	Irritants

Answer Section

Multiple Choice

1. b

   Blister agents are types of chemical weapons. Their effects are like those of a corrosive chemical such as lye or a strong acid. They can cause severe burns to the eyes, skin, and tissues of the respiratory tract.

   Objective: Define chemical agents, give examples of their use as weapons, and explain their effects on the human body.

2. c

   Cyanide is an example of a blood agent. It causes rapid respiratory arrest and death by blocking oxygen absorption in cells and organs through the bloodstream.

   Objective: Define chemical agents, give examples of their use as weapons, and explain their effects on the human body.

Short Answer

3. There are four common types of biological agents: bacteria, viruses, rickettsias, and toxins.

   Objective: Define biological weapons, give examples, and explain how they are spread.

4. There are five main categories of WMDs. B-NICE is a simple way to remember these categories:

   - *Biological*
   - *Nuclear or radiological*
   - *Incendiary*
   - *Chemical*
   - *Explosive*

   Objective: Discuss the five main types of weapons of mass destruction.

5. See table below.

Disease/Agent	Group/Type
Anthrax/Ebola/smallpox	Biological/virus/category A
Botulism/enterotoxin b/ricin	Toxin
Q fever	Rickettsias/category B
Nipah virus/hantavirus	Category C
Sarin, soman, tabun, VX	Nerve agents
Distilled mustard, nitrogen mustard	Blister agents
Cyanide, arsine, hydrogen chloride	Blood agents
Chlorine, phosgene	Choking agents
Mace, pepper spray, tear gas	Irritants

Objective: Define chemical agents, give examples of their use as weapons, and explain their effects on the human body.